Windows Explorer Components

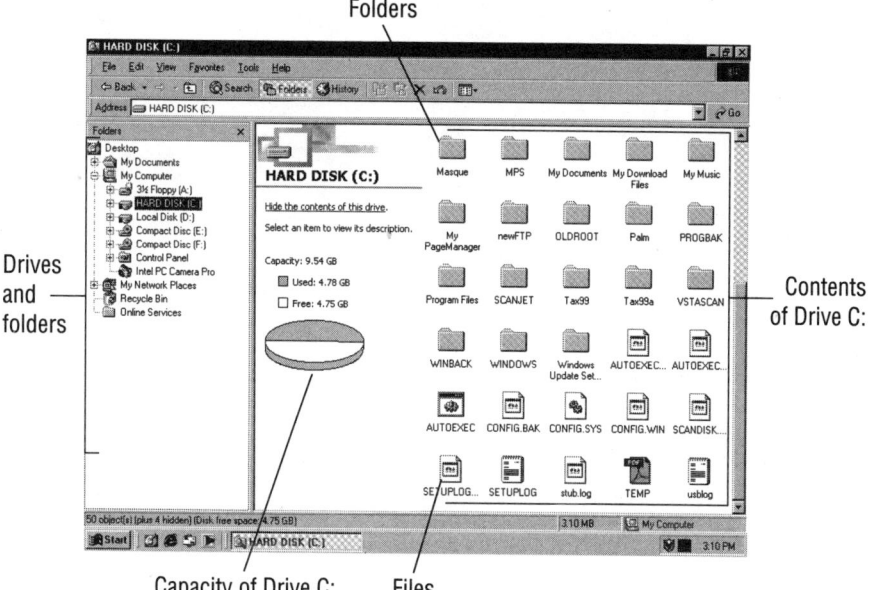

Folders • Drives and folders • Contents of Drive C: • Capacity of Drive C: • Files

Windows Me
Instant Reference

Windows® Me
Instant Reference

San Francisco • Paris • Düsseldorf • Soest • London

Associate Publisher: Jordan Gold
Contracts and Licensing Manager: Kristine O'Callaghan
Acquisitions & Developmental Editor: Ellen Dendy
Customer Service Representative: Jan Fisher, Publication Services, Inc.
Editor: Rob Siedenburg, Publication Services, Inc.
Production Editor: Maureen Elsbernd, Publication Services, Inc.
Technical Editor: Scott Warmbrand
Book Designers: Patrick Dintino, Maureen Forys, Happenstance Type-O-Rama
Graphic Illustrator: Don Waller, Publication Services, Inc.
Electronic Publishing Specialists: David Eynon, Martin D. Stephens, Publication Services, Inc.
Proofreaders: Philip Hamer, Jenny Putman, Eric Hamrin, Jim Rogers, Publication Services, Inc.
Indexer: Ann Rogers
Cover Designer: Design Site
Cover Illustrator/Photographer: Sergie Loobkoff

Library of Congress Card Number: 00-106431
ISBN: 0-7821-2856-4

SYBEX and the SYBEX logo are trademarks of SYBEX Inc. in the USA and other countries. Screen reproductions produced with FullShot 99. FullShot 99 © 1991-1999 Inbit Incorporated. All rights reserved.

FullShot is a trademark of Inbit Incorporated.

Internet screen shots using Microsoft Internet Explorer 5.5 reprinted by permission from Microsoft Corporation.

TRADEMARKS: SYBEX has attempted throughout this book to distinguish proprietary trademarks from descriptive terms by following the capitalization style used by the manufacturer.

The author and publisher have made their best efforts to prepare this book, and the content is based upon final release software whenever possible. Portions of the manuscript may be based upon pre-release versions supplied by software manufacturer(s). The author and the publisher make no representation or warranties of any kind with regard to the completeness or accuracy of the contents herein and accept no liability of any kind including but not limited to performance, merchantability, fitness for any particular purpose, or any losses or damages of any kind caused or alleged to be caused directly or indirectly from this book.

Copyright © 2001 SYBEX Inc., 1151 Marina Village Parkway, Alameda, CA 94501. World rights reserved. No part of this publication may be stored in a retrieval system, transmitted, or reproduced in any way, including but not limited to photocopy, photograph, magnetic, or other record, without the prior agreement and written permission of the publisher. Manufactured in the United States of America

10 9 8 7 6 5 4 3 2

Acknowledgments

Sybex would like to thank all the people who worked on this project, including Faithe Wempen, Jan Fisher, Rob Siedenburg, Maureen Elsbernd, David Eynon, Philip Hamer, Jenny Putman, Martin D. Stephens, Eric Hamrin, Jim Rogers, Don Waller, Steve Sansone, and Dave Powers.

Introduction

Windows Millennium Edition (Me) represents the next evolutionary step in the progression of Windows operating systems. It is bigger, faster, slicker, and more capable than anything that has come before. Windows Me supports more different kinds of hardware and includes much more application software than any previous version of Windows.

Windows Me is tailor-made for home and family use. With its easy-to-follow Wizards, you can set up home networking, Internet connection sharing, and more with very little technical expertise needed. It also provides some great multimedia tools for playing, recording, and editing sounds, music, and video.

What's New in Windows Me?

Windows Me is a natural extension of Windows 98, updating the operating system to include support for all the latest hardware standards and improvements that have developed over the last few years. Windows Me fully supports such technologies as IEEE Firewire, USB, and Universal Plug-and-Play.

There are also a host of new or improved features:

Internet Explorer 5.5 Brings the latest in Web browsers to Windows Me. Internet Explorer 5.5 has the latest security and customization features, and the ability to display all the latest Web content.

Home Networking Wizard Walks you through the process of configuring a PC for network use, making a once-complex process very easy.

Windows Media Player A brand-new, greatly enhanced version of this program offers MP3 and CD audio play, as well as Internet radio and a variety of other audio and video formats.

Windows Movie Maker A handy utility for editing digitized video footage and for combining video or still pictures into multimedia shows with musical sound track and narration.

Internet Connection Sharing Allows you to share a modem or other Internet connection (such as cable modem or ISDN connection) with other PCs in your home. (This feature was included in Windows 98 Second Edition too.)

System Restore Provides a way to return to earlier Windows configurations to correct problems. For example, if you installed a program and then Windows started crashing frequently, you could restore your configuration to the way it was before you installed that program.

INTRODUCTION

Games   Windows Me comes with some new games for your enjoyment, including a challenging new solitaire variation called Spider and several Internet-based games such as Backgammon and Reversi.

Scanner and Camera Wizard   Helps you more easily acquire images from your scanner or digital camera, in most cases allowing you to bypass any proprietary software that came with the device in favor of a standard Windows interface.

How This Book Is Organized

This book presents all the Windows Me features, applications, and configuration options listed in alphabetic order. Most of the entries start with the Windows icon or menu selection you actually use to access the specific feature under discussion. Application toolbars and menu selections are discussed in detail, and configuration options are described in numbered steps for ease of use. A "See also" cross-reference at the end of an entry directs you to other, related entries in the book. If a feature is known by a name other than its official name, you'll find a "See" cross-reference from that name to its official name. You can also access detailed information directly through a complete index.

Conventions Used in This Book

This book uses just a couple of special typographical conventions. Anything that you have to type, such as a command name or a program name, is in **boldface**. Web addresses, also known as URLs, are in a monospace font.

Additional information appears throughout the book in the form of Notes, Tips, and Warnings:

NOTES provide additional information about a specific topic.

TIPS give you clues on how to make better use of a Windows feature, or detail shortcut methods you can use to get the same result.

WARNINGS alert you to the potential dangers of using (or abusing) certain features.

INSTANT REFERENCE

Windows Me

A–Z

Accessibility

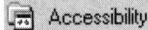 Choose Start ➤ Programs ➤ Accessories ➤ Accessibility to access the Accessibility Wizard, Magnifier, or On-Screen Keyboard.

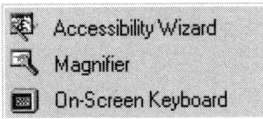

See also Accessibility Options, Accessibility Wizard, Magnifier, On-Screen Keyboard

Accessibility Options

Accessibility Options

Make the computer easier to use for those who are physically challenged—people with reduced vision or hearing impairment, as well as those who have difficulty using the keyboard and the mouse. Choose Start ➤ Settings ➤ Control Panel, and then double-click the Accessibility Options icon to open the Accessibility Properties dialog box.

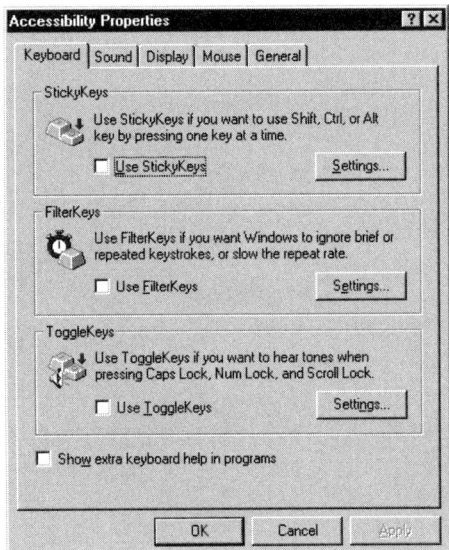

ACCESSIBILITY OPTIONS

NOTE Many of the Accessibility Options have an associated shortcut key that allows you to turn them on and off from the keyboard. These are noted in the following sections.

The Accessibility Properties dialog box has five tabs: Keyboard, Sound, Display, Mouse, and General.

Keyboard Tab

Contains the options that facilitate use of the normal keyboard:

StickyKeys   Allows you to press one of the modifier keys—Alt, Ctrl, or Shift—and another key one at a time instead of simultaneously. If you cannot press two or three keys at a time, you can still handle these keystrokes. To turn on StickyKeys, check the Use StickyKeys box or press the shortcut key and then click Apply. To set more options for StickyKeys, click the Settings button. To set up the shortcut key, click the Settings button to open the Settings for StickyKeys dialog box. Check the Use Shortcut box, and then click OK.

SHORTCUT KEY   Press either Shift key five times.

FilterKeys   Desensitizes the keyboard so that it is less likely to give you unwanted keystrokes. It does this by ignoring repeated or short-duration keystrokes or by slowing the rate at which a keystroke is repeated. These features are valuable if you have tremors or tend to "bounce" keys. To turn on FilterKeys, check the Use FilterKeys box or press the shortcut key and then click Apply. To set more options for FilterKeys, click the Settings button. To set up the shortcut key, click the Settings button to open the Settings for FilterKeys dialog box. Check the Use Shortcut box, and then click OK.

SHORTCUT KEY   Hold right Shift key for 8 seconds.

ToggleKeys   Plays a tone when you turn the Caps Lock, Num Lock, or Scroll Lock keys on or off. You will hear a high-pitched beep when you turn one of them on and a low-pitched beep when you turn one of them off. To turn on ToggleKeys, check the Use ToggleKeys box or press the shortcut key and then click Apply. Click the Settings button to enable or disable the shortcut for ToggleKeys. To set up the shortcut key, click the Settings button to open the Settings for ToggleKeys dialog box. Check the Use Shortcut box and then click OK.

ACCESSIBILITY OPTIONS

SHORTCUT KEY Hold Num Lock key for 5 seconds.

Sound Tab

Contains the options that provide visual aids when Windows generates sounds. These are valuable primarily to people with hearing impairment. The Sound tab has the following options:

SoundSentry Allows you to see when Windows is beeping at you. In place of the audible cue, Windows flashes part of the screen. Click the Settings button to specify which part of the screen you want to flash.

ShowSounds Tells your applications to display a text caption in addition to an audible cue. To select this option, check the Use ShowSounds box.

Display Tab

Allows you to display alternative colors and fonts to make the screens more readable. Check the Use High Contrast box and then click the Settings button to choose the appropriate display options.

SHORTCUT KEY Press Left Alt+Left Shift+Print Screen.

Mouse Tab

Allows you to turn on MouseKeys. When MouseKeys is active, you can use the numeric keypad, which is on the right side of most keyboards, to perform all the functions that can be performed with a mouse. MouseKeys redefines the numeric keypad so that it functions as follows:

- Pressing 5 is the same as clicking the left mouse button once. Pressing 5 twice is the same as right-clicking the mouse.

- Pressing 2, 4, 6, or 8 moves the mouse pointer in the directions indicated by the arrows on the keys.

- Pressing Home, End, Page Up, or Page Down moves the pointer diagonally, according to where each key is positioned on the keypad.

ACCESSIBILITY OPTIONS

- Pressing the minus key (–) and then the 5 key is the same as right-clicking. Pressing the minus key (–) and then the plus key (+) is the same as double-clicking the right mouse button.

- Pressing the plus key (+) is the same as double-clicking the left mouse button.

- Pressing the Ins key is the same as holding down the left mouse button. Press Ins and then press an arrow key to drag a file or a folder.

- Pressing the Del key is the same as releasing the left mouse button after dragging.

- Pressing Ctrl and any number key except 5 jumps the pointer in large increments.

- Pressing Shift and any number key except 5 moves the pointer one pixel at a time.

- Pressing Num Lock switches between MouseKeys and the standard numeric keypad in whatever state (numeric entry or cursor movement) it was in before you started MouseKeys.

SHORTCUT KEY   Press Left Alt+Left Shift+Num Lock

General Tab

Provides additional configuration settings that define how and when the Accessibility Options are available:

Automatic Reset   Sets the length of time that your computer can be idle before the Accessibility Options turn off. This allows two people with different access needs to use the same computer.

Notification   Determines whether the system gives a visual warning, an audio warning, or both when a feature is turned on or off.

SerialKey Devices   Connects an alternative input device to your computer using a serial port. This device sends information to the computer, and that information is then treated as keystrokes and mouse events. Check this box to specify that you want to use an alternative input device and then click the Settings button to select the serial port and baud rate.

See also   Accessibility Wizard, Control Panel, Display, Internet, Internet Explorer, Magnifier, On-Screen Keyboard

Accessibility Wizard

 Gives easy access to several important accessibility features and lets you configure Windows for your level of vision, hearing, and mobility.

Choose Start ➤ Programs ➤ Accessories ➤ Accessibility ➤ Accessibility Wizard to start the Accessibility Wizard. Click Next to begin. Then in the Wizard's first dialog box, press the arrow keys or use the mouse to select the smallest size type that you can read easily and comfortably, and click Next. In the second dialog box, specify the font size you want to use for Windows title bars and menus, and click Next. If you check Use Microsoft Magnifier, a floating window opens at the top of your screen displaying a much enlarged view of the current screen, and you can select the options you want to use with the Magnifier.

In the next dialog box, check those boxes that apply to you, or click the Restore Default Settings button to go back to the original Windows settings. Depending on the choices you make in this dialog box, the Wizard asks you additional questions to help configure your system. Follow the instructions on the screen, and when you complete all the dialog boxes, you will see a final summary dialog box listing your Accessibility selections. Click Finish to put these settings into use, or click Back to refine them.

See also Accessibility Options, Control Panel, Display, Internet Explorer, Magnifier, On-Screen Keyboard

Active Desktop

In Windows, you can use a conventional Windows interface similar to that in earlier versions of Windows, or you can use the Active Desktop. The Active Desktop brings the world of the Web right to the Windows Desktop, allowing you to replace the static Windows wallpaper with a fully configurable, full-screen Web page. The Active Desktop can contain other Web pages, dynamic HTML, and even Java components such as stock tickers and ActiveX controls, and you can add these elements to the Taskbar or to a folder.

To set up your Active Desktop, right-click the Desktop and choose Active Desktop. You will see three options: View As Web Page, Customize My Desktop, and New Desktop Item.

ACTIVE DESKTOP

View As Web Page

Turns on the Active Desktop interface. Selecting this option a second time removes the check mark and turns the Active Desktop off again.

Customize My Desktop

Opens the Display Properties dialog box. You can also right-click the Desktop and select Properties, or if you prefer, choose Start ➢ Settings ➢ Control Panel and select the Display icon. The Display Properties dialog box contains six tabs, but we are concerned with only the two that relate to the active desktop:

> **Background**   Lets you choose an HTML document or a picture to use as your Desktop background. In the Wallpaper box, select the background you want to use, or click Pattern to choose or modify the background pattern. You can also click the Browse button to locate a file or to go directly to a Web site to find the HTML document you are interested in using as a background. To cover your entire Desktop with a small wallpaper image, select Tile from the Display box, or choose Center if you prefer to see the image centered. Click the Apply button to see the effect of your changes before you exit the Display Properties dialog box, or click OK to accept the changes and close the dialog box.

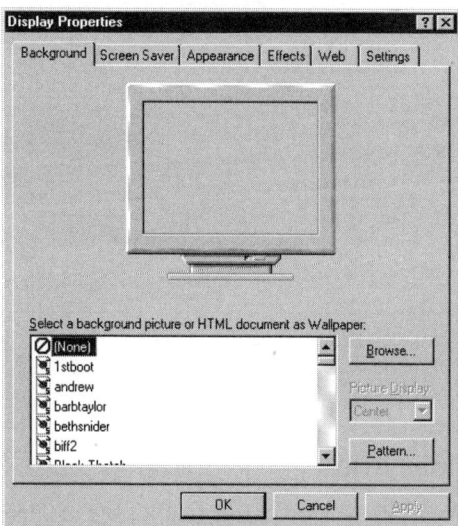

ACTIVE DESKTOP

TIP You can also right-click any Web page graphic that takes your fancy and then click Set As Wallpaper.

Web Lets you select and organize Active Desktop elements. At the top of the tab, you will see a representation of your Desktop, indicating the location of any Active Desktop elements. These same elements are listed in the box below. Make sure that the Show Web Content on My Active Desktop box is selected, so the active elements will appear.

To add a new element, click the New button to run the new Active Desktop Item Wizard, described in the following section.

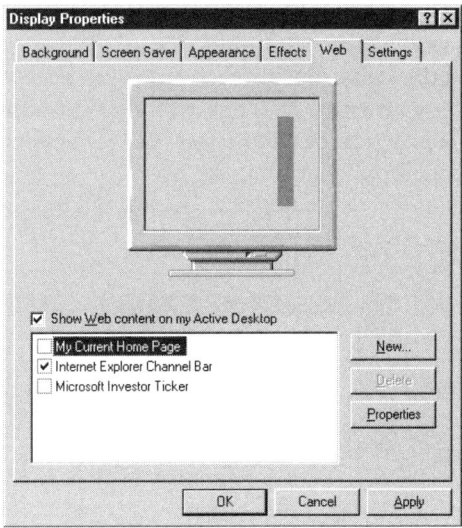

NOTE You can also right-click any link on a Web page, drag it to your Desktop, and then click Create Active Desktop Item Here.

New Active Desktop Item

Runs the New Active Desktop Item Wizard. From here you can enter the URL of a page you want to make into a Desktop item, or you can click the Visit Gallery button to visit the Microsoft Desktop Gallery on the Web, where you can select and download active controls such as a stock ticker, a jukebox, or a clock. On that page, select the active item you want and then click Add to Active Desktop.

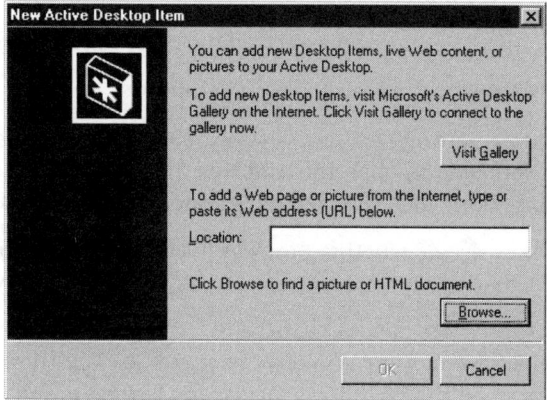

See also   Control Panel, Desktop, Display, Folder Options, Internet Explorer, Start, Taskbar

Add New Hardware

Add New Hardware

Guides you through the process of adding new hardware to your system using the Add New Hardware Wizard. This Wizard automatically makes the appropriate changes to the Registry and to the configuration files so that Windows can recognize and support your new hardware. Be sure you have installed or connected your new hardware before you go any further.

To install a Plug-and-Play device on your system, follow these steps:

1. Turn off your computer.

2. Connect or install the new device according to the manufacturer's instructions.

3. Turn your computer back on to restart Windows. Windows will locate your new hardware automatically and install the appropriate software for you.

If Windows does not find your new Plug-and-Play device, check that it is installed properly, and if you can, confirm that the device actually works and is not defective in some way.

ADD NEW HARDWARE

If the device you want to install is not a Plug-and-Play device, follow these steps instead:

1. Turn off your computer.
2. Connect or install the new device according to the manufacturer's instructions.
3. Turn your computer back on to restart Windows.
4. Choose Start ➤ Settings ➤ Control Panel, and then double-click the Add New Hardware icon to open the Add New Hardware Wizard. Click the Next button. Then click Next again to search for Plug-and-Play devices.
5. You must now decide whether you want Windows to attempt to detect your non–Plug-and-Play hardware or if you want to identify the hardware yourself.

    a. Choose Yes if you want Windows to search for your new hardware. You will be warned that Windows may spend several minutes searching, and that your machine could quit functioning during the search. Click Next. A status monitor indicates the progress of the search. Depending on the amount and type of hardware, the detection process could take several minutes.

    b. If you don't want Windows to try to detect the device, click No and then click Next. A dialog box will prompt you to select the new device from a list. Click the hardware type you are installing, and then click Next.

ADD/REMOVE PROGRAMS

6. From this point on, the dialog boxes depend on the type of hardware you are installing. Simply follow the instructions on the screen to complete the installation.

See also Device Manager, Scanners and Cameras, System

Add/Remove Programs

Add/Remove Programs

Installs or uninstalls individual elements of the Windows operating system itself or certain application programs. Installing or removing application or system software components in this way enables Windows to modify all of the appropriate system and configuration files automatically so that the information in them stays current and correct.

To start Add/Remove Programs, choose Start ➤ Settings ➤ Control Panel, and then double-click the Add/Remove Programs icon to open the Add/Remove Programs Properties dialog box.

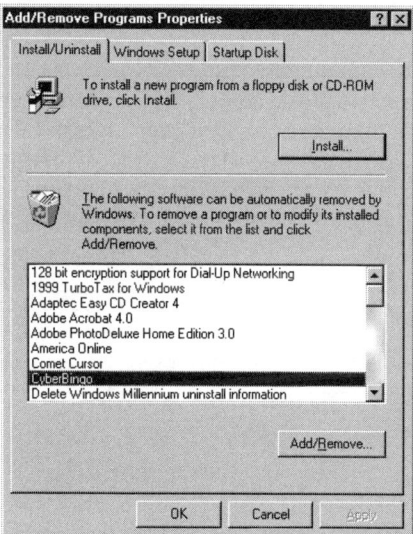

ADD/REMOVE PROGRAMS

Install/Uninstall Tab

To install a new program using the Add/Remove Programs applet, follow these steps:

1. Select the Install/Uninstall tab if it isn't already selected, and then click the Install button.

2. Put the application program CD or floppy disk in the appropriate drive, and click the Next button to display a setup or install message describing the program to be installed.

3. To continue with the installation process, click the Finish button. To make any changes, click Back and repeat the procedure.

To uninstall a program previously installed under Windows, you must follow a different process. The list of programs that have uninstall capability (not all of them do) will appear in the display box of the Install/Uninstall tab. Click the program you want to uninstall, and then click the Add/Remove button. You may see a warning message about removing the application. You will be told when the uninstall is finished. Uninstall may not remove all the files associated with the program. It may leave the program's folder and some data files behind, which you can then delete manually.

NOTE Once you remove an application using Add/Remove Programs, you will have to reinstall it from the original program disks or CD if you change your mind and decide you want to use it again. You can't just restore the files from the Recycle Bin back into their original folders because settings from the Start button and perhaps from the Windows Registry may have been deleted.

WARNING During the Uninstall, you may be asked whether you want to keep or delete a shared file. If in doubt, choose to keep it; it won't hurt anything, and it will ensure that any other programs using that file will still function.

Windows Setup Tab

Some components of the Windows operating system are optional, and you can install or uninstall them as you wish. The Windows Clipboard Viewer is an example. Select the Windows Setup tab to display a list of such components with checkboxes on the left. If the box has a check mark in it, the component is currently installed. If the checkbox is gray, only some elements of that component

ADD/REMOVE PROGRAMS

are installed. To see what is included in a component, click the Details button. Follow these steps to add a Windows component.

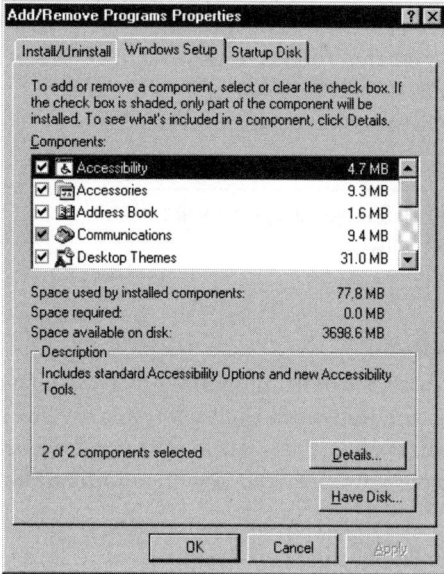

1. Click the feature's checkbox to select it on the Windows Setup tab.

   Or, if the component consists of several elements, click the Details button to display a list of them, and check the boxes you want to install. Then click OK to return to the main listing.

2. Click OK.

3. If prompted, insert the Windows CD and click OK to continue.

To remove a Windows component from your system, follow these steps:

1. Select the component on the Windows Setup tab.

2. Click to remove the checkmark next to the feature.

   Or, if the feature consists of several components, click the Details button, and then remove the checkmark next to the individual pieces of the feature. Click OK to return to the Windows Setup tab.

3. Click OK.

Startup Disk Tab

A startup disk is a floppy disk with which you can start (or *boot*) your computer if something happens to your hard drive. When you originally installed Windows, you were asked if you wanted to create a startup disk. If you didn't do it at that time or if the disk you created then is not usable, you can create one now. Simply insert a disk with at least 1.2MB capacity in the appropriate drive, click Create Disk, and follow the instructions on the screen.

> **NOTE** Almost all floppies these days are double-sided, high-density 3.5" disks with 1.44MB capacity.

Network Install Tab

In some cases, you can also install a program directly from a network using the Network Install tab. If the Network Install tab is not present in the Add/Remove Programs Properties dialog box, this feature may not have been enabled on your computer or on your network. See your system administrator for more details.

If the Install/Uninstall tab is present, your system is currently connected to the network, and you can click Install followed by Next to find the setup program for your network. Follow the instructions on-screen.

Address Book

 Manages your e-mail addresses, as well as your voice, fax, modem, and cellular phone numbers. Once you enter an e-mail address in your Address Book, you can select it from a list rather than type it in every time. To open Address Book, choose Start ➤ Programs ➤ Accessories ➤ Address Book, or click the Address Book icon on the Outlook or Outlook Express toolbar.

Importing an Existing Address Book

Address Book can import information from an existing address book in any of the following formats:

- Windows Address Book
- Microsoft Exchange Personal Address Book
- Microsoft Internet Mail for Windows 3.1 Address Book

ADDRESS BOOK

- Netscape Address Book
- Netscape Communicator Address Book
- Eudora Pro or Lite Address Book
- Lightweight Directory Access Protocol (LDAP)
- Comma-separated text file

To import information from one of these address books, follow these steps:

1. Choose Start ➤ Programs ➤ Accessories ➤ Address Book, or click the Address Book icon on the Outlook Express toolbar.
2. Choose File ➤ Import ➤ Address Book to open the Select Address Book File to Import From dialog box.
3. Select the file you want to import, and click OK.

WARNING If you have Outlook installed, and have the address book set up to automatically share contacts with Outlook, you will not be able to import addresses; the Import command will be unavailable. To stop sharing with Outlook, choose Tools ➤ Options and choose Do Not Share Information Among Microsoft Outlook and Other Applications. Then close the Address Book and reopen it, and you will be able to import.

Address Book Window

The main Address Book window lists the names and e-mail addresses of individuals and groups of individuals, along with business and home phone information if it is available.

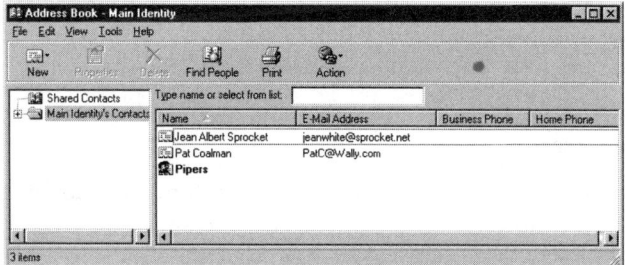

ADDRESS BOOK

The Address Book toolbar contains the following buttons:

 New   Opens a menu containing three options: New Contact, New Group, and New Folder.

 Properties   Displays the Properties dialog box for the selected entry.

 Delete   Removes the selected entry.

 Find People   Opens the Find People dialog box so that you can look up people and businesses using the Internet.

 Print   Prints the address list.

 Action   Opens a menu containing the following options: Send Mail, Send Mail To, Dial, and Internet Call.

Some of these functions are repeated on the Address Book menus, particularly the File, Edit, and Tools menus. The View menu contains options that you can use to configure the toolbar, icons, and entry sort order.

Creating a New Address Book Entry

To add a new entry to your Address Book, click the New button on the Address Book toolbar and choose New Contact, or choose File ➢ New Contact to open the Properties dialog box. This dialog box has the following tabs:

Name   Lets you enter personal information, including the person's first, middle, and last names; a nickname; and an e-mail address.

Home   Allows you to enter additional information about this contact. Enter as much or as little information as makes sense here.

Business   Allows you to enter business-related information. Again, enter as much or as little information as makes sense.

Personal   Allows you to enter personal information, including birthday and anniversary dates.

Other   Offers a chance to store additional information about this contact as a set of text notes.

NetMeeting Lets you enter NetMeeting information such as a person's conferencing e-mail address and server name. If NetMeeting is not installed on your system, this tab will be called Conferencing.

Digital IDs Allows you to specify a digital certificate for use with an e-mail address.

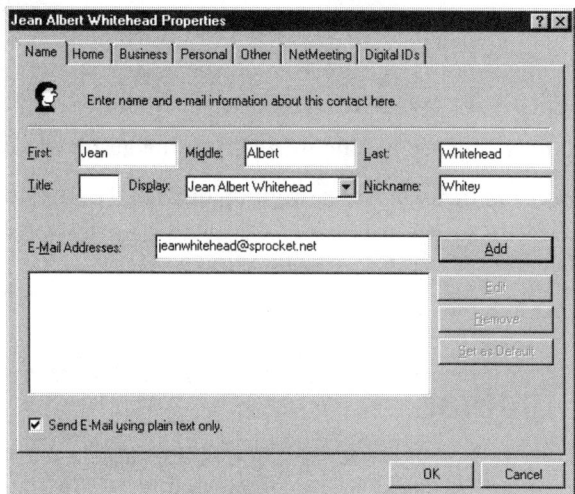

Once you have created a contact entry, when you review an existing contact, you will see essential information presented in a Summary tab in the Properties dialog box.

Setting Up a New Group

You can create groups of e-mail addresses to make it easy to send a message to all the members of the group. You can group people any way you like—by job title, musical taste, or sports team allegiance. When you want to send e-mail to everyone in the group, simply use the group name instead of selecting each e-mail address individually. To create a new group, follow these steps:

1. Click the New button on the Address Book toolbar and select New Group, or choose File ➢ New Group to open the Properties dialog box.

2. In the Group tab, enter the name you want to use for this group into the Group Name field.

3. If you want to add a person to this new group who is not yet in your Address Book, click New Contact to open the Properties dialog box. Enter the information, and click OK.

4. Click Select Members to open the Select Group Members dialog box. Add the names of those people who already have entries in your Address Book into this new group. Click OK when you are done to return to the Properties dialog box.

5. In the Group Details tab, use the Notes field for comments about the group. You might note that they meet at the local bookstore on Thursday evenings at 7:30, for example.

6. When you have finished adding members to the group, click OK.

You will now see the name of this new group displayed in the Address Book main window. To send e-mail to all the group members, select the group name, click the Action button on the toolbar, and select Send Mail.

See also Internet Explorer, Outlook Express, Search

Address Toolbar

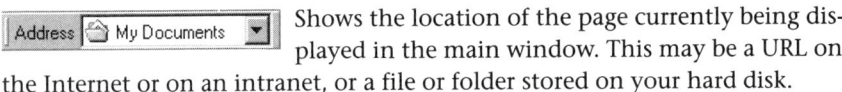

Shows the location of the page currently being displayed in the main window. This may be a URL on the Internet or on an intranet, or a file or folder stored on your hard disk.

To go to another page, click the arrow at the right end of the Address toolbar to select the appropriate entry, or simply type a new location. When you start to type an address that you have previously entered, the AutoComplete feature recognizes the address and completes the entry for you.

The Address toolbar is available in most Windows file management windows, including Explorer, Internet Explorer, My Computer, Control Panel, and others.

See also Explorer, Internet Explorer

Automatic Updates

Automatic Updates

Keeps your copy of Windows Millennium updated with the most recent files from Microsoft. After initial configuration, the feature works behind the scenes, notifying you when an update is ready and installing it, with your approval.

AUTOMATIC UPDATES

After you install Windows, an Update icon appears in your system tray. Click it to view a license agreement for the feature, and accept it.

Then, whenever you are connected to the Internet, the Automatic Update feature periodically checks for updates and downloads them to your PC. When an update is available for installation, the Automatic Update icon reappears in the system tray. Click on it and then follow the prompts to install the update.

You can configure Automatic Update through its icon in the Control Panel. Double-click its icon to open an Automatic Updates box in which you can choose whether to be notified before the download, or whether you wish to turn the feature off completely.

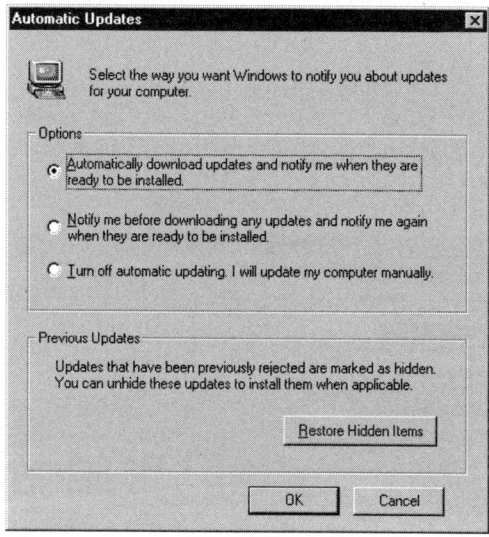

Backup

Previous versions of Windows came with a Backup program, but this version does not. You can, however, buy a third-party backup program, such as BackupExec, at any computer or office supply store.

Briefcase

See My Briefcase

Browse

The Browse button is available in many common dialog boxes when you have to choose or enter a filename, find a folder, or specify a Web address, or URL. Clicking the Browse button or the Find File button opens the Browse dialog box.

You can look through folders on any disk on any shared computer on the network to find the file you want. When you find the file, folder, computer, or Web site, double-click it to open, import, or enter it in a text box.

CALCULATOR

Calculator

Calculator Performs standard arithmetic and scientific or statistical operations. The calculation procedures and the keys available depend on whether you are doing standard or scientific math. Let's take a look.

Calculator Window

Choose Start ➤ Programs ➤ Accessories ➤ Calculator to open the Calculator window. It opens in the view selected when the window was last closed.

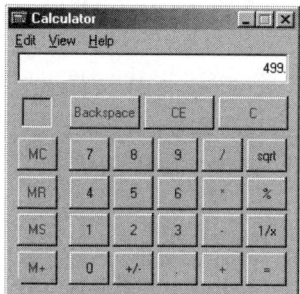

In both Standard and Scientific views, the calculator contains these keys:

Backspace Deletes a single digit.

CE Erases the last entry. You can also press the Delete key on the keyboard.

C Clears a calculation altogether. You can also press the Esc key on the keyboard.

MC Clears a number from the calculator's memory.

MR Recalls the number from the calculator's memory.

MS Stores a number in the calculator's memory, erasing whatever was already in memory. An M appears in the box on the left below the display area.

M+ Adds a number to the number in the calculator's memory.

21

CALCULATOR

TIP Most people click the numbers or operators using the mouse, but if you want to use the numeric keypad for entering numbers and operators, press the Num Lock key on the keyboard. Remember to turn Num Lock off again when you are done.

The Edit and View menus contain simple options. Use Edit to copy and paste, and use View to change from the Standard calculator to the Scientific calculator and back again. As usual, Help is also available.

Performing Standard Arithmetic Calculations

To add, subtract, multiply, divide, and perform other standard arithmetic operations, follow these steps:

1. Enter the first number to be used in the calculation.

2. Click the operator: + to add, – to subtract, * to multiply, / to divide, sqrt to take a square root, % for a percentage of another number, or 1/x to calculate the reciprocal.

3. Enter the next number.

4. Continue to click operators and numbers in the order you want them entered.

5. Click = to get the final answer.

If you want to store a number while you are doing another calculation, use the calculator's memory function. After entering or calculating the first number you want to store, click MS. Do whatever intermediate calculations you want, then click M+ to add result of your calculations to the contents of the calculator's memory. When you are ready to look at the result in the calculator's memory, click MR. You can then clear the calculator's memory by clicking MC.

TIP To subtract a number from the current contents of the calculator's memory, enter the number, click the +/– button to make the number negative, click M+, and then click MR.

Performing Scientific Calculations

To perform scientific calculations such as logarithms, follow these steps:

1. Choose View ➤ Scientific. The Calculator window (shown next) expands to include additional buttons.

22

CALCULATOR

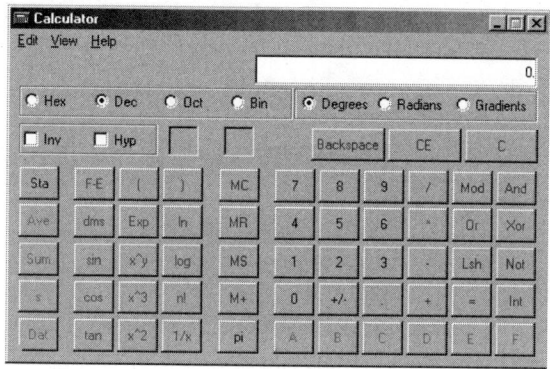

2. Choose a number system in the upper left: Hex (hexadecimal), Dec (decimal), Oct (octal), or Bin (binary).

3. Enter the first number and then click an operator.

4. Continue to enter numbers and operators.

5. Click = for the final result.

TIP To get help on a calculator key, right-click it and then click What's This.

Performing Statistical Calculations

You can apply statistical functions—such as Average, Sum, and Standard Deviation(s)—to a set of numbers entered in Scientific view with the Sta and Dat buttons. Clicking the Sta button opens the Statistics Box, which contains the set of numbers entered with Dat—you must click Sta before you can use the other statistical functions.

Follow these steps to enter a set of numbers that you can then use with the statistical functions:

1. Choose View ➤ Scientific and then enter your first number in the display area.

2. Click Sta to open the Statistics Box and then click Dat to enter the data.

3. Enter the rest of the numbers by typing them over the first number, clicking Dat after each entry.

4. Click Sta to display the statistical data being entered and then click the RET button to return to the calculator.

23

CAPTURING A SCREEN IMAGE

5. When you finish entering your number set, click the statistics functions you want. The results are shown in the display area.

The buttons in the Statistics Box perform the following functions:

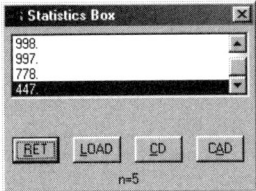

RET Exits the Statistics Box.

LOAD Displays the selected number from the Statistics Box in the Calculator display area.

CD Clears the selected number.

CAD Clears all numbers in the Statistics Box.

Capturing a Screen Image

You can capture screen images—either the entire screen or only the active window—by copying the image to the Clipboard and then pasting it into a document you are creating. Use the following techniques:

- To capture the image of the active window and place it on the Clipboard, press Alt+Print Screen.
- To capture the image of the whole screen, press Print Screen.
- To paste the captured image, open the appropriate document, move the insertion point to the desired location, and choose Edit ➢ Paste or press Ctrl+V.

CD Player

The CD Player from previous versions of Windows has been replaced by the Windows Media Player, an all-purpose player that plays not only CDs but also sound files and video clips.

See Also Windows Media Player, Sounds and Multimedia

Character Map

Displays the set of characters available with a given font. Using the Character Map feature, you can copy special characters not available on a regular keyboard and then paste them into a document. Follow these steps:

1. Choose Start ➤ Programs ➤ Accessories ➤ System Tools ➤ Character Map to open the Character Map dialog box.

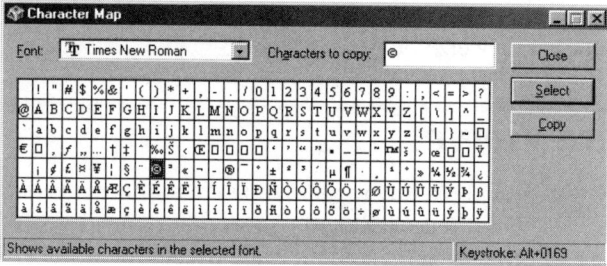

2. Click the Font text box to display a list of the currently available fonts and then select the font you want. Its characters are displayed in the main window.

3. Select the individual characters to copy by clicking a character and then clicking Select (or double-clicking the character). The Characters to Copy box displays the selected characters. Repeat steps 2 and 3 to select more characters.

4. Click Copy.

5. Open the document into which the characters are to be inserted, move the insertion point to the correct location, and choose Edit ➤ Paste, or press Ctrl+V.

TIP To ensure that a character is really the one you want, you can enlarge it by clicking it and holding down the left mouse button.

Clipboard

A temporary storage place for data. You can use the Cut and Copy commands as well as the Windows screen capture commands to place data on the Clipboard. The Paste command then copies the data from the Clipboard to a receiving document, perhaps in another application. You cannot edit the Clipboard contents. However, you can view and save the information stored in the Clipboard by using the Clipboard Viewer, or you can paste the contents of the Clipboard into Notepad.

WARNING The Clipboard holds only one piece of information at a time, so cutting or copying onto the Clipboard overwrites any existing contents. In Microsoft Office 2000 programs, however, there is an enhanced Clipboard that enables you to cut or copy multiple selections.

See also Clipboard Viewer, Notepad

Clipboard Viewer

Provides a way to view and save the contents of the Clipboard. The Clipboard Viewer is not included with the normal Windows installation, but you can add it using the Add/Remove Programs applet.

Choose Start ➢ Programs ➢ Accessories ➢ System Tools ➢ Clipboard Viewer to open the Clipboard Viewer window. It displays the contents of the Clipboard.

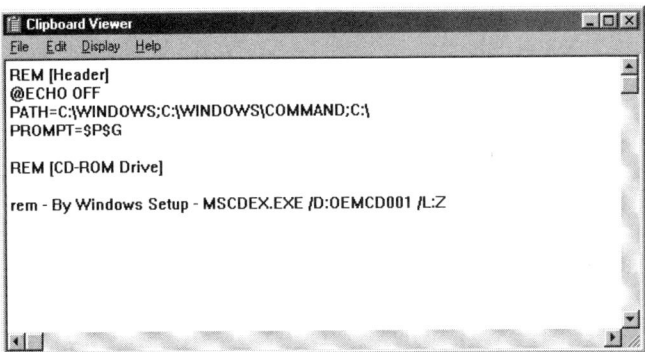

The Clipboard Viewer contains the following menus:

File Allows you to save and open a Clipboard file. Files are saved as .CLP files, which other applications, such as Notepad, cannot easily read.

Edit Allows you to clear the contents of the Clipboard with the Delete command.

Display   Lets you define the current Clipboard contents as text, picture, graphics, or other objects.

See also   Add/Remove Programs, Clipboard

Closing Windows

Closing an application program window terminates the operations of that program. You can close windows in a number of ways:

- Click the Close button in the upper-right corner of the program title bar.
- Click the Control Menu icon (the icon to the left of the program name in the title bar) and then choose Close, or simply double-click the Control Menu icon.

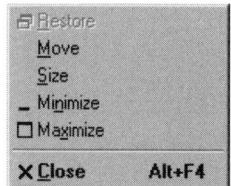

- Choose File ➤ Close or File ➤ Exit within the application.

If the application is minimized on the Taskbar, right-click the application's icon and choose Close, or press Alt+F4.

See also   Shut Down

Communications

   Choose Start ➤ Programs ➤ Accessories ➤ Communications to access all the Windows Me communications tools, including Dial-Up Networking, Direct Cable Connection, HyperTerminal, Home Networking Wizard, and the MSN Messenger Service.

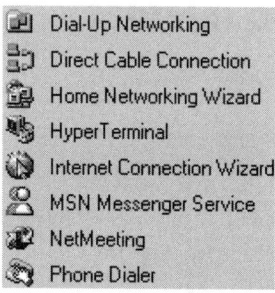

See also   Internet Connection Wizard, Dial-Up Networking, Direct Cable Connection, HyperTerminal, Home Networking Wizard, Modem, Phone Dialer, NetMeeting, MSN Messenger Service

COMPRESSED FOLDERS

Compressed Folders

A new feature in Windows Millennium edition that enables you to view the contents of compressed archives, such as Zip files, as if they were regular folders. This eliminates the need to use a separate unzipping utility program. After you open a compressed archive as a folder, you can simply drag the files out of the folder to extract copies of them.

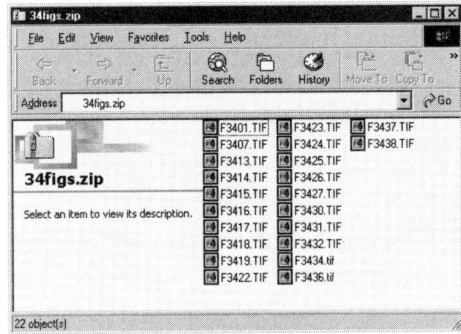

If you double-click a compressed archive file and its content does not appear in a folder, as above, the Compressed Folders feature may need to be enabled in Windows. To do so, use Add/Remove Programs in the Control Panel to add that Windows component.

See Also Add/Remove Programs

Connecting to the Internet

See Internet Connection Wizard

Control Panel

Provides a way to establish settings and defaults for all sorts of important Windows features. To access the Control Panel, choose Start ➤ Settings ➤ Control Panel.

COPYING FILES AND FOLDERS

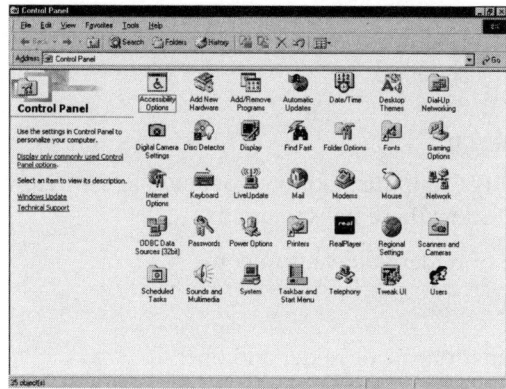

To open an applet, double-click it, or click once on its icon to select it and then choose File ➤ Open.

WARNING Other programs sometimes put icons for their settings in the Control Panel, so the icons you see on your screen may not be exactly the same set as shown here.

The Control Panel window is similar to all folder windows, and you can modify it through the View menu. For detailed information about each Control Panel applet, consult its entry in this book.

See also Folder Options, Printers, Start, Taskbar

Copying Files and Folders

When you copy a file or a folder, you duplicate it in another location and leave the original in place. In Windows, you can copy files and folders in three ways.

Using Drag-and-Drop

To use the drag-and-drop method, you must have both the source and the destination folders open on the Desktop. Press and hold the Ctrl key while holding down the left mouse button and drag the file or folder from one location to another. When the file or folder is in the correct place, release the mouse button and then release the Ctrl key.

COPYING FILES AND FOLDERS

WARNING Be sure to hold down Ctrl. If you do not, the file or folder will be moved rather than copied.

Using the Edit Menu

The Edit menu in My Computer, Explorer, or any folder window provides a Copy and Paste feature. Follow these steps to use it:

1. Select the file or folder you want to copy.
2. Choose Edit ➢ Copy.
3. Find the destination file or folder and open it.
4. Choose Edit ➢ Paste.

You will see the name of the file in the destination folder.

TIP You can select multiple files or folders to be copied by holding down Ctrl and clicking them one after the other. If the files to be copied are contiguous, you can also use Shift to select them.

Using the Right Mouse Button

Right-clicking a file or a folder opens a pop-up menu that you can use to perform a number of functions, including copying. To copy using the right mouse button, follow these steps:

1. Locate the file or folder you want to copy, and right-click to open the pop-up menu. Select Copy.
2. Open the destination folder, click the right mouse button, and select Paste.

You will see the name of the file in the destination folder.

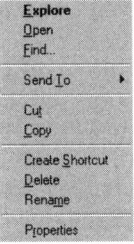

See also Explorer

Copying Floppy Disks

To copy a floppy disk, use the Copy Disk command. The disks used must be of the same type—for example, a 3 1/2" high-density disk must be copied to another 3 1/2" high-density disk. Any information on the receiving disk is replaced with the data from the source disk. Follow these steps:

1. Open My Computer or Explorer and find the floppy disk drives you want to copy to and from.

TIP You can copy to and from the same drive. You will be prompted when to change from the source to the destination disk.

2. Right-click the drive to open the pop-up menu.

3. Choose Copy Disk to open the Copy Disk dialog box:

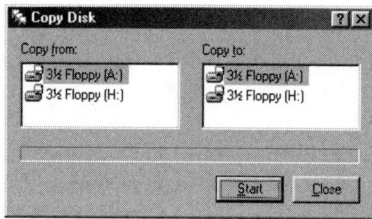

4. On the left, select the disk to copy from. On the right, select the disk to copy to.

5. Click the Start button to begin the copying process. The progress bar at the bottom of the dialog box indicates how much information remains to be copied.

6. If you are working with a single drive, you will be prompted to swap source and target disks as the copy proceeds.

You will see the message "Copy Completed Successfully" when the program has completed copying. Get ready to copy another disk, or click the Close button to close the Copy Disk dialog box.

See also My Computer, Explorer

Creating New Folders

Sooner or later, you will want to add a new folder to a disk or to another folder, and you can do so in Explorer. Follow these steps:

1. In Explorer or My Computer, select the disk or folder in which you want to place a new folder.

2. Choose File ➤ New ➤ Folder. A new folder is added to the disk or the folder you indicated with the name "New Folder" highlighted (shown next).

3. Type a new folder name, something that will act as a reminder as to the files it contains, and press Enter.

You can also right-click the blank part of the Windows Explorer file pane to open a pop-up menu from which you can choose New ➤ Folder.

TIP If you would rather bypass Explorer altogether, you can create a new folder on the Desktop by double-clicking My Documents and then choosing File ➤ New ➤ Folder. Give the folder a new name and then drag it to the Desktop.

See also Explorer

DATE/TIME

Date/Time

Date/Time

The clock that appears in the right corner of the Taskbar displays the system clock, which not only tells you the time, but also indicates the time and date associated with any files you create or modify.

To set the clock, follow these steps:

1. Double-click the time in the Taskbar, or choose Start ➤ Settings ➤ Control Panel and then double-click Date/Time to open the Date/Time Properties dialog box (shown next).

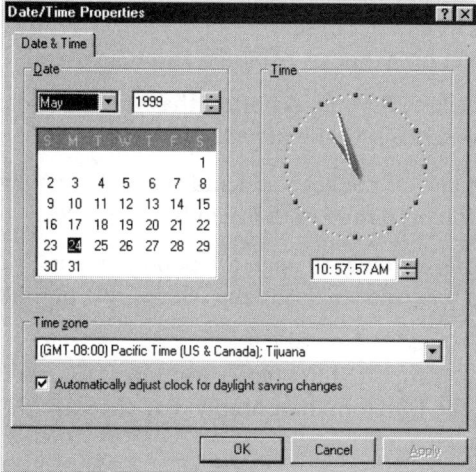

2. To change the time, either drag across the numbers you want to change beneath the clock and type the new time, or highlight the numbers and click the up and down arrows to increase or decrease the values.

3. To change the date, click the drop-down arrow to select the month, use the up and down arrows to change the year, and click the appropriate day of the month.

TIP At any time, you can place the mouse pointer on the time in the Taskbar to display the complete date.

DELETING FILES AND FOLDERS

You can also change the time zone, and automatically adjust the clock for daylight savings time, in the Date/Time Properties dialog box.

NOTE To vary the format of the date and time displayed in the Taskbar, select the Regional Settings applet in the Control Panel.

See also Regional Settings, Taskbar

Deleting Files and Folders

You can delete a file or a folder in several ways. First, select the file or folder you want in My Computer or Windows Explorer, and then do one of the following:

- Choose File ➤ Delete. After you confirm that you want to delete the file or folder, Windows sends it to the Recycle Bin.

- Press the Delete key on the keyboard and verify that you want to delete the selected file or folder. Windows then sends it to the Recycle Bin.

- Right-click the file or folder to open the pop-up menu. Select Delete and then verify that you want to delete the selected file or folder. Off it goes to the Recycle Bin.

- Position the My Computer or Explorer window so that you can also see the Recycle Bin on the Desktop; then simply drag the selected file or folder to the Recycle Bin.

NOTE If you accidentally delete a file or folder, you can choose Edit ➤ Undo Delete, or retrieve the file or folder manually from the Recycle Bin. You cannot retrieve a deleted file or folder if the Recycle Bin has been emptied since your last deletion.

TIP To delete a file without placing it in the Recycle Bin, select the file and then press Shift+Delete. You cannot recover the file if you do this. You will be asked to confirm the deletion.

See also Explorer, Recycle Bin

Desktop

What you see on the screen when you first open Windows. Initially, it contains a set of icons arranged on the left, plus the Taskbar with the Start button across the bottom. As you work with Windows and load application programs, other objects such as dialog boxes and messages boxes are placed on the Desktop.

You can also change the appearance of the Desktop by right-clicking it and selecting Properties. This allows you to change display properties for the Desktop background and screen savers. You can also change the monitor type, font types and sizes, and colors for objects on the screen.

See also

Active Desktop, Control Panel, Display, Folder Options

Desktop Themes

Lets you select a Desktop theme. A theme provides a unified look for your computer's Desktop, icons, font styles, wallpaper, and sounds.

Desktop Themes   Choose Start ➤ Settings ➤ Control Panel and then double-click Desktop Themes to open the Desktop Themes dialog box. To select a new theme, follow these steps:

1. In the Desktop Themes dialog box, choose from the list of themes.

2. Confirm that you want to use all the options listed in the Settings area of the dialog box, or clear the check mark from any options you don't want to use.

3. Click OK to apply the selected portions of the new theme.

4. You can choose Save As to store your newly created theme under a new name so that you can select it again in the future (shown on next page).

Click Screen Saver for a preview of the screen saver used in your chosen theme, and click Pointers, Sounds, Etc. for a preview of the icons, mouse pointer, and sounds used in the theme.

See also   Display, Screen Saver

DEVICE MANAGER

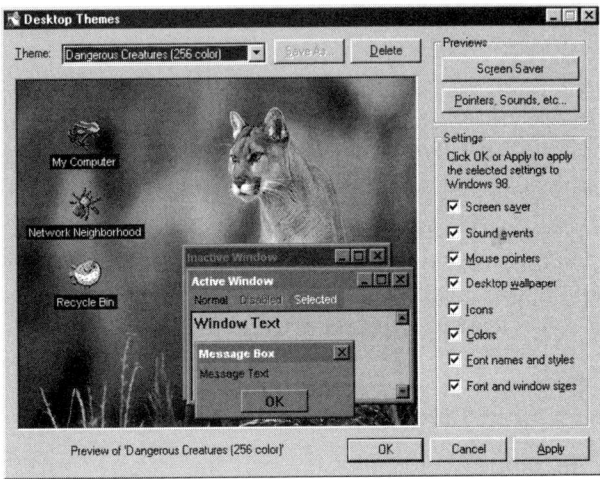

Device Manager

Provides a list of the hardware installed on the PC, along with the status of each device, and offers easy access to each device's properties.

To display the Device Manager, choose Start ➤ Settings ➤ Control Panel and then double-click System, or right-click the My Computer icon on the desktop and choose Properties. Then click the Device Manager tab.

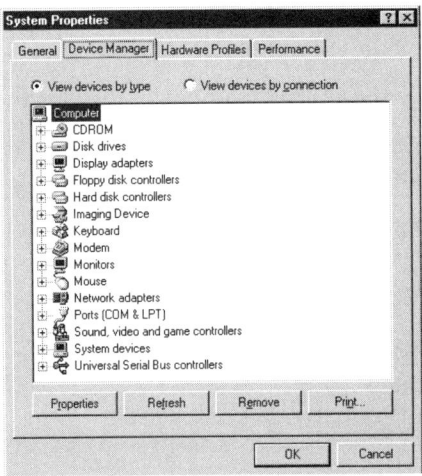

DEVICE MANAGER

Devices are listed by category. Click a plus sign next to a category to see a list of installed devices in it, or double-click the category itself.

Devices that are functioning normally appear on the list with a small icon and their name. If a device has a problem, a yellow circle with an exclamation point appears next to its icon. If a device has been disabled, a red X appears through its icon.

Viewing a Device's Properties

If you are not sure whether a device is functioning, or if you need to know what resources or settings it is using, view its properties. To view a device's properties from Device Manager:

1. Click the device to select it. (You may need to open a category to display the individual device names.)

2. Click Properties. A Properties box for that device opens.

3. Use the controls in the Properties box to specify how the device operates.

Each device has different properties, but almost all have at least a General, Driver, and Resources tab, described in the following sections.

General Tab

The General tab reports the device status. It also contains the following checkboxes:

Disable in This Hardware Profile   Disables the device, freeing up any system resources that were allocated to it. Leave this unmarked in most cases.

Exists in All Hardware Profiles   Makes the installed device available in all hardware profiles, if multiple profiles have been set up. Leave this marked in most cases.

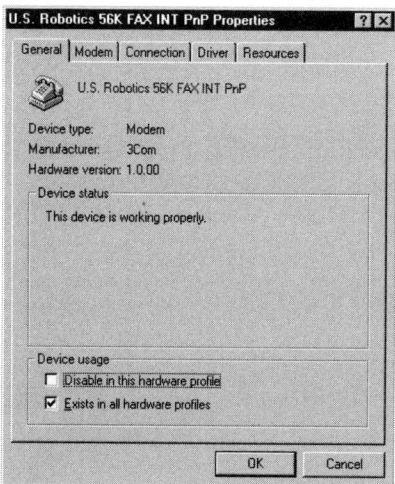

See Also Profiles

Driver Tab

The Driver tab reports information about the driver files in use for the device. It also contains two buttons:

Driver File Details Provides detailed information about the driver files for the device.

Update Driver Runs the Update Device Driver Wizard to locate and install a better driver for the device, if possible. There is usually no need to do this unless you are having a problem with the device.

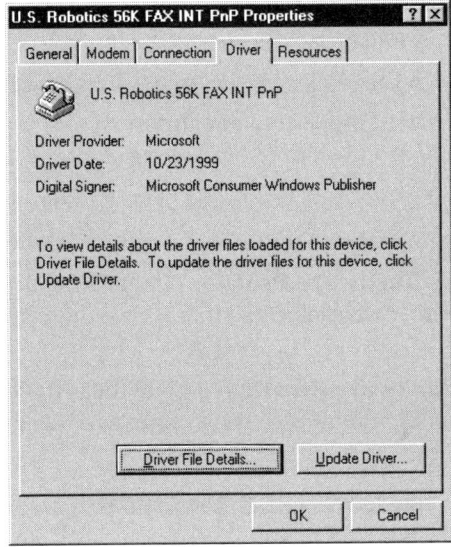

Resources Tab

The Resources tab provides information about the system resources the device is using, such as IRQ (Interrupt Request), I/O Address, and DMA channels. Windows automatically assigns these resources to most devices, so there is no need to change them.

DEVICE MANAGER

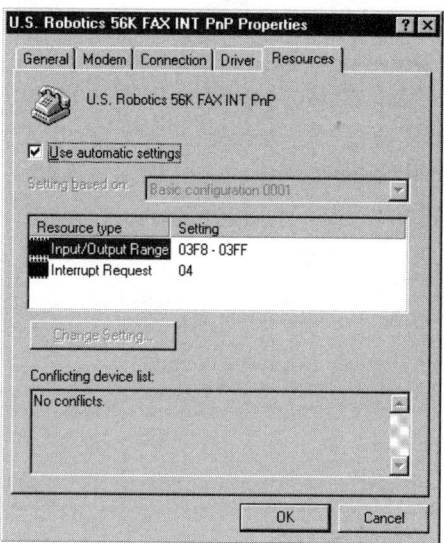

If you do need to change the resource assignments for a device, do the following:

1. Deselect the Use Automatic Settings checkbox.

2. Choose a different configuration from the Settings Based On drop-down list. Find one that reports No Conflicts in the Conflicting Device List section of the dialog box.

3. If none of the settings in step 2 reports No Conflicts, it may be possible to change an individual setting. Click the line in the Resource Type column for the conflicting device, then click Change Setting.

4. Choose a different setting for that resource, and then click OK.

5. Click OK to close the Properties box for the device.

NOTE A message may appear in step 3 that the resource cannot be modified. In that case, check the Conflicting Device List to see what device is at the other end of the conflict, and try to change its setting instead.

DIAL-UP NETWORKING

Removing and Redetecting a Device

Sometimes a problem with a device can be solved by removing the device from Device Manager and letting Windows redetect it. When it is redetected, Windows assigns available resources to it, often eliminating a former resource conflict.

To remove and redetect a device in Device Manager, follow these steps:

1. From Device Manager, select the device to remove.
2. Click Delete.
3. If a confirmation box appears, click Yes.
4. Click Refresh. The device should be redetected.

If the device is not redetected, restart the PC; it might be redetected upon startup.

Dial-Up Networking

 Connects your computer to remote computers, called *servers*, using your modem. This is the most common kind of connection for using the Internet. You use dial-up networking to connect your PC to your Internet Service Provider (ISP).

In addition, if you travel as a part of your job, you can connect your laptop computer to your corporate network right from your motel room. If you telecommute, you can connect to headquarters from your home office. Once you make the connection, you can share information with other computer users back at the office and, at least temporarily, become part of the network to which the remote server is connected.

You can automate the dialing process if you dial one number often, and you can also save telephone numbers and other dialing specifications in a special Dial-Up folder you can use again and again.

NOTE Dial-Up Networking supports conventional modems, ISDN (Integrated Systems Digital Network) connections, and a null-modem connection between serial ports.

DIAL-UP NETWORKING

Installing Your Modem

The first time you open Dial-Up Networking, you will see a different sequence of screens and dialog boxes from those you will see after you install your modem. If you have not installed your modem, the Install New Modem Wizard guides you through the process. You can follow the Wizard, or you can install the modem using the Add New Hardware applet in Control Panel. If you have an external modem, be sure it is connected and turned on before you start.

Creating a New Connection

Once you install your modem, follow these steps to create a new dial-up connection:

NOTE If you have run the Internet Connection Wizard, it prompted you to create a dial-up networking connection, so this may have already been done on your PC.

1. Choose Start ➤ Settings ➤ Dial-Up Networking to open the Dial-Up Networking folder. It displays any connections you already have, as well as the Make New Connection icon.

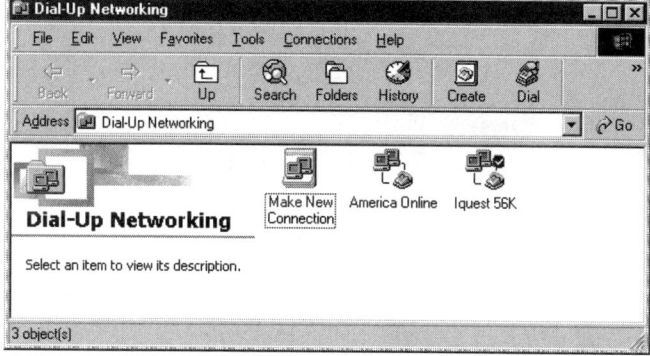

2. Choose Make New Connection to open the Make New Connection Wizard.

3. Type a name to represent the connection you are creating. It makes sense to use the name of the computer you will be accessing using this connection. If you need to change a modem, click the Select a Device drop-down list box. Click the Configure button if you need to change the modem configuration. (If you have not yet installed your modem, you'll also see an Install button here.) Click Next.

41

DIAL-UP NETWORKING

4. Now enter the country code, area code, and telephone number of the remote modem you will be calling. Click Next.

5. Your new connection is created. Click Finish to return to the Dial-Up Networking folder, which now contains an icon for the connection you just created. To dial the connection, simply open the icon representing your new connection.

Dialing an Established Connection

Once you configure a connection to another computer, follow these steps to use it:

1. Choose Start Settings ➤ Dial-Up Networking to open the Dial-Up Networking folder.

2. Double-click the icon for the connection you want to dial to open the Connect To dialog box:

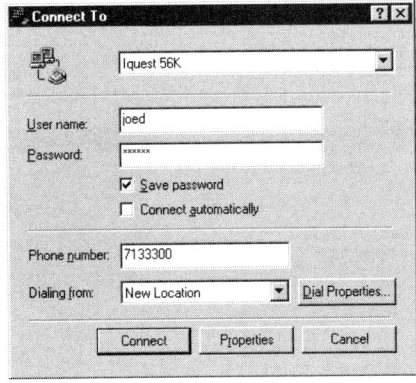

3. If you need to enter a password or change any of the settings, such as the dialing properties accessed from the Dial Properties button, do so now.

4. Click Connect.

With a connection icon selected in the Dial-Up Networking window, you can also click the Dial button on the toolbar or choose Connections ➤ Connect to open the Connect To dialog box.

DIAL-UP NETWORKING

Changing Connection Properties

Sometimes a connection requires non-standard settings in order to work well. Your ISP or network administrator can guide you in determining what properties you need to change for your connection. For example, some connections require a fixed DNS or IP address.

To change settings in the Dial-Up Networking folder, select the connection you want and then choose File ➤ Properties, or right-click the connection and choose Properties to open the Connection dialog box.

General Tab

Use the General tab to change the phone number and the modem or other communications device you want to use with this connection.

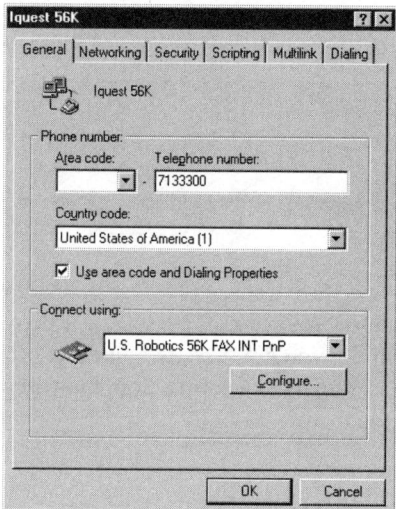

Telephone Number   Change the phone number to dial if needed.

Use Area Code and Dialing Properties   Check this box to include a "1" and the area code when dialing this connection; leave it unchecked if the connection is a local call.

Connect Using   Change the modem to use with this connection if needed.

43

DIAL-UP NETWORKING

Networking Tab

On the Networking tab, you choose what kind of server you're dialing into and what protocols to use. For most Internet connections, the server type is PPP (the default) and the protocol to use is TCP/IP.

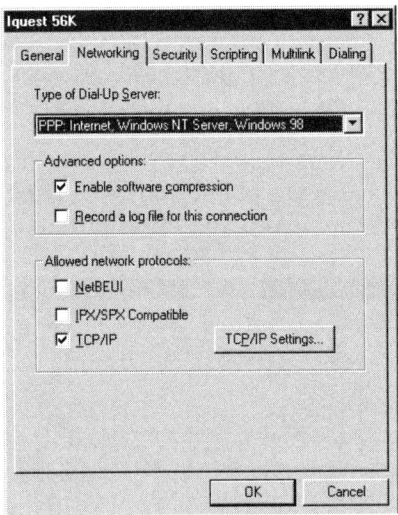

Type of Server   Specifies the type of server that you will access with this connection. If you know the server type, specify it here and you will save time with each connection. If you don't know, Windows cycles through the possibilities until it succeeds in making a connection, but this process does take longer.

Enable Software Compression   Compresses incoming and outgoing data to speed up transmissions.

Record a Log File for This Connection   Creates a text file containing all the status and error messages for the connection session.

Allowed Network Protocols   Allows you to specify the communications protocols you want to use with this connection:

> **NetBEUI** (NetBIOS Extended User Interface)   Connects to Windows NT, Windows for Workgroups, and other Microsoft server products.
>
> **IPX/SPX Compatible** (Internet Packet Exchange/ Sequenced Packet Exchange)   Connects to Novell NetWare products, as well as to Windows NT servers.

TCP/IP (Transmission Control Protocol/Internet Protocol) Connects to Unix systems, corporate intranets, and the Internet. To use TCP/IP, click the TCP/IP Settings button to specify additional protocol parameters. Defining these TCP/IP parameters is beyond the scope of this book, because they will be different for each network server. See your System Administrator for more information.

Security Tab

On the Security tab, you can change your username and password, and specify whether to use any special security options. (Most servers don't require this.)

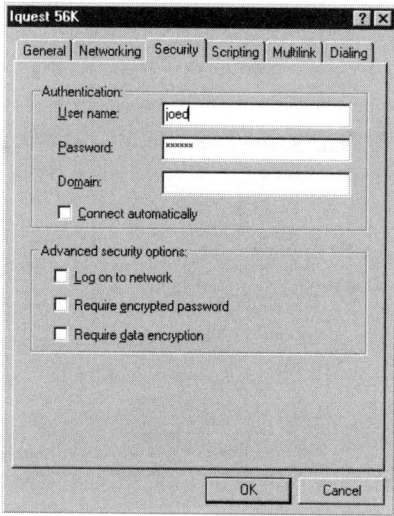

Authentication   Change your username and password here if needed, and enter a domain name if required by the server.

Connect Automatically   Mark this checkbox if you want the connection to be established automatically whenever a program tries to access the server (or the Internet).

Advanced Security Options   Mark any of these checkboxes as needed if the server to which you are connecting uses any of these advanced security measures.

Scripting

Enter a script to use here if your network requires you to use a login script. This is more common with corporate network connections than with Internet access.

DIAL-UP NETWORKING

Multilink

If you have access to additional communications devices, you can select the Multilink tab to add them to this particular connection, possibly increasing your overall connection speed.

Multilink Channel Aggregation (MCA) lets you combine different physical communications channels to increase bandwidth. For example, two lines with 56-Kbps modems, when combined, produce one 128-Kbps channel, which is suitable for high-bandwidth applications such as videoconferencing. This works only if you have a suitable server to connect to, such as a Windows NT Server or a Windows 2000 Server.

Dialing Tab

The Dialing tab enables you to specify how and when this dial-up connection will be established.

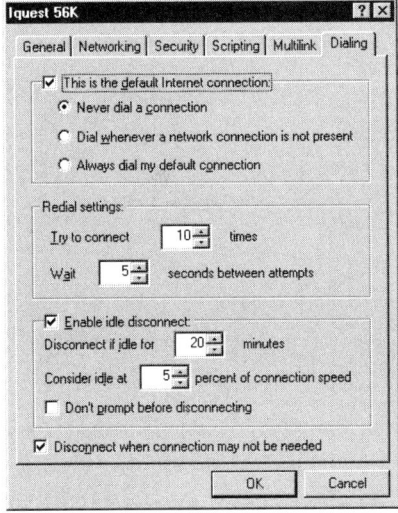

This is the Default Internet Connection Mark this checkbox if this dial-up connection is your primary one for connection to the Internet. Then choose an option button beneath it to specify how automated the connection should be.

Redial Settings Specify how many times the connection will retry itself in the event of a busy signal or connection error.

Enable Idle Disconnect Turn this feature on to allow the connection to disconnect after a certain period of inactivity. This is useful if you are billed by the hour for your Internet service, or if it's a long-distance call.

Disconnect When Connection May Not Be Needed Turn this on to disconnect whenever another source is available. For example, if network access to the Internet becomes available on the PC, it would hang up the modem connection to the Internet.

Changing General Dial-Up Networking Settings

The preceding section discussed making changes to individual dial-up connections. To change the settings for all your connections, from the Dial-Up Networking window choose Connections ➢ Settings to open the Dial-Up Networking dialog box at the General tab.

The General tab has two settings:

Show an Icon on Taskbar after Connected Adds an icon for a connection on the right of the Windows Taskbar. Pointing to this icon displays the current status of the connection.

Show a Confirmation Dialog after Connected Displays a short message confirming that the connection is complete.

The Security tab contains three checkboxes, one to disable the sending of LAN Manager passwords, one that requires a secure Virtual Private Network (VPN) connection, and one to accept only 128-bit security when required (such as for sensitive banking transactions on the Internet).

Connecting to the Internet with Dial-Up Networking

You can use Dial-Up Networking to connect your computer to an Internet service provider (ISP) and thence to the Internet.

1. Establish an account with an ISP in your area. If your company already has a direct connection to the Internet, you don't need this step.
2. Install and configure your modem or other communications equipment. If your company has a direct connection, use the Network applet in the Control Panel to bind the TCP/IP protocol to your network interface card (NIC).
3. Use Dial-Up Networking to create a new connection to the number provided by your ISP.
4. Dial your ISP.

See also Add New Hardware, Internet Explorer, Modem, Network, Internet Connection Wizard

Direct Cable Connection

 Connects your computer with another computer so that you can transfer files between them. The computers are connected by a cable attached to either the serial ports or the parallel ports. Both computers must use the same type of port. You might use a direct cable connection when you connect your laptop to your desktop system at the end of the week to download all the data you have collected.

If the desktop computer is also connected to the company network, Direct Cable Connection allows the laptop to access the network through the desktop system.

NOTE You can also use an infrared connection between two systems. When Direct Cable Connection asks you to specify the port, select the infrared communications port and click the Next button.

Follow these steps to establish a direct cable connection:

1. Connect a cable to either the serial ports or the parallel ports of both computers.

2. Choose Start ➢ Programs ➢ Accessories ➢ Communications ➢ Direct Cable Connection to open the Direct Cable Connection dialog box.

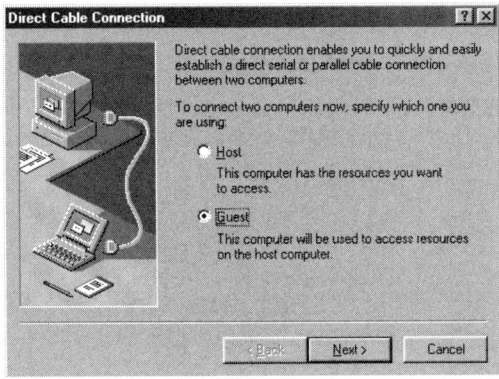

DISK CLEANUP

3. Decide which computer will be the *host* and which will be the *guest*. If you are the host computer, the other computer will access information or services on your computer. If you are the guest computer, you will access the other computer for the services or information you need. Click either Host or Guest and then click Next.

4. Select the port you are using to connect the computers, or click Install New Ports to add a new port. Both computers must use the same type of port (serial or parallel). Click Next, and a final screen tells you that you have successfully set up the computer. If you are a host computer and want guests to use passwords, click Use Password Protection. Click Finish.

TIP You'll want to set up the host computer first and then configure the guest computer.

5. Repeat steps 2 through 4 on the second computer, choosing Guest in step 3.

Once you complete the direct cable connection, the guest computer can access any shared resources on the host computer, including hard disks, CD-ROMs, printers, and faxes, as well as any shared resources on the network to which the host computer is attached.

TIP If you have the choice, use the parallel port with Direct Cable Connection; it will be quite a bit faster. However, you will need to temporarily disconnect the printer from the parallel port if your printer is hooked up to it. Don't forget to turn off both devices before disconnecting any cables.

See also Dial-Up Networking, Infrared, Modems, Network

Disk Cleanup

A quick and convenient way to make more space available on your hard disk. Choose Start ➤ Programs ➤ Accessories ➤ System Tools ➤ Disk Cleanup to open the Select Drive dialog box. From the list, select the drive you want and click OK, and Disk Cleanup begins calculating what can be deleted. Its results appear in a window like the one shown next.

DISK CLEANUP

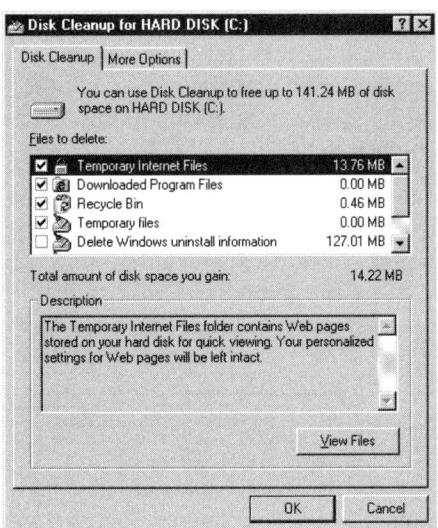

Alternatively, you can open Explorer or My Computer, right-click the disk you want to work with, and then choose Properties from the pop-up menu. On the General tab, click the Disk Cleanup button.

The Disk Cleanup dialog box has two tabs:

Disk Cleanup   Displays the amount of free space that could be recovered by deleting temporary files in certain categories, including Internet files and downloaded program files, or by emptying the Recycle Bin on your Desktop. As you check the boxes to delete files, a running counter tells you how much disk space will be recovered. Click View Files to open an Explorer window so you can check the files a little more closely before you delete them from your hard disk.

More Options   Lets you remove applications or Windows components that you don't use or configure System Restore to use less disk space. Click either of the first two Cleanup buttons to open the Add/Remove Programs applet and then select the Windows Setup tab to remove Windows components you don't use, or select the Install/Uninstall tab to remove application programs you don't use. Click the Clean Up button under System Restore to open the System File Properties box.

See also   Add/Remove Programs, Disk Defragmenter, Maintenance Wizard, Scheduled Tasks

Disk Defragmenter

Keeps your hard-disk performance at its peak by finding fragmented files on your system and rewriting them in contiguous, continuous areas of your hard disk.

As files on your computer grow, they will not fit back into their original locations on your hard disk, so Windows divides the files into pieces and spreads the files over several disk locations. This is how Windows is designed to work and how the system manages constantly changing file sizes. An unfortunate side effect is that, as a file is divided into more and more pieces, finding and retrieving the whole file when you open an application takes longer and longer.

Disk Defragmenter works behind the scenes. Although the files on your hard disk have actually moved, you will still find them in the same folders. Follow these steps to use the Disk Defragmenter:

1. Choose Start ➤ Programs ➤ Accessories ➤ System Tools ➤ Disk Defragmenter to open the Disk Defragmenter dialog box.

2. Choose the disk you want to defragment and click the Settings button to open the Disk Defragmenter Settings dialog box.

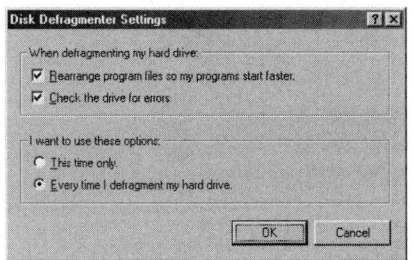

This dialog box contains the following options:

Rearrange Program Files so My Programs Start Faster Tells Disk Defragmenter to position your most frequently used applications files sequentially on the hard disk for faster loading and therefore faster program starting.

Check the Drive for Errors Specifies that Disk Defragmenter test your files and folders for errors before it defragments the drive.

3. You can also specify that Disk Defragmenter use these settings every time you defragment your hard drive or for this time only. Click the OK button when you have made your selections.

4. If you click the OK button, Disk Defragmenter starts work. Buttons are available so that you can stop or pause Disk Defragmenter. Click Show Details to see how Disk Defragmenter is proceeding; once in this display, click the Legends button for an explanation of the symbols in the display. Click the Hide Details button to return to the smaller display.

DISK SPACE

You can certainly perform other work on the computer while Disk Defragmenter is running, but the response time will be much slower, and each time you write a file to your hard disk Disk Defragmenter will start over. The best time to run Disk Defragmenter is while you are out for lunch, or you can use the Task Scheduler to run the program during the night.

See also Maintenance Wizard, ScanDisk, Scheduled Tasks

Disk Space

To find out how much disk space a file or folder occupies, select it (hold down the Ctrl key to select more than one) in My Computer or Explorer. If the window's status bar is turned on in the View menu, the number of objects selected and the amount of disk space they occupy are displayed at the bottom of the window.

Alternatively, you can choose File ➤ Properties or right-click a file or folder and select Properties. The General tab displays the amount of disk space or, in the case of a folder, its size plus the number of files or other folders it contains.

To see how much disk space remains on the entire disk, select the disk name in My Computer or Explorer and then choose File ➤ Properties or right-click and choose Properties. The Properties dialog box displays both the amount of used space and the amount of free space. The status bar of My Computer also displays the free space and capacity of a disk drive.

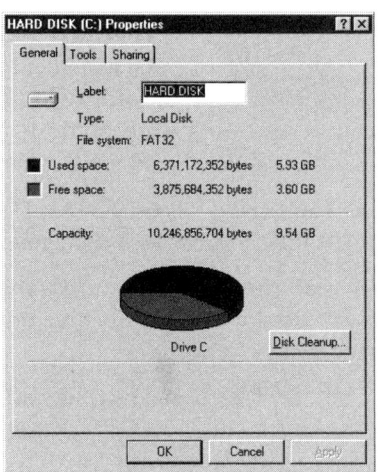

See also Explorer, My Computer

DISPLAY

Display

 Controls how the objects on your screen—patterns, colors, fonts, sizes, and other elements—look. Choose Start ➤ Settings ➤ Control Panel and Display then double-click Display to open the Display Properties dialog box.

The Display Properties dialog box has six tabs: Background, Screen Saver, Appearance, Effects, Web, and Settings.

 TIP You can also open the Display Properties dialog box by right-clicking the Desktop and selecting Properties.

Background Tab

You can choose an HTML document or a picture to use as your Desktop background. In the Wallpaper box, select the background you want to use, or click Pattern to choose or modify the background pattern. You can also click the Browse button to locate a file or to go directly to a Web site to find the HTML document you are interested in using as a background.

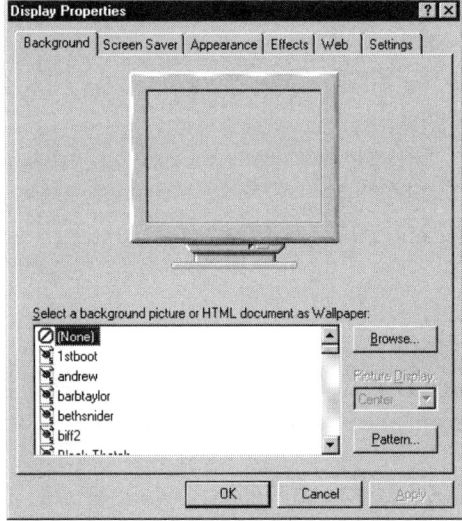

To cover your entire Desktop with a small wallpaper image, select Tile from the Display box, or select Center if you prefer to see the image centered. Stretch stretches the image to fill the desktop with a single copy.

Click the Apply button to see the effect of your changes before you exit the Display Properties dialog box, or click OK to accept the changes and close the dialog box.

DISPLAY

Screen Saver Tab

A screen saver provides a constantly changing image on the screen to prevent a fixed image from being burned into the screen. When activated, the screen saver automatically appears after the computer is unused for a period of time. You can turn on, preview, and select a screen saver from the Screen Saver tab, which contains the following options:

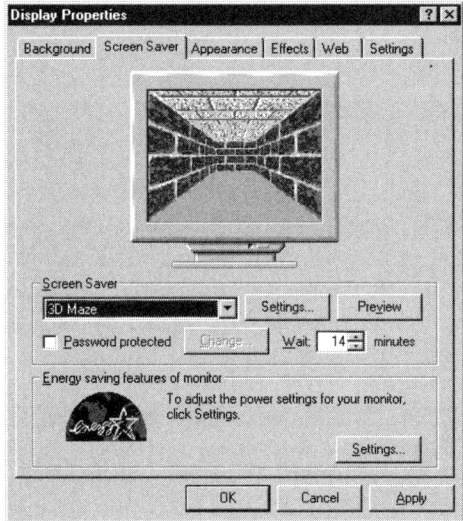

Screen Saver   Lists the available screen savers. Click the one you want to preview in the display box.

Settings   Determines the speed and density of the pattern of the screen saver.

Preview   Displays the screen saver in full-screen view. To return to the dialog box, move the mouse or press any key.

Password Protected   Requires a password for access beyond the screen saver. Windows will not clear the screen saver until the correct password is given.

Change   Allows you to change the password. It is available only when Password Protected is enabled. You must be able to confirm the old password to change to a new password.

Wait   Sets the amount of time before the screen saver is activated.

DISPLAY

If you have a PC and monitor with built-in energy-saving features, click the Settings button to open the Power Management Properties dialog box. You can also access this dialog box directly from the Power Management applet in the Control Panel.

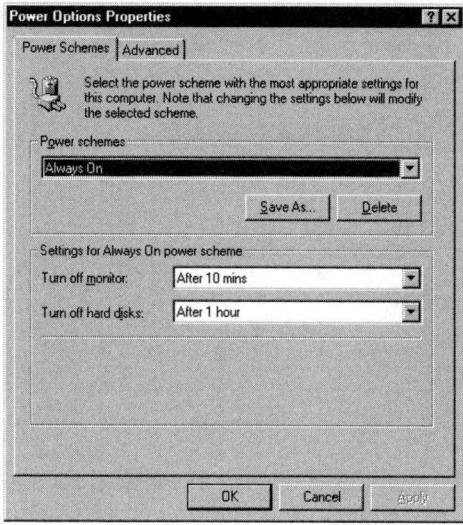

You may not see all the options described here if your hardware does not support these power-saving features.

You can set the length of idle time after which you want Windows to turn off your monitor and your hard disk. Time periods extend from After 1 Minute to Never, which effectively disables the power-management features on your computer.

If you have a laptop that supports the feature, you can click the Hibernate tab to specify that your laptop goes into hibernation when you close the lid. When you put your computer into hibernation, everything in memory is saved to the hard disk so that when you turn your computer on again, all the applications and documents that were open when you closed the lid are reloaded.

Once you choose the appropriate settings for your system, you can save them as a named Power Scheme or, in other words, as a group of preset options. Click the Save As button in the top part of the Power Management Properties dialog box to do so.

DISPLAY

Appearance Tab

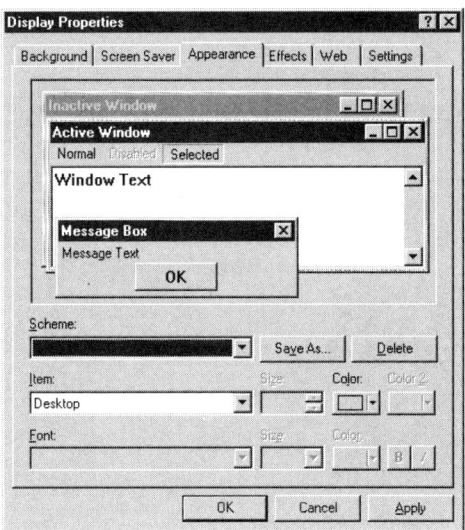

The display window at the top of this tab shows how the major Windows elements, such as window borders, fonts, and colors, are currently configured. You can change all these elements using the following options:

Scheme Lists the preset schemes that change the appearance of windows, dialog boxes, and message boxes. You can select a scheme from the list or create your own.

Item Allows you to select a single item and customize its appearance. Depending on the item, you can change the size or the color.

Font Sets the font for the selected item, when appropriate. The following options are available:

  Size Sets the point size.

  Color Sets the color of the text.

  B Boldfaces the text.

  / Italicizes the text.

Effects Tab

Lets you work with Desktop icons and certain visual effects. Use the Desktop Icons box at the top of this tab to select a new icon or return to the default icon for My Computer, My Documents, My Network Places, and the full and empty Recycle Bin. You can also specify that your Desktop icons be hidden when the Desktop is viewed as a Web page.

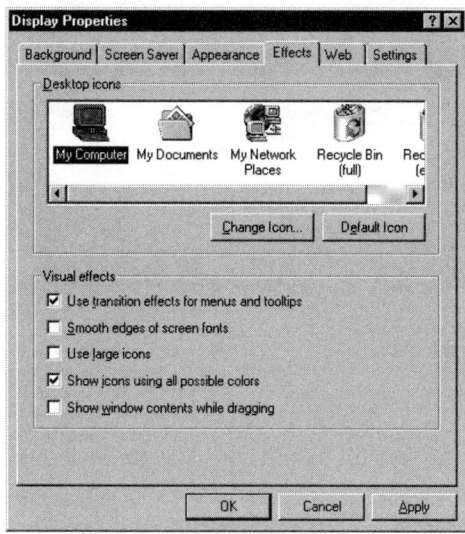

You can also turn the following visual effects on or off: Use Large Icons, Show Icons Using All Possible Colors, Use Menu Animations, Smooth Edges of Screen Fonts, and Show Window Contents While Dragging.

Web Tab

Let's you select and organize Active Desktop elements. At the top of the tab, you'll find a representation of your Desktop, indicating the location of any Active Desktop elements. These same elements are listed in the box below. Check the Show Web Content on My Active Desktop box if you want the active items to be enabled.

DISPLAY

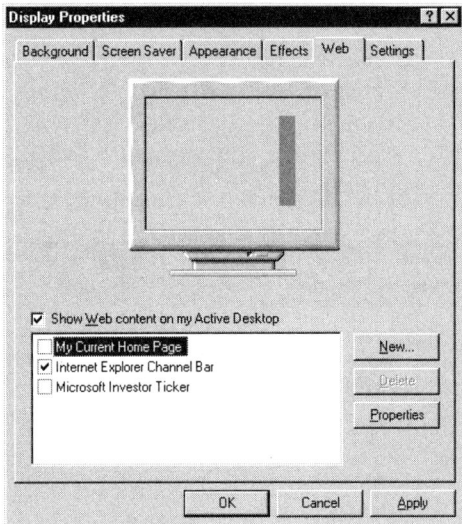

See Also   Active Desktop

Settings Tab

Allows you to vary the resolution and color palette that your monitor and display adapter card use.

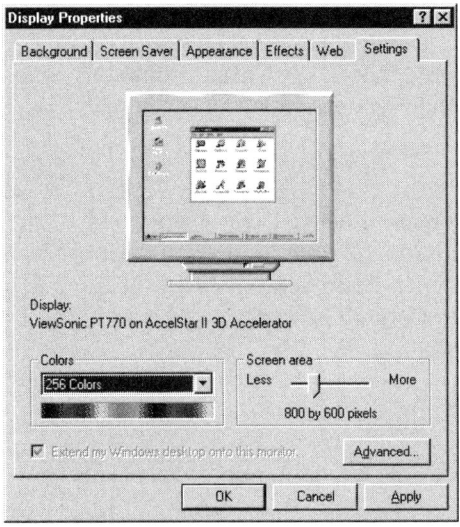

DRAG-AND-DROP

The following options are available:

Colors   Establishes the color palettes that your monitor and display adapter support—either 16-Color or 256-Color for lower resolution monitors and either High Color or True Color for higher resolutions.

Screen Area   Sets the resolution of your monitor, in terms of pixels.

Click the Advanced button to open a dialog box specifically for your own display adapter and monitor. In this dialog box, you will find tabs relating to the adapter card settings, your monitor, hardware graphics acceleration, and color management.

See also   Active Desktop, Desktop, Folder Options, Power Options, System

Documents

Choosing Start ➢ Documents displays a list of all the documents you have created or edited recently. If you select a document from the list, Windows opens the document in the appropriate application, making this a quick way to continue working on an interrupted project.

Windows maintains this list of documents and preserves it between Windows sessions even if you shut down and restart your computer. The last 15 documents are preserved in this list, but some of them may look more like applications or folders than documents.

To clear the list of documents and start the list over, choose Start ➢ Settings ➢ Taskbar and Start Menu. Select the Advanced tab and click the Clear button. Once you do this, only one entry will remain in the list—the shortcut to the My Documents folder.

See also   My Documents, Start, Taskbar and Start Menu

DOS

See   MS-DOS Prompt

Drag-and-Drop

You can use drag-and-drop to move, copy, activate, or dispose of files and folders on the Desktop and in many accessory and application windows. Place the mouse pointer on a file, press the left button, and drag the file or folder to another disk or folder. Position the pointer over the destination and release the mouse button. The result depends on the file or folder being dragged and the destination:

Dragging a file or folder to another folder on the same disk moves it (hold down the Ctrl key if you want to copy the file or folder).

Dragging a file or folder to another disk copies it.

Dragging a file to a shortcut printer icon on the Desktop prints the document.

Dragging a file or folder to the Recycle Bin disposes of it.

See also   Explorer, My Computer

Drive Converter

In previous versions of Windows, there was a Drive Converter (FAT32) program, accessible from the System Tools submenu, that converted a FAT16 system to FAT32, an improved disk format that supports larger hard disk partitions and faster file access.

In Windows Millennium edition, there is still the capability, but it must be run from a command prompt. If you want to convert a hard disk that uses FAT16 to FAT32, follow these steps.

WARNING   You can't do these steps from an MS-DOS prompt started from within Windows; you must start your PC in real mode, without entering Windows's graphical user interface.

1. Restart the PC, and at the Starting Windows message (which roughly corresponds to the single beep you hear at startup), press F8 to display the Startup menu.
2. Choose Command Prompt Only from the menu.
3. When the command prompt appears (C:\>), type **CD \Windows\Command** and press Enter.
4. Type **CVT X:** where *X* is the drive letter to convert.
5. Press Enter.
6. Follow the onscreen prompts to convert the drive.

DRIVESPACE

Note that you cannot convert a drive that has been compressed with DriveSpace or DoubleSpace.

See also DriveSpace, MS-DOS Prompt

DriveSpace

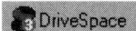

 WARNING Manages drives that have been compressed with DoubleSpace or DriveSpace. (DoubleSpace was an earlier version of DriveSpace that came with MS-DOS version 6.20.) Windows Millennium Edition's version of DriveSpace is for management of existing compressed drives only; it does not compress or uncompress drives. Microsoft is discontinuing the use of DriveSpace compression in Windows because it is incompatible with FAT32, and FAT32 is the preferred file management system for modern drives.

The DriveSpace Dialog Box

Choose Start ➤ Programs ➤ Accessories ➤ System Tools ➤ DriveSpace to open the DriveSpace dialog box.

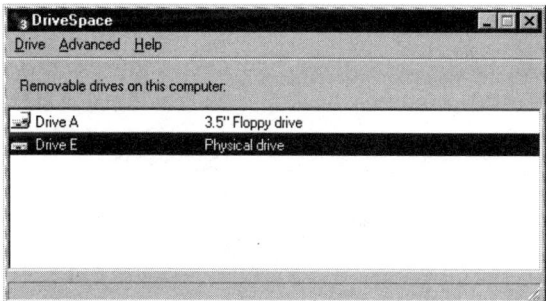

A list of drives appears beneath the menu bar. This list includes removable drives (because you could insert a disk that was compressed into one of them), plus any compressed hard drives. Select the drive you want to work with and choose a command from the Drive menu or Advanced menu to act upon it.

DRIVE SPACE

Drive Menu

The Drive menu contains these options:

Adjust Free Space Allows you to change the distribution of free space between a compressed drive and the host drive. This command appears only if a compressed drive is selected.

Format Formats a compressed drive.

Exit Closes the program.

Advanced Menu

The Advanced menu contains these options:

Mount Connects a compressed-volume file to a selected drive. This is used with floppy disks that contain a compressed-volume file.

Unmount Removes a compressed drive from its volume file.

Delete Removes a compressed drive.

Settings Allows you to choose the compression method and whether to automatically mount new compressed devices. See the following section for details.

Refresh Updates the DriveSpace window.

Disk Compression Settings

To look at or change the compression-specific configuration parameters, choose Advanced ➤ Settings to open the Disk Compression Settings dialog box (shown next).

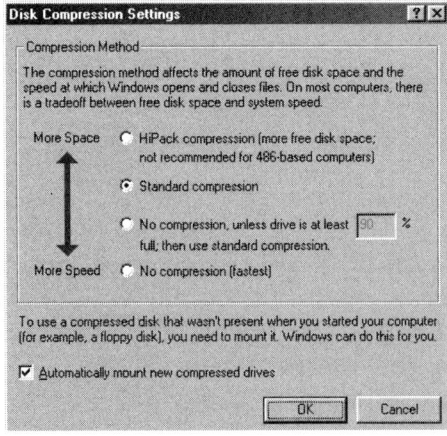

DRIVE SPACE

In this dialog box, you control the tradeoff between speed, which is maximized by using no compression of any kind, and disk space, which is maximized by using the most complex (and therefore slowest) compression techniques. No single answer is correct here; you choose the settings that make the most sense for the way you work with your computer.

The Disk Compression Settings dialog box contains the following options for controlling the compression method:

HiPack Compression   Uses the most compute-intensive compression method to gain the largest amount of free disk space possible on your system.

Standard Compression   Uses a less intensive compression method to provide free disk space.

No Compression Unless Drive Is At Least X% Full   Does no compression until the amount of material stored on the drive reaches a preset level, at which point the standard compression technique is automatically invoked.

No Compression   Provides the fastest speed, but performs no compression.

You can also check a box to automatically mount new compressed drives. You need this when you have a compressed disk that wasn't mounted when the computer was booted—a floppy disk, for example. With this option checked, the disk will be automatically mounted when it is inserted.

See also   Drive Converter, Help, ScanDisk

E-Mail

See Outlook Express

Entertainment

 Choose Start ➤ Programs ➤ Accessories ➤ Entertainment to access the Windows Entertainment applications. These include Media Player, Sound Recorder, and Volume Control.

See also CD Player, Sound Recorder, Sounds, Volume Control, Windows Media Player

Explorer

The Windows Explorer (to use its full name) is *the* place to go when working with files and folders in Windows. The Explorer lets you look at your disks, folders, and files in a variety of ways and helps you perform such tasks as copying, moving, renaming, and deleting files and folders, formatting floppy disks, and so on.

Explorer Menus

To access Explorer, choose Start ➤ Programs ➤ Windows Explorer, or right-click the Start button and choose Explore. You may want to create a shortcut for Explorer on the Desktop or in the Start menu itself since Explorer is used so often.

The Explorer menus give you access to all common functions. However, for some menu selections to work, you may first have to select an appropriate object in the main Explorer window. The type of object you select determines the available options. You may, therefore, not see all these options on any given menu, and you may see some options not listed here. You will also find similar menus in My Computer, the Recycle Bin, and Network Neighborhood.

File Menu

Displays basic file-management options. It allows you to do the following:

- Open a folder or file.
- Explore the contents of a selected computer, disk, or folder.
- Print a file or get a Quick View of the contents of a file (not shown on the menu unless it is available).
- Set parameters for sharing a folder with other users.
- Send a file to a floppy disk, as an e-mail or fax using Windows Messaging, to My Briefcase, or to another destination.
- Create a new folder or shortcut.
- Make a shortcut to a file or folder.
- Delete or rename a file or folder.
- Display a file's properties.
- Close a file or a folder.

If you are working with the Printers folder, you will also see Capture Printer Port and End Capture options.

Edit Menu

Allows you to work with the contents of a folder or file. It allows you to do the following:

EXPLORER

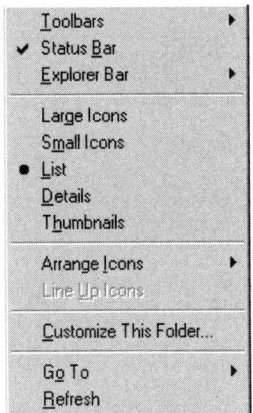

- Undo the previous action.
- Cut, copy, and paste folders and files.
- Paste a shortcut within a folder.
- Select all files and folders.
- Copy or move selected files or folders to another folder.
- Select all files except those already selected, which become deselected.

View Menu

Allows you to change the window to include or exclude the toolbars, status bar, and Explorer bar. You can choose how the files and folders are displayed:

- As a Web page
- With large icons or small icons

- In a list
- With details, describing the size and type of a file and the date modified

You can arrange icons by name, type of file or folder, size, or date created or last modified. You can also arrange icons into columns and rows. Refresh redisplays your screen. Customize This Folder lets you change the appearance of the folder. Go To lets you choose to go back, forward, or up one level.

Favorites Menu

The Favorites menu is the same as the one in Internet Explorer. It lists the favorites you've defined (plus some default ones to get you started). You can add to and manage your favorites list with the Add to Favorites and Organize Favorites commands, respectively.

Tools Menu

Helps you map and disconnect network drives, and synchronize content. It also contains the important Folder Options command, which lets you customize how Windows Explorer looks and operates.

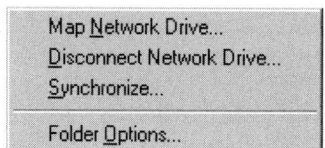

Help Menu

Provides access to the Windows Help system.

EXPLORER

TIP Some functions available from the Explorer menus are also available as buttons on the toolbar.

Explorer Toolbar

The following buttons are available on the standard Explorer toolbar:

 Back Displays the item you last displayed. Click the small down-pointing arrow just to the right of this button to see a list of all the items you have displayed in this Explorer session. You can click an item to go to it directly, rather than clicking the Back button as many times as necessary.

 Forward Displays the item you were viewing before you went back to the current item. Click the small down-pointing arrow just to the right of this button to display a list of items. Click an item to go to it directly.

 Up Moves up the directory tree in the left Explorer window, changing the contents displayed in the right window as it goes.

 Search Opens the Search pane to the left of the main window, which you can use to search for files on your hard disk or for information on the Internet.

 Folders Displays or hides the Folders pane to the left of the file listing.

NOTE If you hide the Folders pane, the window looks just like the My Computer window. In fact, My Computer and Windows Explorer are the same program, except that My Computer doesn't show the Folders pane by default.

 History Displays a pane from which you can view all the places you've been (on the Web) over various time periods (one week, two weeks, and so on). This is great for remembering the name of a site you want to return to.

EXPLORER

Move To Allows you to move the selected files or folders to a different location. Clicking the button opens a browsing window from which you can select the destination.

Copy To Just like Move To, except it copies.

Delete Places the selected file or folder in the Recycle Bin.

Undo Cancels the previous action. The label changes, depending on what you did last—for example, Undo Delete or Undo Copy.

Views Changes the way information is displayed in the right-hand Explorer window. Click the button to display a menu you can use to select the various displays.

Large Icons Displays larger-sized icons representing the contents of the selected folder or disk.

Small Icons Displays smaller-sized icons in a horizontal, columnar list representing the contents of the selected folder or disk.

List Displays the contents as small icons, but in a vertical rather than horizontal orientation.

Details Displays the contents in a detailed list with additional information about the file size, file type, and modification date.

Thumbnails Displays graphic files as small previews, and all other files as icons.

TIP In the Details view, you can change the column sizes by dragging the column break. You can also sort the Details view by clicking a column heading. It acts as a toggle switch. The first time you click, you'll see an ascending sort; the second time, a descending sort.

The Explorer also contains three other toolbars:

Address Displays the location of the item currently displayed by the Explorer. The arrow at the right end of the Address toolbar opens a drop-down list of items. Select one item to open it.

EXPLORER

Links   Displays a set of hyperlinks to various parts of Microsoft's Web site. You can also access these links from the Links selection in the Favorites menu.

Radio   Lets you set the volume and select a radio station to play over your Internet connection.

TIP   You can mix and match all these separate toolbars using the Toolbars, Status Bar, and Explorer Bar selections from the View menu.

You will also see a single status line across the bottom of the main Explorer window. It displays messages about your actions and lists information on disk storage space, including the number of items in a folder and the occupied and free disk space.

Explorer Window

When you run the Explorer, all items that make up your computer are listed in the left pane. Some objects have a plus sign (+) next to them, indicating that the object contains other objects that are not currently visible. To display the contents of such an item in the right pane, click the item, not the plus sign.

When you click the plus sign associated with an object, you display all the subelements, usually folders, in the left window, where they become part of the overall tree structure. The plus sign becomes a minus sign (–) when an object's contents are expanded. This tree structure is a graphical representation of how the files and folders on your system are related; the name of each folder appears just after its icon. If you have more files and folders than will fit in the Explorer window, use the scroll bars—one in the left pane and one in the right—to scroll the display up and down.

EXPLORER

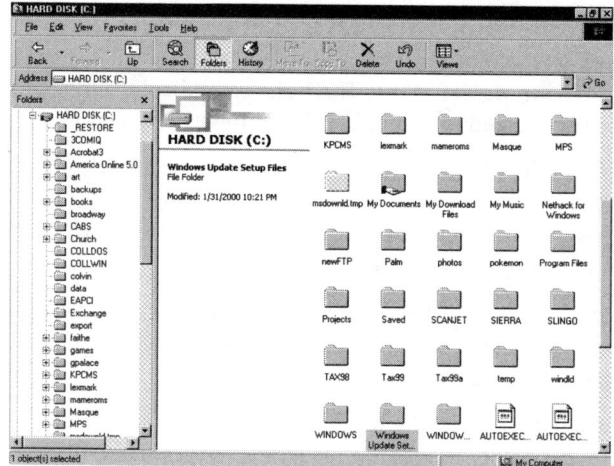

 TIP To collapse everything, click the minus sign next to My Computer.

Customizing a Folder

You can change the appearance of a folder in two ways:

- You can add a background picture (in the same way that you can add wallpaper to your Desktop).

- You can create an HTML document and completely customize the appearance of the folder.

Choose View ➤ Customize This Folder to open the Customize This Folder Wizard with these options:

Choose or Edit an HTML Template   Lets you choose a layout for the folder based on an HTML template.

Modify Background Picture and Filename Appearance   Lets you select a picture that will be displayed as wallpaper when you open this folder.

Add Folder Comment   Lets you enter text that will appear along with the folder name in views where there is room for a comment.

Remove Customization   Lets you return this folder to its original look and feel.

EXPLORER

Selecting a Drive and Choosing a File or a Folder

When you open the Explorer, all the disks and folders available on your computer are displayed in the left pane. The right pane displays the contents of the disk or folder you selected on the left. Follow these steps to find a file or a folder:

1. Scroll up and down using the left scroll bar. On the left, you can see all the disks on your computer, plus those that are shared on your network, and all the folders within each disk. On the right, you will see all the folders and files within the selected disk or folder.

2. If the drive you want is not visible, you may have to expand the My Computer icon by clicking its plus sign. Normally, you will be able to see a floppy disk and at least one hard disk.

3. Click a disk or folder in the left pane to display its contents in the right pane. When a folder is selected, its icon changes from a closed folder to an open one. If the folder you select contains other folders, they will be listed in the right pane, followed by any files within the folder.

4. Once you find the file or folder you want, open it and get to work.

NOTE One of the beauties of Explorer is its ability to drag a file or a folder from the right pane to any object in the left pane. If you do this within the same disk drive, you *move* the object to the new location. If you press Ctrl while dragging, or drag to an object outside the current disk, you *copy* the object you are dragging.

TIP When you right-click a file, the pop-up menu duplicates many functions found in the File and Edit menus, giving you the ability to open the file, send a copy as a fax or e-mail or to another disk, cut or copy it, create a shortcut for it, delete or rename it, or display the Properties dialog box for it. Right-clicking a folder gives you the same options plus Explore (which displays its contents on the right), Find (which opens the Find dialog box), and Sharing (which sets parameters for allowing the folder to be shared). Right-clicking a disk icon also allows you to format a disk.

See also Clipboard, Clipboard Viewer, Closing Windows, Copying Files and Folders, Copying Floppy Disks, Creating New Folders, Favorites, Formatting Disks, Help, Internet Explorer, Mapping Network Drives, My Computer

Favorites

Contains selections you can use to track your favorite Web sites. You can open your favorite Web sites from many places within Windows. You can use the Favorites menu in Windows Explorer, My Computer, Internet Explorer, Network Neighborhood, and Control Panel; even the Recycle Bin has a Favorites menu.

 There is also a Favorites button in most windows that opens the Favorites list as a separate pane to the left of the main window. You can also open this pane by choosing View ➤Explorer Bar➤Favorites.

Add to Favorites

Choose Favorites ➤ Add to Favorites to bookmark a Web site so that you can find it again quickly and easily. Once you place the address, or URL, for the site in this list, you can revisit the site simply by selecting it from the Favorites menu. The result is the same as if you had typed the whole URL into the Address toolbar and pressed Enter.

When you add an address to the Favorites list, you can choose a folder in which to add it. You can have unlimited folders within the Favorites list. See the following section for details.

Organizing Favorites

Choose Favorites ➤ Organize Favorites to group your Web sites into an arrangement that makes sense to you. A single long list is certainly not the most efficient organization.

The Organize Favorites dialog box contains the following buttons:

Create Folder   Lets you create a brand-new folder for storing your favorites.

Move to Folder   Lets you reorganize the folders within your Favorites folder.

FOLDER OPTIONS

Rename Lets you change the name of the selected item.

Delete Removes the selected item.

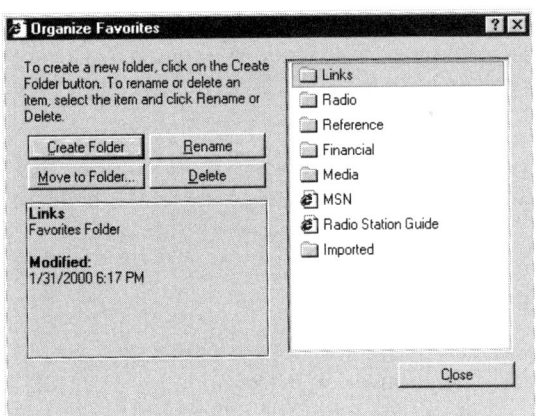

See also Explorer, Internet Explorer

Folder Options

Folder Options...   In Explorer, choose Tools ➤ Folder Options to open the Folder Options dialog box, in which you specify how your folders will look and work. You can also double-click the Folder Options icon in the Control Panel if you prefer. The Folder Options dialog box contains three tabs: General, View, and File Types. When you open the Folder Options dialog box in My Network Places or the Recycle Bin, you will see two tabs: General and View.

General Tab

Defines how the following systemwide settings work on your computer:

Active Desktop Allows you to choose between Active Desktop, in which the desktop acts more like a Web page, and Classic desktop, which acts more like earlier versions of Windows.

Web View Chooses between enabling Web content in folders (such as a description pane to the left of a file listing) and displaying folder content in the traditional Windows manner.

FOLDER OPTIONS

Browse Folders   Lets you choose between opening each folder in a new window and keeping the same window open and changing its content.

Click Items As Follows   Lets you choose between single-clicking and double-clicking as the default method of activating objects. Double-clicking, the default, is the traditional Windows way; single-clicking is more like on a Web page.

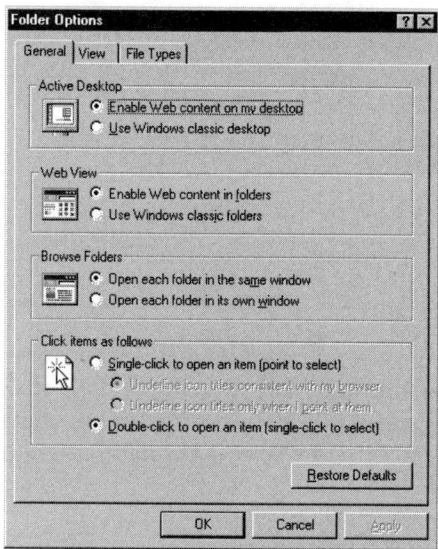

View Tab

Controls advanced settings for files and folders. The Folder Views box contains two options you can use to make all the folders on your system look and work in the same way:

Like Current Folder   Uses the current settings in effect in the View menu (except for the toolbar settings) on all folders on your computer.

Reset All Folders   Uses the original View menu settings in effect when the program was first installed.

FOLDER OPTIONS

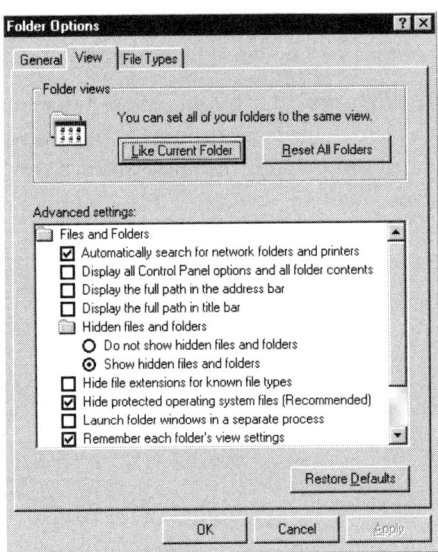

The Advanced Settings box contains a set of checkboxes for certain display options, such as how to treat hidden files, whether file attributes are shown in the Details view, and so on. Check the box to turn that option on, and clear the box to turn it off again. Click the Restore Defaults button to put everything back into its original state.

File Types Tab

Displays all the file types currently registered with Windows. This is how Windows knows which program to use to open specific data files. When you select a file type in the list, the File Type Details box displays a short summary of which filename extension belongs to that type and the name of the program used to open it.

To change or delete one of the existing types, select it in the Registered File Types box, and then choose Change or Delete.

To change a file extension's association (for example, to use a different graphics program to open a certain type of graphic), do the following:

1. Select the file type on the Registered File Types list.

2. Click the Change button to change the new type's properties. The Opens With dialog box appears.

3. Select the program you want that file type to open with, and click OK.

FONTS

WARNING If you change an extension's associated program, you will not be able to delete that file until you have clicked Restore to restore its default association.

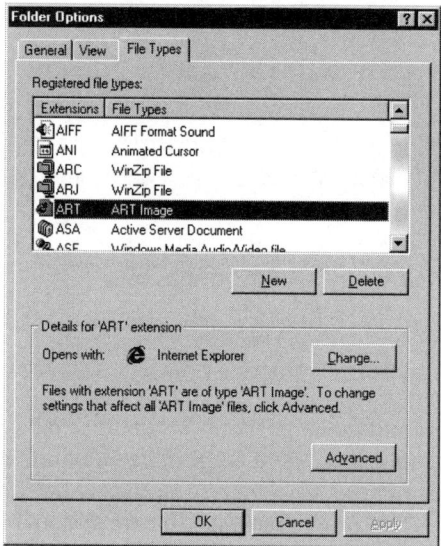

Fonts

Fonts   The styles of type used when Windows displays or prints text. Windows maintains a library of fonts available to all applications that run under it. Choose Start ➤ Settings ➤ Control Panel and then double-click Fonts to open the Fonts folder. This displays all the fonts installed on your computer.

Windows applications use primarily two types of fonts:

- TrueType fonts (represented by a pair of *T*s in the icon)

- Other fonts (represented by an *A* in the icon), such as printer fonts, which are bitmapped, or vector fonts

FONTS

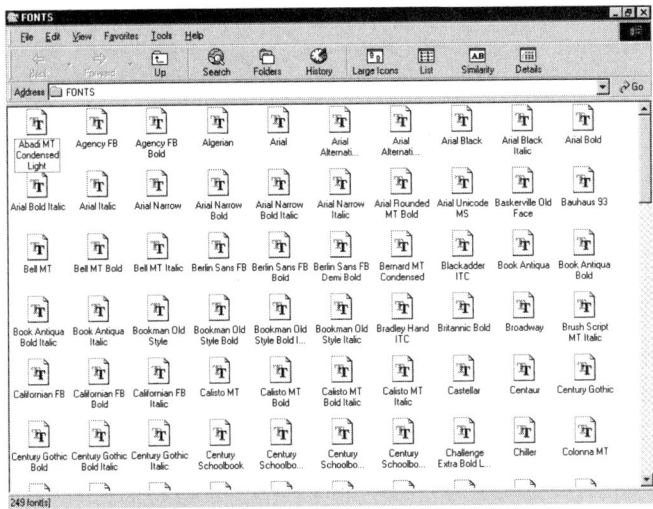

In addition to the standard Large Icons, List, and Details views found in the View menu of the Fonts folder, there is a unique and quite useful view for fonts called List Fonts by Similarity. Clicking the Similarity button on the toolbar displays the same view. This shows the fonts that are reasonably alike, which can be handy if you know approximately how the font should look and want to see variations. Another useful and unique option in the View menu is View ➢ Hide Variations. If you have a lot of fonts, this option helps reduce the selection to only the main fonts by hiding bold, italics, and so on.

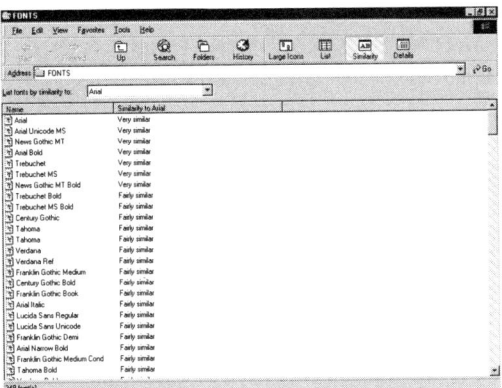

FONTS

Controlling Which Fonts Are Used in Windows

The defaults for the size and type of fonts used in the Windows windows and dialog boxes are set in the Display Properties dialog box. You can vary the font and size for text objects and in menus, message boxes, and title bars.

Right-click the Desktop and choose Properties from the pop-up menu to open the Display Properties dialog box, or choose Start ➤ Settings ➤ Control Panel ➤ Display. You use the Appearance and Settings tabs to control the size of fonts on the screen and the size and typeface of fonts for selected objects on the screen.

Adding a New Font to Your Computer

If you have acquired some new fonts, you can add them to those that come with Windows Me by following these steps:

1. Choose Start ➤ Settings ➤ Control Panel ➤ Fonts to open the Fonts folder.
2. Choose File ➤ Install New Font to open the Add Fonts dialog box.
3. Select the drive and then select the folder that contains the new font.
4. Click the font you want to add. Hold down the Ctrl key and then click to select more than one font.

Displaying and Printing Font Samples

Once you have collected a large number of fonts, remembering what each one looks like can be difficult. Fortunately, the Windows Font Viewer can help. To use it, follow these steps:

1. Open the Fonts folder.
2. Double-click any font in the folder to open that font in the Font Viewer. Open additional Font Viewer windows if you want to compare two or more fonts.
3. To print an example of the font, click the Print button in the Font Viewer; alternatively, right-click the font in the Fonts folder and select Print from the pop-up menu.

See also   Character Map, Display

79

Formatting Disks

Unless you purchase formatted disks, you must format a floppy disk before you can use it the first time. Formatting a new disk places information on the disk that Windows needs to be able to write and read files and folders to and from the disk. Formatting a used disk erases all the original information it contained and turns it into a blank disk, so be sure that you are formatting the right disk.

To format a floppy disk, follow these steps:

1. Place the floppy disk you want to format in the disk drive.

2. From My Computer, select the disk drive containing the disk for formatting and then choose File ➤ Format to open the Format dialog box. You can also right-click the disk drive in My Computer or Explorer and choose Format.

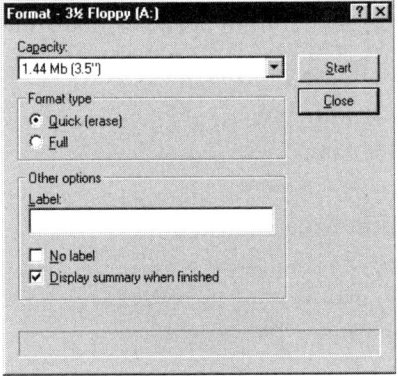

3. Enter or confirm the following specifications:

   Capacity Specifies the maximum amount of data that the disk can hold. To select a different capacity, click the down arrow and then select an option from the list.

   Format Type Controls the type of formatting. Choose Quick (erase) if the disk contains no bad sectors. Choose Full if you want Windows to check for bad sectors and attempt to repair them, or if it is a brand-new, unformatted disk.

   Label Allows you to place a name on a disk so that it can be more easily identified in the future.

No Label Places no name on the disk and removes any that was previously there.

Display Summary When Finished Displays a short report describing the space available on the disk and listing any bad sectors.

4. Click the Start button when you are ready to begin formatting the floppy disk. Clicking Close closes the dialog box without saving the specifications you have made.

See also Explorer

FTP

An abbreviation for File Transfer Protocol, a part of the TCP/IP communications protocol used on the Internet. It is also the name of a program used to transfer files to or from a remote computer using this protocol. FTP supports file transfer for a wide range of types and formats including ASCII, binary, and the IBM format known as EBCDIC. You can also list files and directories. The FTP program in Windows is a text-based program you run from the MS-DOS prompt. It's not pretty, but it certainly works.

To run the FTP program, follow these steps:

1. Choose Start ➢ Programs ➢ MS-DOS Prompt.
2. At the MS-DOS command prompt, type **FTP** and press Enter.

The normal FTP command prompt is `ftp>`. Type **?** or the word **help** to display a complete list of the FTP commands. Although a large number of commands is available, most are used for troubleshooting and need not concern us here. You can become quite an FTP expert with only the few commands shown in Table F.1.

TABLE F.1: Frequently Used FTP Commands

Command	What It Does
open	Establishes a connection to a remote computer
ascii	Sets the file-transfer type to ASCII
binary	Sets the file-transfer type to binary
get	Transfers the specified file from the server to your own computer
put	Transfers the specified file from your own computer to the server
quit	Closes the connection to the remote computer and terminates the FTP session

FTP

Once you close the FTP session, you will find yourself at the MS-DOS prompt once again. To close a full-screen session and return to the Windows Desktop, press Ctrl+Esc; to close an MS-DOS window, simply click the Close button in the top-right corner of the window.

Because many of the files on FTP servers were originally created using one of the variations of the Unix operating system, you may encounter unfamiliar filename extensions, and you may find that some files are compressed to minimize both hard-disk space and download time.

See also Internet Explorer

GAMING OPTIONS

Gaming Options

Gaming Options

Configure and test peripherals such as flight yokes, joysticks, gamepads, and the like. Choose Start ➤ Settings ➤ Control Panel ➤ Gaming Options to open the Game Controllers dialog box, which has three tabs:

Controllers   Lists the controllers on your system along with their current status.

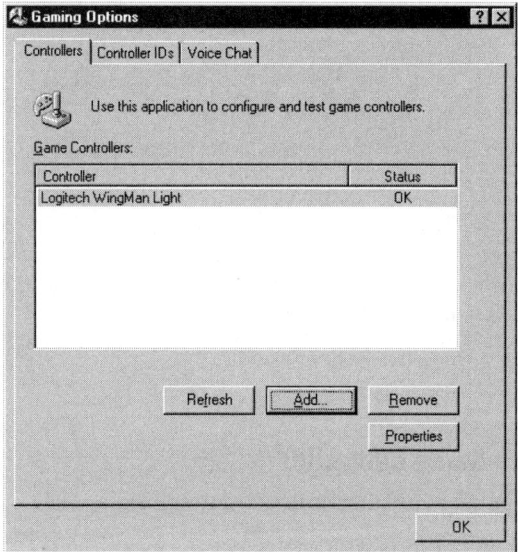

Controller IDs   Lists the ID assignment for each installed controller and enables you to change it if needed.

VoiceChat   Lists any installed games that are DirectPlay compatible, so you can enable VoiceChat for them if desired.

Adding a Game Controller

If your game controller is installed (probably connected to a game port on your sound card), but does not appear on the list, you will need to add it.

1. In the Gaming Options window, select the Controllers tab.
2. Click Add.

83

GAMING OPTIONS

3. Select your game controller from the list that appears.

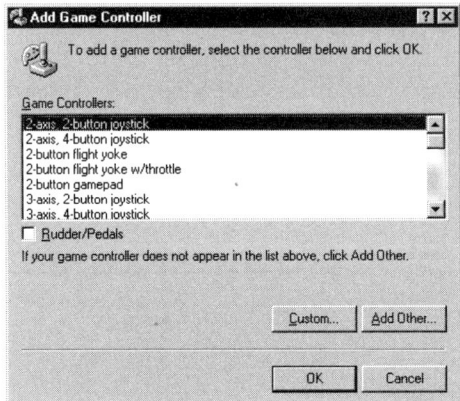

NOTE If your exact model does not appear, you can choose a generic description of it (such as 4-button flight yoke), or you can click Add Other to add drivers for it from a disk that came with the device.

4. Click OK.

Calibrating Your Game Controller

To calibrate your game controller, follow these steps:

1. In the Gaming Options window, select the Controllers tab.
2. Select the device you want to calibrate and then click Properties. The properties for the device appear.
3. Click the Settings tab.
4. Click the Calibrate button.
5. Follow the on-screen prompts to calibrate the controller. Depending on its buttons and movements, the instructions may vary.
6. Click OK to close the game controller's properties.

GAMES

Testing Your Game Controller

After calibrating the controller, you should test it to make sure it is working correctly. To test the controller, do the following:

1. In the Gaming Options window, select the Controllers tab.

2. Select the device you want to calibrate and then click Properties. The properties for the device appear.

3. Click the Test tab.

4. Move the joystick or yoke and note the position of the crosshair in the box.

5. Press the buttons on the controller and note whether the button indicators light up on-screen.

6. If the test is successful, click OK. If not, return to step 3 of the preceding set of steps. (Calibrating Your Controller)

Games

Windows Millennium edition includes many more games than earlier versions of Windows. Not only are the old favorites included (Solitaire, Minesweeper, Hearts) but also a whole group of Internet games such as Backgammon and Reversi, so you can play online against opponents all over the world.

To get to the games, choose Start ➤ Programs ➤ Games, and then click the game you want to play. If you get stuck, click Help for instructions on how to play.

If you choose one of the Internet games, an MSN Gaming Zone box pops up, offering to connect you to a gaming server. Click Play, and follow the prompts.

HARDWARE

Hardware

See also Add New Hardware

Help

Windows Millennium Edition contains an extensive Help system that provides you with online assistance at almost any time. You can use the Windows Help and Support window to gain access to a huge amount of information.

Choose Start ➢ Help to open the main Help and Support window shown here.

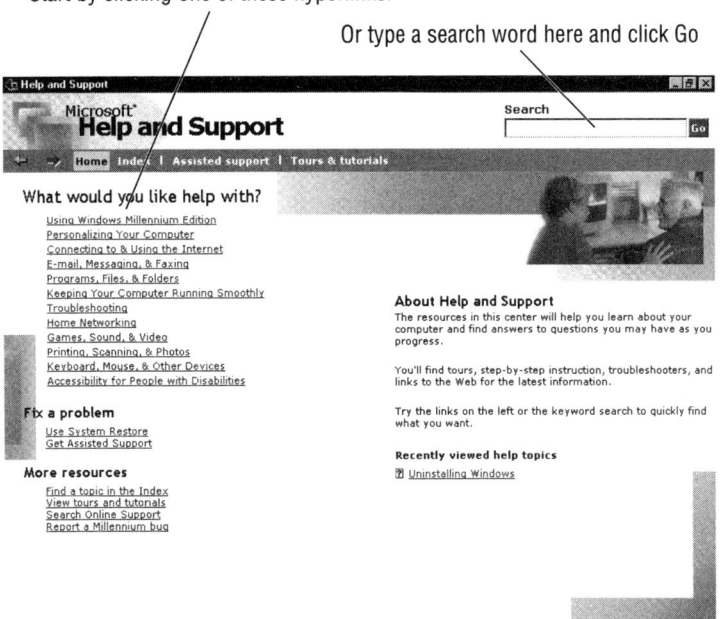

Start by clicking one of these hyperlinks.

Or type a search word here and click Go

TIP Each popular Windows application also contains a Help menu you can use to display information specific to that program.

There are five main areas available in the Help system: Home, Index, Search, Assisted Support, and Tours & Tutorials.

Browsing the Help System

The opening page of the Help and Support system is the Home page. You can return to it at any time by clicking Home on the navigation bar at the top of the window.

From the Home screen, you can start browsing the Help system by topic. If you have used earlier versions of Windows, you may recognize this feature as the Help Contents. Click a hyperlink for the general information you need, then click another hyperlink to further narrow it down until you come to the article you want to read.

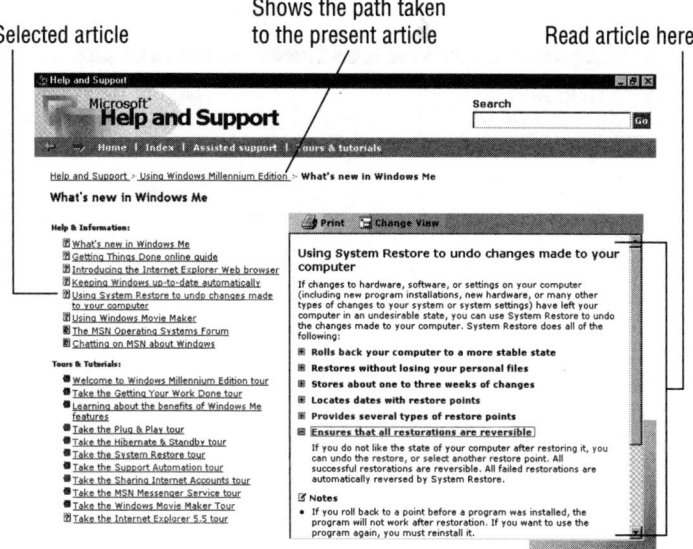

Selected article | Shows the path taken to the present article | Read article here.

Click the plus sign next to a heading in the right pane to expand the text beneath it.

Click the Print button to print the displayed text.

Click the Change View button to toggle between the large default window in the navigation pane on the left and a smaller version which shows only the text window on the right.

The hyperlinks in the navigation pane (the left pane) have symbols next to them to tell you where the hyperlink will take you:

HELP

 Takes you to a Help topic stored on your PC's hard drive.

Takes you to a Tour, which is like an article but multimedia and more involved.

Takes you to a Web page on the Internet.

Searching Help

Search To search the Help system for a certain keyword, type it in the Search box and press Enter or click Go. A list of articles matching that topic appears on the left, and you can click a hyperlink to read an article on the right.

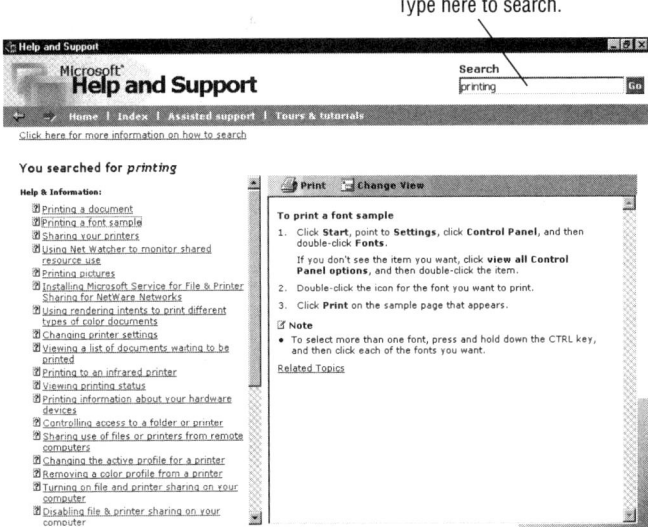

Using the Help Index

Index To look up a term in the alphabetical index, click Index at the top of the Help window. Then type the first few letters of the word to jump to that place on the alphabetical list. When you find the word you want, double-click it, and a list of articles matching that word appears. To display the article you want, double-click it.

HELP

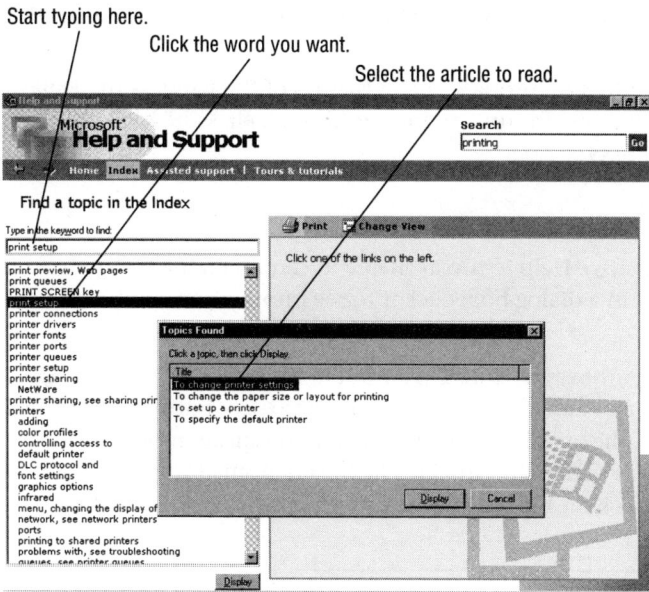

Using Assisted Support

Assisted support Click Assisted Support to display a list of support hyperlinks. These are broken down into three types:

Contact Support Tells you how to contact Microsoft to get help.

Support Communities Lists places online where you can get help from other users.

More Resources Lets you check the status of help requests you've filed with Microsoft (under Contact Support), and check your system information.

Click on any hyperlink to open the associated Web page or Windows dialog box.

Help Tours and Tutorials

Tours & tutorials Windows Millennium comes with a wide variety of tours and tutorials to help you get up to speed on its features. Most of these are multimedia—that is, they involve text, pictures, and sounds—and in some cases videos. If you don't have sound support, you may miss out on part of the benefit.

Click the Tours & Tutorials link at the top of the window to display a list of tours and tutorials. To run any tour or tutorial, click the hyperlink for it and follow the prompts.

Help in a Dialog Box

Context-sensitive Help is also available in certain dialog boxes. You may see a Help button in a dialog box; click it to see information specific to that dialog box.

Other dialog boxes have a Help button in the upper-right corner (look for the button with a question mark on it) next to the Close button. When you click this Help button, the question mark jumps onto the cursor; move the cursor to the entry that you want help with and click again. A small window containing the Help text opens; click the mouse to close this window when you are done.

TIP You can also right-click certain objects to open a small menu containing the single selection What's This. Click What's This to display a small window of Help text for that object.

Home Networking Wizard

 Automates the process of setting up a PC to work in a networked situation, such as a peer-to-peer network in a home or small business. Corporations with large networks will still probably want to set up their networks in custom ways with configuration by professionals, but home users will find this utility more than adequate.

Choose Start ➤ Programs ➤ Accessories ➤ Communications ➤ Home Networking Wizard to start the Wizard. Then answer each question and click Next to go on until you reach the end. The exact steps depend on your answers to the questions.

The Home Networking Wizard will help you install the needed drivers for your network and will set up your dial-up connection to your Internet Service Provider. The Wizard will turn on Internet Connection Sharing for other PCs in your home if needed so that PCs can share Internet access across your network.

Some of the questions it asks include:

- How to connect to the Internet. If you already have a dial-up or network connection, you can choose it; otherwise, you can set up a new one.
- Which network interface card (NIC) should be used to share that Internet connection with other PCs on your home network.
- Whether the connection should be established automatically when another PC wants to use the Internet.
- What name you want to use to identify this PC to the network.
- What workgroup you want the PC to be a part of.
- Which files and printers you want to make available for sharing.
- Whether you need to make a setup disk to set up non-Windows Millennium Edition PCs to be in your home network.

HyperTerminal

HyperTerminal A utility program you can use to connect to another computer—perhaps one that uses a different operating system, such as Unix—or to an information service such as the book catalog at your local library. You can use this type of connection to download or transfer files.

This kind of connection is not as popular as it once was, because the Internet can be used to do almost everything people once did with terminal programs such as HyperTerminal. However, you might occasionally find a system that requires a terminal program instead of the Internet. For example, a company with very high security needs might want you to dial directly into their server instead of going through the Internet.

Creating a New HyperTerminal Connection

To create the phone numbers and specifications for initiating a HyperTerminal connection, follow these steps:

1. Choose Start ➢ Programs ➢ Accessories ➢ Communications ➢ HyperTerminal. HyperTerminal runs, and a Connection Description dialog box appears.

HYPERTERMINAL

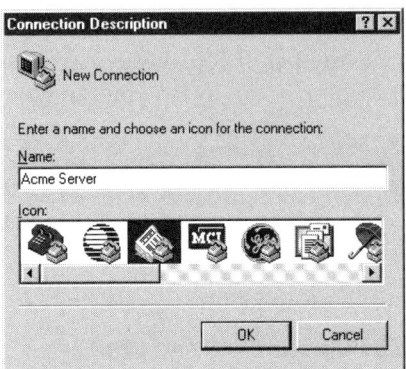

2. Enter the descriptive name you want to assign to this connection and then choose one of the icons from the selection displayed at the bottom of the dialog box. Click OK to open the Connect To dialog box.

3. Verify the country/region and area code, type the telephone number you want to use with this connection, and confirm your modem type. Click OK to open the Connect dialog box.

4. Check the phone number for this connection. If it is incorrect, click Modify to change it. To look at or change any of the settings associated with the phone line or with dialing, click Dialing Properties.

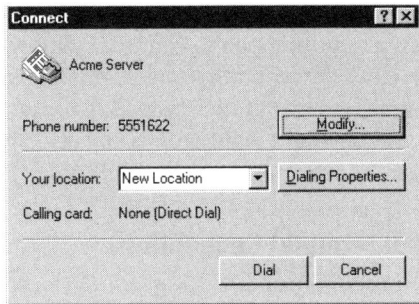

6. When you are ready to make the connection, click Dial. You will be connected to the computer, and a named window for the connection will open. If you do not want to dial right now, click Cancel, and the named window for the connection will be displayed.

HYPERTERMINAL

The next thing that you see in the window will depend on the service or computer you have connected to. You may be asked to select a terminal type, to enter a password, or to make a selection from a menu. When you are finished, use the appropriate command to log off the remote computer before you close the HyperTerminal window. If prompted to save your connection, choose Yes or No. If you choose Yes, you will be able to reopen it later using the following procedure.

Reopening a Saved Connection

To reestablish a connection you have previously set up in HyperTerminal, do the following:

1. Choose Start ➤ Programs ➤ Accessories ➤ Communications ➤ HyperTerminal. HyperTerminal runs, and a Connection Description dialog box appears.
2. Choose Cancel. A blank HyperTerminal screen appears.
3. Choose File ➤ Open. The Open dialog box appears.
4. Choose the saved connection you want, and click Open.
5. If a box appears asking whether you want to save your existing connection, choose No.
6. Choose Dial to redial the saved connection.

Working with a Connection

The HyperTerminal toolbar offers features you can use while connected to a remote PC, or while preparing to connect, as follows:

New   Creates a new connection.

Open   Opens an existing HyperTerminal Connection folder.

Call   Opens the Connect dialog box so that the number can be dialed. Click Dial to proceed.

Disconnect   Terminates the connection.

HYPERTERMINAL

Send Transmits a file to the remote computer or service. Select the protocol from the drop-down list.

Receive Allows you to specify the name of a folder in which to store a file received from the remote computer. Select the protocol used by the sending computer from the drop-down list.

Properties Opens a Properties dialog box that contains two tabs, Connect To and Settings, which you can use to modify information about this HyperTerminal connection.

In addition to the normal menu selections, the menus in a HyperTerminal connection window also contain several unique options, as shown in Table H.1.

TABLE H.1: Unique Options in HyperTerminal Menus

Menu	Option	What It Does
File	New Connection	Opens the Connection Description dialog box in which you can create a new connection
Edit	Copy	Copies the selected contents of the terminal window to the Clipboard
	Paste to Host	Sends the contents of the Clipboard to the remote computer's terminal window
Call	Call	Calls a remote computer
	Wait for a Call	Waits for a call from a remote computer
Transfer	Send File	Sends the selected binary file to the remote computer
	Receive File	Receives the selected binary file from the remote computer
	Capture Text	Sends the contents of a HyperTerminal session to a text file
	Send Text File	Sends the selected text file to the remote computer
	Capture to Printer	Sends the contents of a HyperTerminal session to the default printer at the end of the session

Imaging

Imaging   A Windows application you can use to look at and modify graphical images. You can then use these graphical images as wallpaper for your Desktop, or you can use them in your e-mail messages. You can load images as files, or you can scan them directly into Imaging. You can even convert from one graphics file format to another. Imaging manages three types of files:

TIFF   This is the default file type and the file type that most scanners create. You can edit and annotate TIFF files, you can change their color palette, and you can compress the files to save hard-disk space.

AWD   You can edit and annotate AWD files, but because they are in black and white, you can't change colors. When you add annotations, you must make them permanent when you close the file. AWD files are automatically compressed.

BMP   You can edit and annotate BMP files, but when you add annotations, you must make them permanent when you close the file. You can use only single-page BMP files, and file compression is not available.

Choose Start ➤ Programs ➤ Accessories ➤ Imaging to open the Imaging dialog box. If the program is not listed there, add it with Add/Remove Programs in the Control Panel.

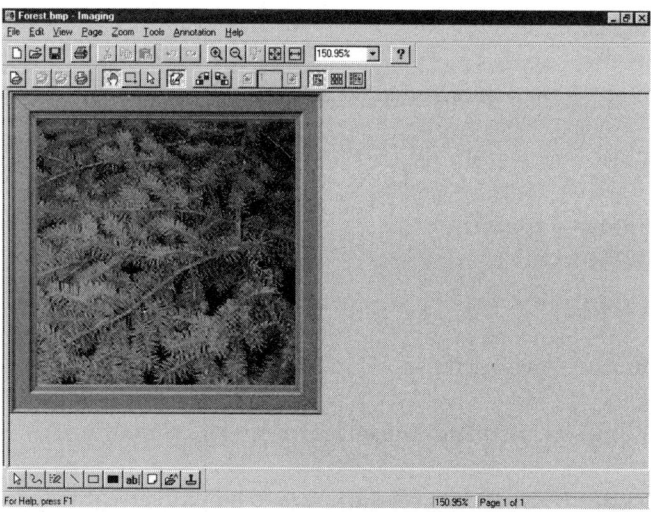

IMAGING

 NOTE The graphics file format defines the way in which graphical data are stored in a file. Imaging can read graphics files in three popular formats: TIFF, AWD, and BMP. A BMP file is a Windows bitmapped image; almost all the Windows applications can create and display images stored in this format. A TIFF file contains a tagged image file format graphic; most screen-capture, illustration, scanning, and word-processing applications can handle TIFF files. AWD files are Windows files that contain a black-and-white graphic used to store fax messages; they cannot contain a color or a grayscale image.

Imaging Toolbars

As you might imagine, Imaging has several toolbars with related functions grouped. To turn each of these toolbars on or off independently, choose View ➤ Toolbars.

Standard Toolbar

Contains those functions associated with opening, closing, and saving images; cutting and pasting; and zooming in and out:

New   Creates a new blank document.

Open   Opens an existing document.

Save   Stores the current document.

Print   Prints the current document.

Cut   Moves the selected item to the Clipboard.

Copy   Copies the selected item to the Clipboard.

Paste   Inserts the contents of the Clipboard in the upper-left corner of the window.

Undo   Reverses the last action.

Redo   Reverses the last Undo action.

Zoom In   Expands the image to twice its current size.

Zoom Out   Contracts the image to half its current size.

IMAGING

Zoom to Selection   Zooms in on the current selection.

Best Fit   Scales the image to fit the window.

Fit to Width   Scales the image to fit the width of the window.

Zoom   Selects a predefined zoom factor.

Help   Opens the Help system for the program.

Imaging Toolbar

Contains the buttons that let you work with your image and with the other toolbars:

Scan New   Opens your scanner's interface to scan a new picture.

Insert Scanned Page   Uses your scanner's interface to scan a new picture and insert it in the current one.

Append Scanned Page   Uses your scanner's interface to scan a new picture, and appends it to the current file.

Rescan Page   Uses your scanner's interface to scan the same page again.

Drag   Selects the dragging tool.

Select Image   Selects the Image Selection tool.

Annotation Selection   Selects the Annotation Selection button on the Annotation toolbar.

Annotation Toolbar   Displays or hides the Annotation toolbar.

Rotate Left   Rotates the current image 90 degrees to the left.

Rotate Right   Rotates the current image 90 degrees to the right.

Previous Page   Displays the previous page in sequence.

Page   Displays the specified page.

Next Page   Displays the next page in sequence.

IMAGING

 One Page View   Displays the current document one page at a time.

 Thumbnail View   Displays the pages of the current document as a set of thumbnails. A thumbnail is a small image used as a preview before displaying the full-sized image.

Page and Thumbnail View   Displays the pages of the current document as pages and as a set of thumbnails.

NOTE   When you right-click any of the buttons on the Standard, Imaging, or Scanning toolbars, you open a pop-up menu you can use to turn the other toolbars on or off. Similar options are available when you choose View ➤ Toolbars. When you right-click the buttons on the Annotation toolbar, a menu gives you access to a Properties dialog box where you can fine-tune how the Annotation tool works. For example, right-click the Text button and select Properties to open the Text Properties dialog box. Here you can select font type, font size, and font style, as well as color and other effects such as strikethrough or underline.

Annotation Toolbar

Contains a set of annotation and drawing tools:

Annotation Selection   Selects the annotation marks for moving, changing, or deleting.

Freehand Lines   Draws freehand lines.

Highlighter   Creates a highlighter.

Straight Line   Draws a straight line.

Hollow Rectangle   Draws a hollow rectangle.

Filled Rectangle   Draws a solid rectangle.

Text   Places text in the window.

Attach-a-Note   Places a sticky note in the window.

Text from File   Inserts text from a specified file into the window.

Rubber Stamp   Selects the Rubber Stamp tool.

You can think of these annotations as being on a separate transparent overlay on top of the image. You can merge them into a permanent image, but once you do, you cannot edit or change the annotations.

Imaging Menus

Many menu items duplicate functions available from the toolbars. But in addition to the standard Windows menu selections, some Imaging menus contain several options with specific uses, as Table I.1 shows. And as you would expect, the Help menu is always available.

TABLE I.1: Unique Imaging Menu Items

Menu	Option	What It Does
File	New	Opens a dialog box with five tabs you can use to create a new blank document.
	Color Management	Specifies how image colors will appear on your monitor or, if you want to proof colors, how they would appear on another device.
	Send	Lets you include an image as part of an e-mail message.
View	Scale to Gray	Displays black-and-white pages as grayscale (which makes them easier to read).
	Full Screen	Displays the current document as a full-screen image with no window borders, menus, or toolbars. Click the Full icon to return to the normal display.
	Toolbars	Turns the Imaging toolbars on or off.
Page	Properties	Displays the properties associated with the current document.
Tools	General Options	Specifies how documents are initially displayed and whether scroll bars are used.
	Scan Options	Sets the scanner configuration.
	Thumbnail Options	Specifies the size and aspect ratio for thumbnails.
Annotation	Make Annotations Permanent	Merges the underlying image with the annotations.

See also Add/Remove Programs

Infrared

Windows supports infrared communications between two computers, between a computer and the network, and between a computer and a printer. All must be equipped with the appropriate infrared (IR) hardware.

NOTE Infrared communication is a method of wireless transmission that uses part of the infrared spectrum to transmit and receive signals. Data can be transmitted between nodes—for example, a computer and a printer—as much as 80 feet apart along an unobstructed path. Infrared beams cannot pass through masonry walls.

To install the appropriate device driver, follow these steps:

1. Choose Start ➤ Settings ➤ Control Panel ➤ Add New Hardware to open the Add New Hardware Wizard. Then click Next twice to enable the Plug and Play detection.

2. When the Wizard asks whether you want to let Windows search for your non–Plug and Play hardware, click No and then click Next.

3. Select Infrared from the list of hardware types, and click Next to open the Add Infrared Device Wizard. Click Next to begin it.

4. Here you specify manufacturer information about your IR device. If the device is built-in, select Infrared COM Port or Dongle. If you have an adapter, choose the name of the manufacturer and the model for your adapter. Click OK.

5. Choose the infrared transceiver type, and click Next.

6 Choose the COM port it resides on, and click Next.

7. Accept the default virtual COM and LPT ports, and click Next.

8. When prompted by the Add Infrared Device Wizard, click Finish to complete the installation. If the Wizard did not display New Hardware Found messages in step 4, restart your computer. If the Wizard did display the messages, you do not need to restart your computer.

9. To activate the IR device, select the Infrared icon in Control Panel. If there is no Infrared icon, choose View ➤ Refresh, or press F5 to force the icon to appear.

INTERNET CONNECTION SHARING

When a compatible infrared device is within range, a Wireless Link icon appears on the Desktop, and an Infrared icon appears on the taskbar.

To use an infrared connection to transfer files to an infrared-connected source, select the files, then drag and drop them on the Wireless Link icon on the Desktop, or right-click them and choose Send To ➢ Infrared Recipient.

TIP To print to an infrared printer, be sure the printer is within range and is assigned to the infrared printer port; then simply print as you normally would.

See also Add New Hardware, Direct Cable Connection, Copying Files and Folders, Printers

Installing Applications

You can install applications from floppy disks and CD-ROMs using the Add/Remove Programs applet in the Windows Control Panel. You can also choose Start ➢ Run to invoke an individual Install or Setup program.

See also Add/Remove Programs, Run

Internet Connection Sharing

Allows all the client computers on a home or office network to access the Internet through a single host computer and a single Internet connection. The Internet connection can be by conventional analog modem, two-way cable modem, ISDN (Integrated Services Digital Network), ADSL (Asymmetric Digital Subscriber Line), or dial-up adapter.

One easy way to set up Internet Connection Sharing is to run the Home Networking Wizard, described under that heading in this book.

Another way is to use the Internet Connection Sharing Wizard, as described in the following steps:

1. Make sure all the computers are connected to your network.

2. Make sure the Internet connection on the machine containing the modem to share is up and running. Use the Internet Connection Wizard if needed.

3. Install Internet Connection Sharing. To do so, do the following:

INTERNET CONNECTION WIZARD

- Choose Start ➤ Settings ➤ Control Panel, and open the Add/Remove Programs applet.
- Click the Windows Setup tab, click Internet Tools, and click Details.
- Select Internet Connection Sharing, click OK, and follow the instructions in the Internet Connection Sharing Wizard.

When a client connects to the Internet via the Connection Sharing computer, Internet Connection Sharing replaces the client's Internet Protocol (IP) address with the host's IP address, makes the connection, and automatically routes information from the Internet back to the client computer.

See also Internet Explorer, Modem, Internet Connection Wizard, Home Networking Wizard

Internet Connection Wizard

Walks you through the steps of setting up your Internet connection. All you need is an account with an ISP (Internet Service Provider), and you're all set. You can start the Internet Connection Wizard in several ways:

- Click the Connect to the Internet icon on the Desktop of a PC that has no Internet connection set up yet.
- Start Internet Explorer on a PC that has no Internet connection set up yet.
- Choose Start ➤ Programs ➤ Accessories ➤ Communication ➤ Internet Connection Wizard.
- Choose Start ➤ Settings ➤ Control Panel ➤ Internet Options to open the Internet Properties dialog box, and then select the Connections tab and click the Setup button.
- In Internet Explorer, choose View ➤ Internet Options to open the Internet Options dialog box, and then select the Connections tab and click the Connect button.

No matter which method you use, the Welcome dialog box gives you three choices:

I Want to Sign Up for a New Internet Account (My Telephone Line Is Connected to My Modem) Select this first option if you do not

INTERNET CONNECTION WIZARD

already have an account. The Wizard takes you through the steps of finding an ISP and starting an account, and it sets up the dial-up link for you.

I Want to Transfer My Existing Internet Account to This Computer (My Telephone Line Is Connected to My Modem) Establishes a connection to an existing Internet account. Select this option to set up a connection to your existing Internet account or to revise the settings for your current account.

I Want to Set Up My Internet Connection Manually, or I Want to Connect through a Local Area Network (LAN) Allows you to set up your account configuration manually.

Click Tutorial to learn more about the Internet, or click Cancel if you want to close the Internet Connection Wizard without setting up your account.

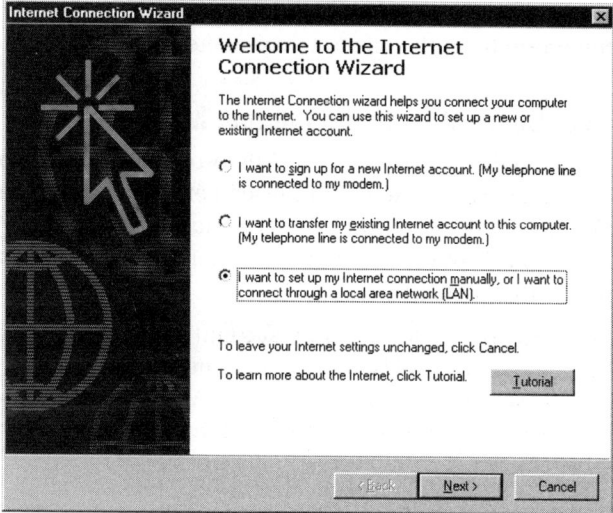

Creating a New Connection to the Internet

To create a new dial-up connection to the Internet, start the Internet Connection Wizard, and then follow these steps:

1. In the opening dialog box, choose the first option to select an ISP and set up a new Internet account, then click Next.

103

2. The Wizard dials out on your modem, connects to the Microsoft Internet Referral Service, and downloads information on ISPs. Not all the ISPs available in your area will be listed here; most of those listed are actually nationwide services.

3. Select one of the ISPs and click Next. The information shown in the next two dialog boxes depends on which of the ISPs you chose in the last step.

4. Enter your name, address, and phone number into the next dialog box and click Next.

5. Choose a billing option from those shown on the screen and click Next.

6. Choose a method of payment, enter the details of your credit card, and click Next.

7. The Internet Connection Wizard connects to the ISP, selects a user ID and password, and completes the configuration of your Internet connection. Follow the prompts on the screen to complete your setup.

Setting Up Your Connection to the Internet Manually

You don't have to use the ISPs listed by the Microsoft Internet Referral Service. If you want to use an ISP whose name is not listed here—perhaps a local ISP known for offering a particularly good service or an ISP recommended by a friend—choose the *third* option on the Internet Connection Wizard opening dialog box and follow these steps:

1. Call the ISP and arrange for a dial-up account that will give you e-mail and Internet access. Some ISPs also assign space on their systems so you can create a small Web site of your own. The ISP will send you details of the servers they operate; you will need that information to complete the steps outlined below.

2. Start the Internet Connection Wizard and, in the opening dialog box, select the third option to set up a connection manually.

3. Choose the method you want to use to connect to the Internet. Most people will check the option I Connect through a Phone Line and a Modem. Click Next.

4 If prompted, choose which modem to use and click Next.

5. In the next dialog box, enter the phone number to dial to make the connection to your ISP. Then click Next.

INTERNET EXPLORER

6. In the next dialog box, enter your username and password information. These will be provided by your ISP—and remember to enter them in the same case, either uppercase or lowercase, as specified by your ISP. Click Next.

7. Enter a name for this connection (choose something easy to remember). Click Next.

8. You'll be asked if you want to set up an Internet e-mail account. Click Yes and then Next to specify whether you want to use an existing account or create a new one. If you opt to continue using an existing account, you will be asked to confirm your e-mail account settings. If you establish a new account, you will have to enter this information from scratch. Click Next.

9. Finally, click the Finish button to complete the configuration and close the Wizard.

See also Internet Connection Sharing, Internet Explorer, Modem

Internet Explorer

Internet Explorer

The application that displays Web pages from the Internet or from your corporate intranet. In many ways, Internet Explorer resembles Windows Explorer; it is a *viewer* that presents information in a structured way. Internet Explorer is an easy-to-use program that hides a large part of the complexity of the Internet and Internet operations.

You can start Internet Explorer in several ways:

- Click the Internet Explorer icon on the Desktop.
- Choose Start ➤ Programs ➤ Internet Explorer.
- Open an Internet file from inside Windows Explorer or My Computer.
- Enter an Internet address, or URL, in the Browse dialog box.
- Open an Internet address from within an Outlook Express e-mail message by clicking the underlined address.
- Choose Go ➤ Home Page in Windows Explorer, My Computer, or any other application that has a Go menu.

105

Internet Explorer Toolbars

The Internet Explorer toolbars—Standard Buttons, Links, Address Bar, and Radio—contain buttons that act as shortcuts to many items in the program's menus. The Explorer Bar, which is actually a special pane in the Internet Explorer main window, contains tools to help you navigate the Internet quickly and easily.

Standard Buttons Toolbar

Contains buttons you can use as shortcuts to some of the most often used Internet Explorer menu items:

Back Displays the page you last displayed. Click the small down-pointing arrow just to the right of this button to see a list of all the items you have displayed in this Internet Explorer session. You can click an item to go to it directly, rather than clicking the Back button as many times as necessary.

Forward Displays the page you were viewing before you went back to the current item. And just like the Back button, when you click the small down-pointing arrow just to the right of this button, you can display a list of items. Click an item to go to it directly.

Stop Cancels the downloading of the current page.

Refresh Updates the current page by downloading it again.

Home Opens your home page—the Web page you see when you start Internet Explorer.

Search Opens the Explorer Bar on the left side of the Internet Explorer window and displays the search options.

Favorites Opens the Explorer Bar on the left side of the Internet Explorer window and displays the contents of your Favorites menu.

History Opens the Explorer Bar and displays the contents of your History folder.

Mail Opens a drop-down list of mail options, including sending a new message or opening your e-mail program to read your new mail.

INTERNET EXPLORER

 Print   Prints the current Web page.

 Edit   Opens the current page in your Web page editor. This button has a drop-down list from which you can choose an editing program.

 Discuss   Connects you to a discussion server. If you have none set up, the Add or Edit Discussion Servers Wizard runs.

 Messenger   Runs MSN Messenger, a chat program. If you have not used it before, it opens a configuration window for the program.

 WARNING   With screen resolutions of 800 × 600 and less, the buttons may not all fit on the toolbar at once. You can click the >> button at the end of the toolbar to see and use whatever extra buttons do not fit. You can also choose View ➤ Toolbars ➤ Customize and choose No Text Labels from the Text Options box. This makes the buttons smaller, so more can fit.

Links Toolbar

All buttons on the Links toolbar are links to different parts of Microsoft's Web site; you can also access these links by choosing Favorites ➤ Links. Microsoft does an excellent job of keeping the information at these links up to date, so you will probably see something different each time you visit.

Address Toolbar

Shows the location of the Web page currently being displayed in the main Internet Explorer window; this may be a URL on the Internet, a URL on your intranet, or a file on your hard disk. To go to another Web site, enter its URL in the Address toolbar and either press Enter or click the Go button at the end of the Address toolbar.

 TIP   When you start to type in an address that you have previously entered, Internet Explorer's AutoComplete feature recognizes the URL and completes the entry for you.

107

INTERNET EXPLORER

Clicking the arrow at the right side of the Address toolbar opens a drop-down list of addresses you have previously entered using the Address toolbar. To open one, select it.

Radio Toolbar

The Radio toolbar lets you connect to a Microsoft Web site where you can choose a radio station to listen to as you work at your computer. Other buttons on the Radio toolbar let you adjust the station's volume, and there is a handy mute button you can use, should the boss put in an unscheduled appearance. To get the full benefit from this Internet Explorer option, you really do need a fast Internet connection (greater than 56K).

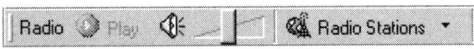

NOTE Windows Media Player also plays radio stations, and it does so with more options and features.

Explorer Bar

When you click the Search, Favorites, or History button on the main Internet Explorer toolbar or select one of these commands from the View ➤ Explorer Bar menu, the Explorer Bar appears as a special pane on the left side of the main Internet Explorer window. The information this pane displays depends on which toolbar buttons you clicked. You can now make choices from the information in the left pane and see the results in the pane to the right.

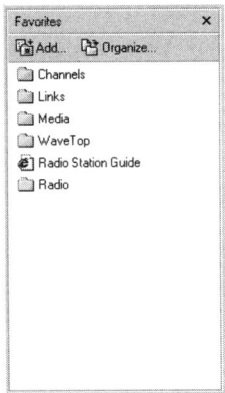

To close the Explorer Bar, click the Close button in the top-right corner of the Explorer Bar, or click the appropriate toolbar button a second time.

INTERNET EXPLORER

Internet Explorer Menus

You can use the buttons on the Internet Explorer toolbars, or you can use menu items to get the job done. The Internet Explorer menus give you access to all the common functions; however, for some menu items to work, you may first have to select an appropriate object in the main Internet Explorer window. The options that become available depend on the type of object you select.

File Menu

Displays basic file and URL management options and allows you to open a file by specifying a name and URL or location. You can save or print the current file, send the current page or its URL as an e-mail message, or create a Desktop shortcut to it. You can also look at the properties for the current object, and choose to work offline. Finally you can use Import and Export to swap lists of favorites (or bookmarks as they are called in the Netscape world) between Internet Explorer and Netscape Navigator.

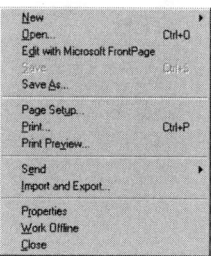

Edit Menu

In addition to the items found in any Windows Edit menu, the Internet Explorer Edit menu includes Find (On This Page), which searches for specific characters on the current page.

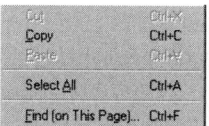

View Menu

Lets you hide or display all Internet Explorer toolbars and the Explorer Bar, change the size or style of the fonts, cancel the downloading of the current Web page, reload the current Web page, display the current Web page as HTML source code, and switch to full screen mode.

INTERNET EXPLORER

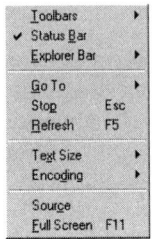

Favorites Menu

This menu is divided into two parts. You use the first part to manage your favorite Web sites with Add to Favorites and Organize Favorites. You use the second part for fast access to groups of Web sites with Links, Media, and Radio.

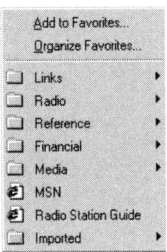

TIP The Internet Explorer logo, shown at the right end of the menu bar, is animated when Internet Explorer is sending or receiving information. You can click this logo to go to Microsoft's Web site.

Tools Menu

Gives you fast access to other Windows elements such as Mail and News, and the MSN Messenger service; lets you synchronize online and offline contents so you can be sure you are using the most up-to-date material when working offline; and gives you access to the setup parameters described in detail in the "Internet Options" section elsewhere in this book.

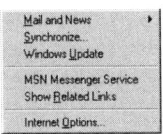

INTERNET EXPLORER

Help Menu

Gives you access to the Internet Explorer Help system through Contents and Index; contains information of special interest to those changing from Netscape Navigator; guides you through an online tutorial with Web Tour; helps locate information on technical problems with Online Support; and lets you send your opinions right to Microsoft with Send Feedback.

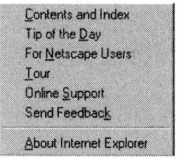

Internet Explorer Window

The major part of the Internet Explorer window consists of the document window where Web pages are displayed. As you move the mouse cursor around the page, it turns into a small hand whenever it passes over a link to another page. The page may be on the same Web site or on an entirely different Web site. Simply click the link to open the new page.

The last line of the Internet Explorer main window holds the status bar, which displays information about the current state of Internet Explorer. Icons you might see at the right end of the status bar include a padlock, indicating you are connected to a secure Web site, or a network cable with a red X superimposed on top, indicating that you are working offline.

You can right-click many of the objects displayed in the main Internet Explorer window to open a pop-up menu. The choices on the pop-up menu depend on the type of object you choose:

- If you right-click a blank part of the window, the pop-up menu contains items relevant to the complete page. You can open the next or the previous page, add the current page to your Favorites menu, display the page as HTML source code, and so on. If the page contains a background image, you can save the image to a file or use it as your Desktop wallpaper.

- If you right-click a link, the pop-up menu lets you open the link; save, print, or copy the address information to the Clipboard; and add the address to your Favorites menu.

INTERNET EXPLORER

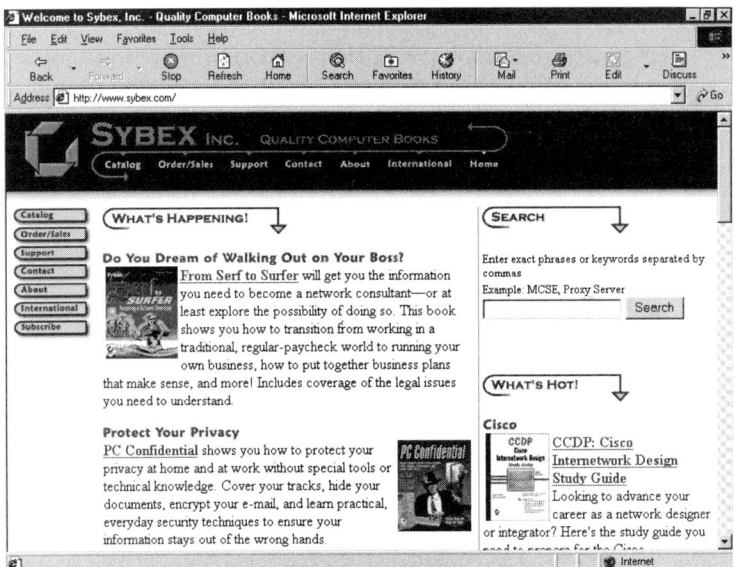

- If you right-click a graphic, the pop-up menu lets you save the image in a file, use the image as your Desktop wallpaper, or copy the image to the Clipboard.

- If you right-click selected text, you can copy the text to the Clipboard or print the text.

Configuring Internet Explorer

To view or set the many configuration options for Internet Explorer, choose Tools ➢ Internet Options to open the Internet Options dialog box. Or you can choose Start ➢ Connections ➢ Control Panel ➢ Internet Options. The Internet Options dialog box has six tabs. For a complete discussion of all the settings on these tabs, see the "Internet Options" entry elsewhere in this book.

Returning to Your Favorite Pages

One of the most common problems associated with using the Internet is finding your way back to something—a Web page or even a complete Web site—that you want to revisit.

INTERNET EXPLORER

TIP If you want to return to a Web site you visited during your current Internet Explorer session, click the Back and Forward buttons on the Internet Explorer toolbar. But by far the easiest way to keep track of interesting Web sites is to add them to your list of favorite sites.

Add to Favorites

When you want to bookmark a Web site so that you can find it again quickly and easily, choose Favorites ➤ Add to Favorites to open the Add Favorites dialog box.

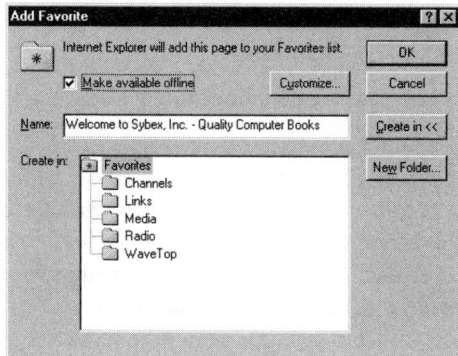

Once you place the address or URL for a site in this list, you can revisit the site simply by selecting it from the Favorites menu; the result is the same as if you had typed the whole URL into the Address toolbar and pressed Enter or clicked Go.

Click the New Folder button if you want to make a brand-new folder for some of your favorite Web sites. When you create a new folder within your Favorites folder, you also create a submenu on the Favorites menu for that same folder.

You can also display your Favorites menu from the Explorer Bar: simply click the Favorites button. In addition, you can choose View ➤ Explorer Bar ➤ Favorites. To close the Favorites folder, click the Close button in the upper-right corner, or click the Favorites button on the toolbar a second time.

Organize Favorites

Keeping a single long list is certainly not the best way to organize your favorites. To group Web sites in some sort of arrangement that makes sense to you, choose Favorites ➤ Organize Favorites to open the Organize Favorites dialog box, which contains the following buttons:

INTERNET EXPLORER

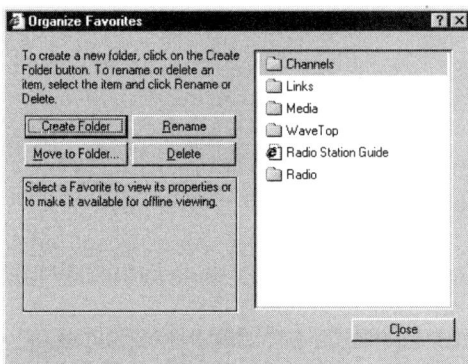

Create Folder Lets you create a brand-new folder for storing your favorites.

Move to Folder Lets you reorganize the folders within your Favorites folder. You can also move any item within the Organize Favorites dialog box by dragging it to a different folder. Or you can right-click a favorite, choose Cut from the pop-up menu, browse your way to the folder where you want to move the favorite, right-click inside that folder, and choose Paste from the pop-up menu.

Rename Lets you change the name of the selected item. You can also press F2 to edit the name.

Delete Removes the selected item.

> **TIP** You can open your favorite Web sites from many places within Windows. You can choose Start ➤ Favorites, or you can use the Favorites menu in Windows Explorer, My Computer, Internet Explorer, Network Neighborhood, or Control Panel; even the Recycle Bin has a Favorites menu.

Going Back with History

Once you access a Web site using Internet Explorer, its address (or URL) is stored in your History folder. You can use this list of all the sites you have visited to return to any one of them quickly and easily.

INTERNET EXPLORER

 TIP When several people use the same computer by logging on with different usernames and passwords, Internet Explorer creates a separate History folder for each of them.

To access the information in your History folder, choose View ➢ Explorer Bar ➢ History, or click the History button on the Internet Explorer toolbar. The Explorer Bar opens on the left side of the main Internet Explorer window. There you will see a complete list of all the Web sites you have visited, arranged in alphabetic order and grouped by week.

Click a week to expand the entries it contains. If you see a folder icon to the left of the URL, you can click that URL to see a list of all the pages you visited at that Web site. When you click an element from the History folder, the Web site opens in the right side of the main Internet Explorer window.

You can also view the contents of your History folder by date, site, most visited, or by order visited today, and you can search for specific text, all from within the History window. The results are displayed in the History window for quick and easy access.

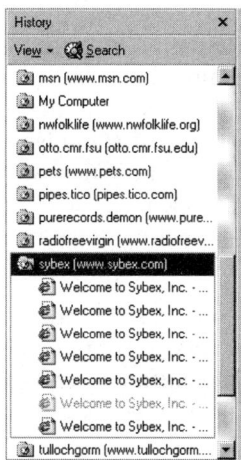

To close the History folder, click the Close button in the upper-right corner, or click the History button on the toolbar a second time.

Searching the Web

At times, you'll want to use the Internet to find specific information on a topic. You can use Internet Explorer as an aid in that search in a couple of ways. The first way is to perform a straightforward search. Follow these steps:

1. In Internet Explorer, click the Search button on the toolbar.

2. When the Explorer Bar opens on the left side of the main Internet Explorer window, click New and select the type of search you want to perform:

   - Find a Web Page
   - Find a Person's Address
   - Find a Business
   - Previous Searches
   - Find a Map
   - Find in Encyclopedia
   - Find in Newsgroups

3. If you are looking for information on a specific subject, enter the text into the Find a Web Page Containing box and click Search. Internet Explorer submits your search to eight major Internet search engines simultaneously, including InfoSeek, AltaVista, GoTo, and NorthernLight. Click the Next button to see search results from the next search engine. When you click a search result, the Web page opens in the right-hand pane of Internet Explorer. You can also use the drop-down menu to go directly to the results from your favorite search engine.

The second kind of search can be even faster and involves the Internet Explorer Address toolbar. Type the word or phrase that you want to find into the Address toolbar, and click the Go button. Internet Explorer locates the information you are looking for. In the list of results, click a link to display the Web page.

TIP To search the Web from the Start menu, choose Start ➤ Find ➤ On the Internet.

Browsing Offline

You can browse the Web with Internet Explorer without being connected to the Internet. This is because many of the files that you open while browsing the Web are stored in the Temporary Internet Files folder on your hard disk. Choose File ➢ Work Offline, and Internet Explorer will not attempt to connect to the Internet when you select a resource, but will display the copy in the Temporary Internet Files folder instead. To go back to online browsing, choose File ➢ Work Offline a second time.

You can also use File ➢ Save As to save complete Web pages to a folder on your hard disk. This is a little different from reviewing items in your History folder, because pages saved to your hard disk will not expire like the items in your History folder.

Speeding Up Internet Explorer

The text component of a Web page downloads quickly, but some of the other common elements, such as graphics, sound files, and animations, can take quite a long time to download.

Of course, there is nothing you can do to change the way a Web site is constructed, but you can stop certain types of files from being downloaded to Internet Explorer. You can essentially tell Internet Explorer to ignore all graphics files or all video clips and just collect the text. Here are the steps:

1. In Control Panel, click Internet Options, or choose Tools ➢ Internet Options within Internet Explorer to open the Internet Options dialog box.

2. Select the Advanced tab.

3. Scroll down the list box until you see the Multimedia settings, most of which are selected by default.

4. Deselect all the items you want to exclude from the Web pages you download to your system.

5. Click OK to close the Internet Options dialog box.

Remember that these options stay in effect for all subsequent Internet Explorer sessions until you change their settings.

INTERNET OPTIONS

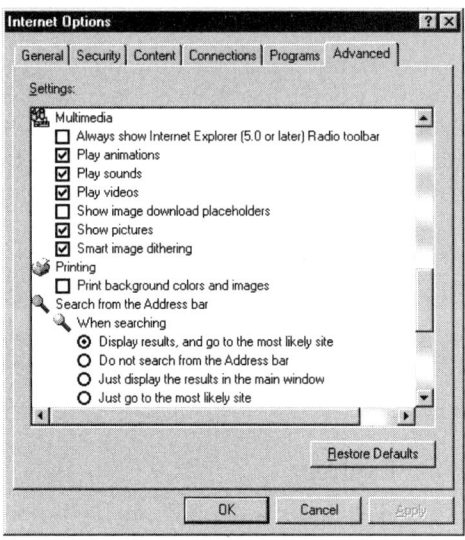

See also   Active Desktop, Dial-Up Networking, Explorer, Internet Connection Wizard, Internet Options, Modem, NetMeeting, Outlook Express, Users, Windows Radio

Internet Options

In Windows, you can view or change the configuration options relating to the Internet in two ways:

Internet Options

In Internet Options, in the Control Panel

In Internet Explorer

To open the Internet Properties dialog box, choose Start ➢ Settings ➢ Control Panel ➢ Internet Options, or open Internet Explorer and choose Tools ➢ Internet Options. The Internet Properties dialog box has six tabs.

General Tab

Contains these groups of settings:

Home Page   Lets you choose which Web page opens each time you connect to the Internet. The home page is the first Web page you see when you start Internet Explorer. Click Use Current to make the current

INTERNET OPTIONS

page your home page, click Use Default to return to the default setting, and click Use Blank to start each Internet session with a blank screen. To use a different Web page as your home page, type the URL into the Address box.

Temporary Internet Files   Lets you manage those Web pages that are stored on your hard disk for fast offline access. If these files are occupying too much hard-disk space, click the Delete Files button to remove them. To control how these files are stored on your hard disk, click Settings to open the Settings dialog box. Click the option that applies to when you want Internet Explorer to check for newer versions of these stored Web pages. You can use the slider to specify how much hard-disk space is given over to these temporary Internet files. Click Move Folder if you want to use a different folder to hold your temporary Internet files; you must remember to restart your computer after making this change so that the new folder is used in place of the default. Click View Files to open an Explorer window listing all the Web and graphics files in the folder, or click View Objects to open an Explorer window listing all the other Web-related files such as ActiveX controls and Java-related files.

History   Contains a list of the links you have visited, so that you can return to them quickly and easily. You can specify the number of days you want to keep pages in the History folder. If you are running low on hard-disk space, consider reducing this number. To delete all the information currently in the History folder, click the Clear History button.

Colors   Lets you choose which colors are used as background, links, and text on those Web pages for which the original author did not specify colors. By default, the Use Windows Colors option is selected.

TIP   You can always change the Windows colors. In Control Panel, click Display and then select the Appearance tab.

Fonts   Lets you specify the font style and text size to use on those Web pages for which the original author did not make a specification.

INTERNET OPTIONS

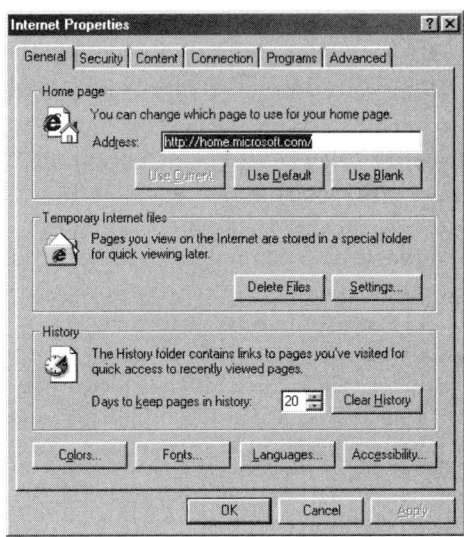

Languages Lets you choose the character set to use on those Web pages that offer content in more than one language. English is rapidly becoming the most common language in use on the Internet, so you may not use this option often.

Accessibility Lets you choose how certain information is displayed in Internet Explorer, including font styles, colors, and text size. You can also specify that your own style sheet is used.

Security Tab

Lets you specify the overall security level for each of four zones. Each zone has its own default security restrictions that tell Internet Explorer how to manage dynamic Web page content such as ActiveX controls and Java applets. The zones are as follows:

Internet Sites you visit that are not in one of the other categories; default security is set to medium.

Local Intranet Sites you can access on your corporate intranet; default security is set to medium-low.

INTERNET OPTIONS

Trusted Sites   Web sites for which you have a high degree of confidence that they will not send you potentially damaging content; default security is set to low.

Restricted Sites   Sites that you visit, but do not trust; default security is set to high.

To change the current security level of a zone, just move the slider to the new security level you want to use:

High   Excludes any content capable of damaging your system. Cookies are disabled, so some Web sites will not work. This is the most secure setting.

Medium   Opens a warning dialog box in Internet Explorer before running ActiveX or Java applets on your system. This is a moderately secure setting that is good for everyday use.

Medium-Low   Same as Medium, but without the prompts.

Low   Does not issue any warning, but runs the ActiveX or Java applet automatically. This is the least secure setting.

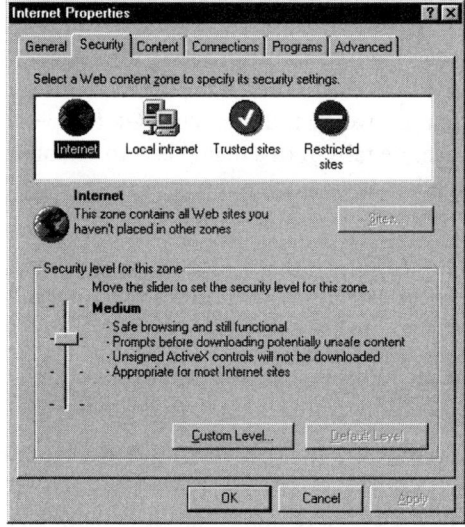

Click the Custom Level button to create your own security settings. You can individually configure how you want to manage certain categories, such as ActiveX controls and plug-ins, Java applets, scripting, file and font downloads, and user authentication.

121

INTERNET OPTIONS

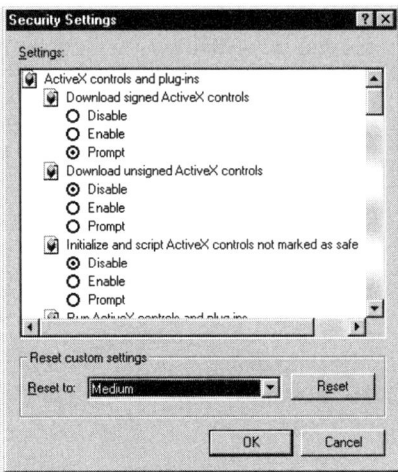

Content Tab

Contains settings you can use to restrict access to sites and specify how you want to manage digital certificates:

Content Adviser   Lets you control access to certain sites on the Internet and is particularly useful if children have access to the computer. Click Settings to establish a password, and then click OK to open the Content Advisor dialog box. Use the tabs in this dialog box to establish the level of content you will allow users to view:

Ratings   Lets you use a set of ratings developed by the Recreational Software Advisory Council (RSAC) for language, nudity, sex, and violence. Select one of these categories, and then adjust the slider to specify the level of content you will allow.

Approved Sites   Lets you create a list of sites that are always viewable or always restricted regardless of how they are rated.

General   Specifies whether people using this computer can view material that has not been rated. Users may see some objectionable material if the Web site has not used the RSAC rating system. You can also opt to have the Supervisor enter a password so that users can view Web pages that may contain objectionable material. You can click the Change Pass-

INTERNET OPTIONS

word button to change the Supervisor password. Remember that you have to know the current Supervisor password before you can change it.

Advanced Lets you look at or modify the list of organizations providing rating services.

Certificates Lets you manage digital certificates used with certain client authentication servers. Click Certificates to view the personal digital certificates installed on this system, or click Publishers to designate a particular software publisher as a trustworthy publisher. This means that Windows applications can download, install, and use software from these agencies without asking for your permission first.

Personal Information Lets you look at or change the settings for Windows AutoComplete and your own personal profile. Click AutoComplete to change the way that this feature works within Windows, or click My Profile to review the information sent to any Web sites that request information about you when you visit their site.

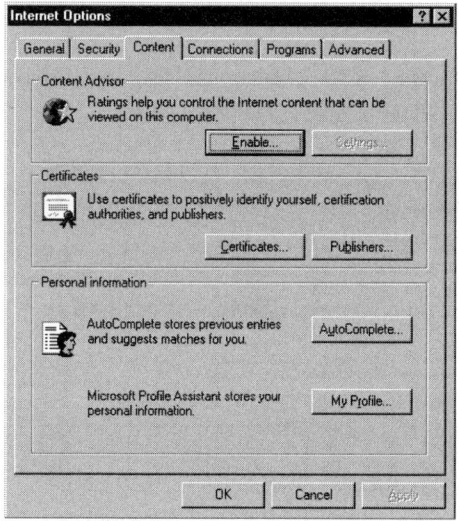

Connections Tab

Allows you to specify how your system connects to the Internet. Click the Setup button to run the Connection Wizard and set up a connection to an Internet service provider (ISP). (See the "Internet Connection Wizard" entry for complete details.) If you use a modem, click the Settings button to open the My Connection Settings dialog box, where you can specify all aspects of the phone connection to your ISP.

INTERNET OPTIONS

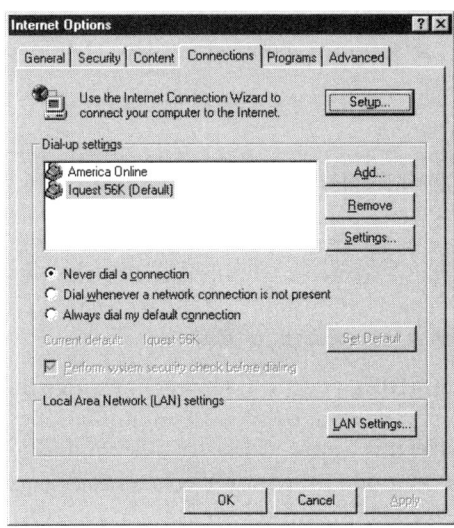

Programs Tab

Lets you set your default program choices for HTML editor, e-mail, newsgroup reader, Internet call, calendar, and contact list.

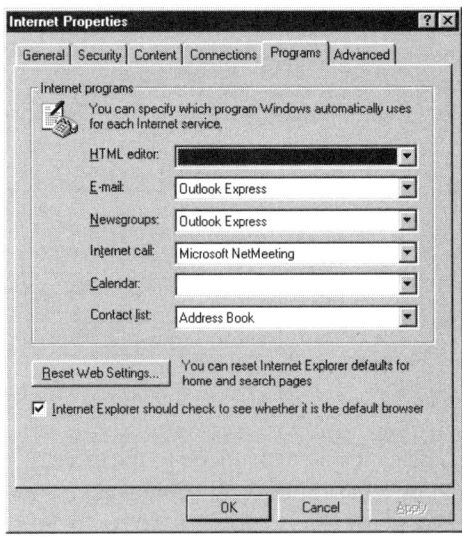

INTERNET EXPLORER

Finally, you can specify that Internet Explorer checks to see if it is configured as the default browser on your system each time it starts running.

Advanced Tab

Lets you look at or change a number of settings that control much of Internet Explorer's behavior, including accessibility, browsing, multimedia, security, the Java environment, printing and searching, the Internet Explorer toolbar, and how HTTP 1.1 settings are interpreted. Click a checkbox to turn an option on; clear the checkbox to turn the option off.

Changes you make here stay in effect until you change them again, download an automatic configuration file, or click the Restore Defaults button, which returns the settings on the Advanced tab to their original values.

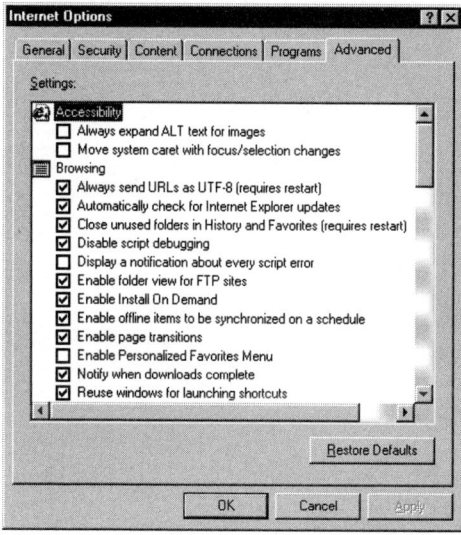

See also Address Book, Disk Cleanup, Display, Internet Connection Wizard, Internet Explorer, Modem, NetMeeting, Outlook Express

Interrupting Printing

You may find that you want to interrupt the printing of a document, perhaps to change the type of paper or to print a different set of pages. Follow these steps to stop a print job:

1. Double-click the Print icon on the Taskbar to display the printer's print queue.

2. After selecting the document, choose Document ➢ Cancel Printing to stop printing permanently, or choose Document ➢ Pause Printing to temporarily interrupt printing.

Keyboard

Keyboard

Most of the time, you will work with your keyboard without giving it a second thought, but the Keyboard applet in the Control Panel allows you to set several important defaults for keyboard properties, such as the language displayed and at what speed a key must be pressed to be recognized as a repeat key.

To look at or change the keyboard properties, choose Start ➢ Settings ➢ Control Panel ➢ Keyboard to open the Keyboard Properties dialog box. It has two tabs: Speed and Language.

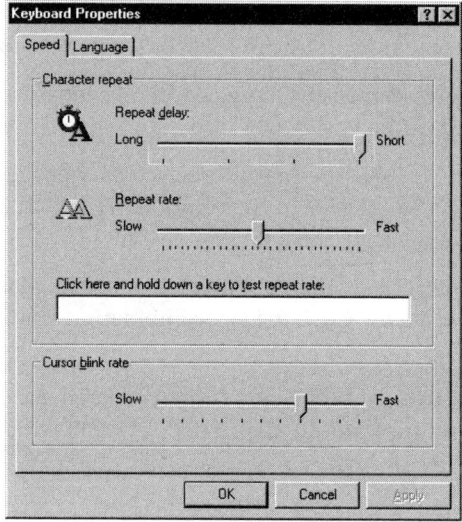

The Speed tab contains the following options:

Repeat Delay Sets the length of time you must hold down a key before the repeat feature kicks in. Drag the slider between Long and Short to get the time you want.

Repeat Rate Sets the speed at which a character is repeated while a key is held down. Adjust the slider between Slow and Fast to get the repeat rate you want.

Click Here and Hold Down a Key to Test Repeat Rate Tests the repeat delay and repeat rate speeds that you have chosen.

KEYBOARD

Cursor Blink Rate   Sets the rate at which the cursor blinks, making the cursor easier to spot in some instances. As you adjust the slider, the sample cursor to the left blinks at the selected rate.

The Language tab contains the following options:

Language and Layout   Displays the language and keyboard layout loaded into memory when the computer is first started. Double-click the highlighted language or layout to open the Language Properties dialog box and select another keyboard layout.

Add   Adds a language and keyboard layout to those loaded into memory when the computer is booted.

Properties   Allows you to change the keyboard layout default. For example, you can choose from at least five keyboard layouts for the United States.

Remove   Deletes the selected language and keyboard layout. It will no longer be loaded into memory when you boot the computer.

Set as Default   Makes the currently selected language and keyboard layout the default to be used when the computer is started. Not available unless more than one language is installed.

Switch Languages   Switches between two or more language and layout settings, as listed above. Click the key combination you want to use to switch the default.

Enable Indicator on Taskbar   Displays a language on the right of the taskbar. Click this indicator to open a dialog box in which you can switch language defaults quickly.

See also   Accessibility Options

Linking and Embedding

Methods you can use to insert information or objects from one document or source into another. You can link or embed text, graphics, sound, and video objects. You can create linked and embedded elements in one application and then insert them in documents that you created with a different application. For example, you might link or embed a graph created by Excel into a Word document along with your company logo created in Paint.

When you *link* an object, any updates to the original object are reflected in the linked object. Windows does not make a copy of the original object in the new document—only a link address, or reference, to it. When you want to change a linked object, you must change the original; those changes are then reflected in the linked copy. Windows enables you to do this easily by displaying the menus and toolbars of the program that created it.

When you *embed* an object, a copy of the object is inserted in the new document, along with all the information it needs to be maintained—for instance, a reference to the program that created it. The embedded copy is totally separate from the original object. Updates to the original are not reflected in the embedded copy. When you begin to edit an embedded object, the menus and toolbars of the program that created it are loaded and made available to you.

Inserting Linked or Embedded Information

To link or embed one document into another, follow these steps:

1. Open the first application and select the information you want to embed or link into the other document.
2. Choose Edit ➤ Copy.
3. Open the document into which you want to link or embed this information. Click the location in this document where you want the information to be placed.
4. Choose Edit ➤ Paste Special, and then click the format that you want to use. If you want to embed the document, select Paste from the Paste Special dialog box. If you want to link the document, select Paste Link.

Modifying a Linked File

To edit a linked file, you must edit the original information, since there is no copy. Follow these steps:

1. Double-click the linked copy to open an editing window that contains the original object with the toolbars and menus of the program that created it.

2. Make your changes to the original.

3. When you are finished modifying the original, click outside the linked object. You will be returned to the original window with the linked copy, where all the changes will be reflected.

Modifying an Embedded Object

To edit an embedded object, you use the program that originally created the object. When you first begin to edit the object, a special editing window will surround it, and the program's menus and tools will be displayed. Follow these steps:

1. Double-click the embedded object. If it was created by another program, that program's menus and toolbars will be displayed.

2. Make the changes you want.

3. When you are finished, click outside the embedded object to close the program that created the object and return to the original window.

TIP Not all programs support linking and embedding. If it is not supported in an application, the Paste Special command will not appear on the Edit menu.

Log Off

Windows maintains a set of user profiles, each containing a different username and password, and different Desktop preferences and Accessibility options. When you log on to Windows , your profile ensures that your Desktop settings—including elements such as your own Desktop icons, background image, and other settings—are automatically available to you.

LOG ON

Windows contains an option you can use to log off and log on again as another user quickly and easily. Click the Start button, and then click Log Off *username*. In the Log Off Windows dialog box, click Yes. This closes all your programs, disconnects your system from the network, and prepares the system for use by other users.

See also Accessibility Options, Log On, Passwords, Profiles, ShutDown, Users

Log On

To use Windows, you must first log on as a user. Windows maintains a set of user profiles, each containing a different username and password, and different Desktop preferences and Accessibility options. This allows several people to use the same computer at different times, and Windows loads a different user profile for each user.

When you log on to Windows and are prompted to enter your username and password, your profile is loaded to ensure that your Desktop settings—including elements such as your own Desktop icons, background image, and other settings—are automatically available to you.

Unfortunately, you can also press the Esc key to bypass this logon screen and completely circumvent all aspects of Windows logon security. This makes Windows a particularly unsecure system.

If you are connected to a local area network and Windows is configured for that network, you will also be prompted to enter your network password.

NOTE The sequence of dialog boxes that prompt for your username and password the first time you start Windows will be different from those you see in later sessions. Subsequent sessions will involve fewer steps because you won't be asked to confirm your password.

See also Accessibility Options, Log Off, Passwords, Profiles, Shut Down, Users

Magnifier

 Enlarges a portion of the screen to make it easier to read. Choose Start ➤ Programs ➤ Accessories ➤ Accessibility ➤ Magnifier to open the Magnifier Settings dialog box. At the same time, a portion of the Desktop displays a large image of the dialog box; to make this area of the screen larger, simply drag the boundary of the enlarged display to a new location.

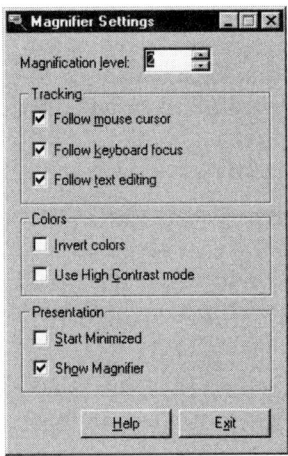

Use the checkboxes in the Magnifier Settings dialog box to control how the Magnifier works on your system, including the size and position of the magnification window, the level of magnification, and the screen colors. You can also control several tracking options, including whether the magnified area follows the mouse cursor, follows the keyboard focus, or follows the insertion point as you enter text. Click the Minimize button in the dialog box to minimize the dialog box while you are using the Magnifier. You can set it to start up minimized by marking the Start Minimized checkbox.

To turn the Magnifier off when you finish using it, click the Exit button in the Microsoft Magnifier dialog box, or right-click the Magnifier taskbar and choose Close.

See also Accessibility Options, Display

Mail

Mail An icon in the Control Panel that opens an Accounts window, in which you can configure the various e-mail accounts set up on your PC. You can get to this same dialog box from within your e-mail program (Outlook or Outlook Express) by choosing Tools ➢ Accounts.

Maintenance Wizard

Optimizes your system for best performance. The Maintenance Wizard can help make your programs run faster, free up precious hard-disk space, and optimize system performance.

The Wizard actually does its work by running three other Windows system utilities—Disk Defragmenter, ScanDisk, and Disk Cleanup—in concert with Task Scheduler, which controls when the other utilities run on your system. To run the Maintenance Wizard, follow these steps:

1. Choose Start ➢ Programs ➢ Accessories ➢ System Tools ➢ Maintenance Wizard. The Wizard welcome screen gives you two choices:

    Express Uses the most common optimization settings.

    Custom Allows you to select the tune-up settings.

2. Choose Express and click Next. The next screen lets you schedule when the Maintenance Wizard will run on your system. Select a time when your computer will be switched on, but you won't be using it, such as in the middle of the night, very early in the morning, or during your lunch break.

3. In the final screen, you will see a list of the optimizations that the Wizard plans to execute on your system. Check the box at the bottom of the screen to run these optimizations when the Wizard closes.

4. Click Finish to close the Wizard.

MAP NETWORK DRIVE

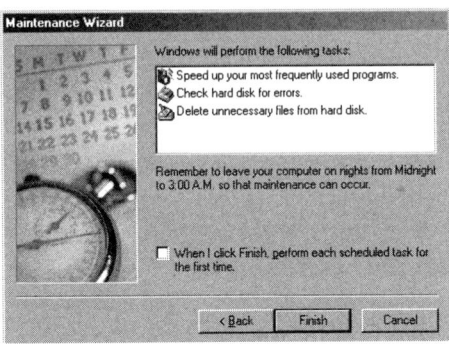

If you choose Custom in the Wizard welcome screen, you can also specify in more detail how Disk Defragmenter, ScanDisk, and Disk Cleanup will operate on your system.

See also   Disk Cleanup, Disk Defragmenter, ScanDisk, Scheduled Tasks

Map Network Drive

Map Network Drive... Gives a unique name on your computer to a shared drive on another computer, and enables you to access its data. For example, you could map the C:\My Documents folder on another computer to drive letter F: on your system, to avoid confusion with your own C:\My Documents folder. Mapping a drive letter allows you to access the drive's data from within an application in programs that do not directly support network file access. The tools to map network drives are available in Explorer, My Computer, and My Network Places.

NOTE   You do not have to map a network drive to be able to access the data it contains; if it is a shared drive, you can access it through My Network Places.

Mapping a Network Drive

Follow these steps to map a drive to your computer:

1. Choose Start ➤ Programs ➤ Accessories ➤ Windows Explorer to open Explorer.

2. Choose Tools ➤ Map Network Drive to open the Map Network Drive dialog box. The Drive list box contains the suggested name of the drive.

3. Click the arrow to open the list box, and then select the name of the drive or type a new name. The list contains the names already assigned to other drives.

4. Click the Path box and type two backslashes followed by the path to the disk you are mapping, such as \\computer\drive, or click Browse to browse for it.

TIP If you have already mapped the drive, click the arrow on the right of the list box and select the name you want.

The next time you open My Computer, Explorer, or My Network Places, the mapped drive will be displayed as a drive on your computer, and you will see the folders available within the selected drive.

Disconnecting a Network Drive

When you disconnect (or unmap) a mapped resource, you remove it from the list of resources and free up its drive letter. Follow these steps to disconnect a network drive:

1. Choose Start ➤ Programs ➤ Accessories ➤ Windows Explorer to open Explorer.

2. Choose Tools ➤ Disconnect Network Drive to open the Disconnect Network Drive dialog box, which lists all mapped drives on your computer.

3. Select the network drive you want to disconnect and click OK. The mapped resource is removed from those available to you.

Maximize/Minimize Buttons

Allows you to change the size of an application window. As always in Windows, you can approach this in a couple of ways.

MICROSOFT NETWORK (MSN)

The Maximize button is in the upper-right corner of an application window, and when you click it, the window expands to full-screen size. Once the window has expanded, the Maximize button changes to the Restore button, which you can then use to shrink the window back to its original starting size.

You can also place the mouse pointer on the window border, and when the two-headed arrow appears, drag the border in the direction in which you want to change its size.

 Use the Minimize button to place an open application on the Taskbar; click the Taskbar icon when you are ready to work with the application again.

See also   Taskbar

Microsoft Network (MSN)

Originally conceived as a members-only online service, MSN is now both an Internet Service Provider (ISP) and a provider of free content on the Web. You do not have to use MSN for your ISP in order to use the MSN content.

Signing Up for MSN Internet Access

 If you want to use MSN as your ISP, you can easily sign up for the service right on your own PC. Connect your modem to the phone line, close any other applications, and double-click the Set Up MSN Internet Access icon. Then follow the onscreen prompts. Be ready to supply your name, address, phone number, a credit card number and expiration date, a username, and a password during the registration process. Follow the instructions on the screen to complete your registration.

Once you are registered, you can use MSN the same as any other Internet Service Provider.

 NOTE   MSN uses an 800 number to sign you up as a member. After you register, you are supplied with a different telephone number.

Connecting to MSN Internet Content

MSN online content is available to everyone, not just to MSN subscribers. To start browsing MSN, open your Web browser and go to www.msn.com.

See also   Internet Explorer, Online Services

Modems

Modems

Allows you to look at or change the settings Windows uses with your modem. Choose Start ➤ Settings ➤ Control Panel ➤ Modems to open the Modems Properties dialog box. It contains the General and Diagnostics tabs.

If you have no modem installed yet, choosing the Modems icon in the Control Panel opens the Add New Modem Wizard, which you can work through to set up your modem.

General Tab

Used to add or remove modems, or to edit the properties of a modem. All the currently installed modems appear on a list.

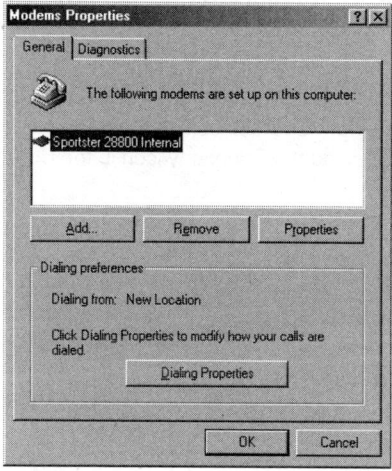

You have the following options:

Add   Guides you through the installation of a new modem. Be sure to physically connect the modem to your computer and turn it on so that Windows can sense its presence. You can also specify that you will select the modem from a list, rather than having Windows search for it.

Remove   Removes the selected modem's drivers from Windows.

Properties   Displays the modem's Properties dialog box, which has two tabs:

137

MODEMS

General   Allows you to specify the port used for the modem, the speaker volume, and the maximum modem speed to use, which is scaled according to your modem's capabilities.

Connection   Sets the number of data bits, the parity, and the stop-bits settings, and specifies certain call preferences, including whether to wait for a dial tone before dialing out and how long to wait before canceling an unconnected call. Click the Port Settings button to open the Advanced Port Settings dialog box, where you can set levels for both the receive and the transmit buffers: use lower levels if you are having connection problems and higher levels to boost performance. Click the Advanced button to open the Advanced Connection Settings dialog box, where you can establish error control, flow control, and other hardware settings.

Dialing Properties   Specifies how your calls are actually made, including the rules for using the area code when dialing, how to dial an outside line, and how to turn off call-waiting services. You can also specify a calling card for use with long-distance calls.

NOTE   These Dialing Properties controls are the same as the ones you can set directly by double-clicking the Telephony icon in the Control Panel.

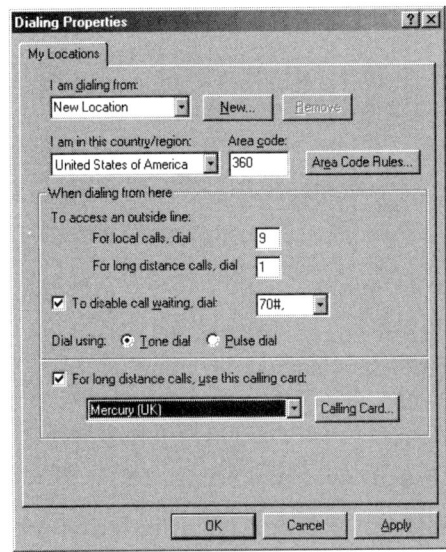

Diagnostics Tab

Identifies which devices are assigned to specific ports, and tells what drivers each modem or port is using. This tab can also be used to check whether a modem is functioning correctly, even if you do not have a phone line to hook up to it at the moment. It has three buttons:

Driver Shows the selected device driver filename, its size, and the date the device was installed.

More Info Shows detailed port information for the selected device and the modem command set. Use this button to test a modem's operation. If at least some of the results come back with "OK" then the modem is working.

Help Provides access to the Windows Help system and the Modem Troubleshooter.

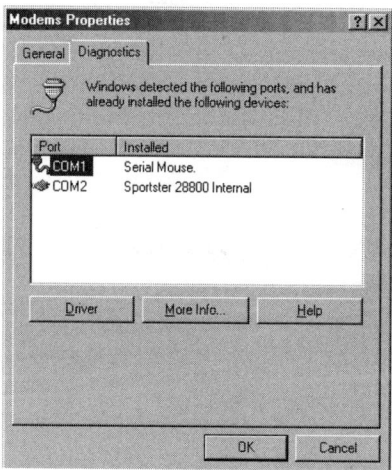

See also Add New Hardware, Dial-Up Networking, Help, Internet, Internet Explorer, Outlook Express

Mouse

Changes your mouse settings. Choose Start ➤ Settings ➤ Control Panel ➤ Mouse to open the Mouse Properties dialog box, which contains three tabs.

Mouse

MOUSE

If you make changes to the settings in any of these tabs, click the Apply button to make sure your changes are implemented, and then click OK.

Buttons Tab

Sets the mouse button configuration and speed with these options:

Button Configuration   Allows you to switch functions from the default right-handed use of the mouse buttons to left-handed. When you select Left-Handed, the left button then performs secondary functions, such as displaying the pop-up menu and performing special drag functions. The right button performs the primary functions of selecting and dragging.

Double-Click Speed   Allows you to set and then test the speed between clicks at which a double-click is recognized. You can increase or decrease the speed with which you must press the mouse button for it to be recognized as a double-click.

ClickLock   Allows you to drag with the mouse without holding down the mouse button. To turn the feature on, select its checkbox; click Settings to control its properties. With ClickLock on, holding down the mouse button briefly locks the mouse button "on," and clicking the mouse button again turns the lock off.

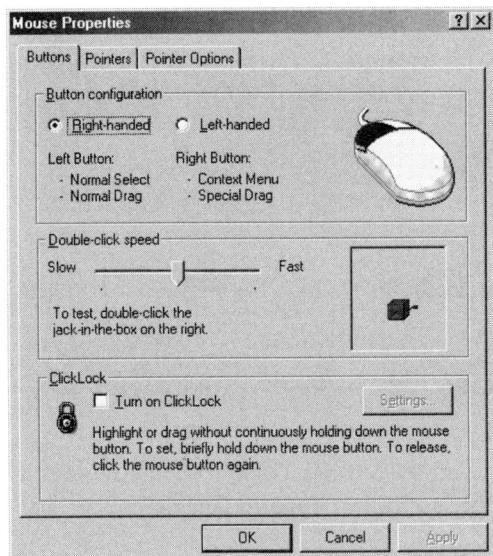

Pointers Tab

Allows you to change the appearance of the mouse pointer. For example, you can change the pointer used to indicate that Windows is busy from an hourglass to a symbol or caricature of your choice from those provided.

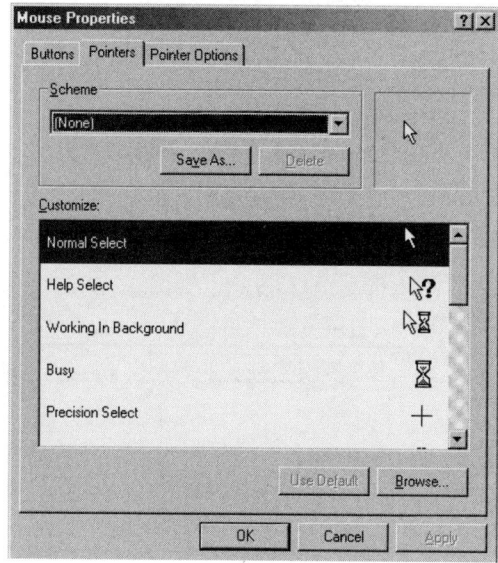

The Scheme box contains the list of pointer schemes available in Windows. By selecting one, you'll see the set of pointers in the scheme displayed in the box below. You can create additional schemes by replacing the individual pointers. Click the Browse button and select the .ANI or .CUR files you want. Once you assign the new pointers to the scheme's functions, click Save As to name and save your new scheme. Clicking Delete removes a scheme, and clicking Use Default restores the original default pointers.

Pointer Options Tab

Controls the pointer speed and the presence of a pointer trail, which makes the mouse pointer much easier to see on LCD screens. If you select a pointer trail, you can choose whether it is a long or a short trail. This tab also contains some additional features, such as Snap To and Hide Pointer While Typing.

MOVING AND ARRANGING ICONS

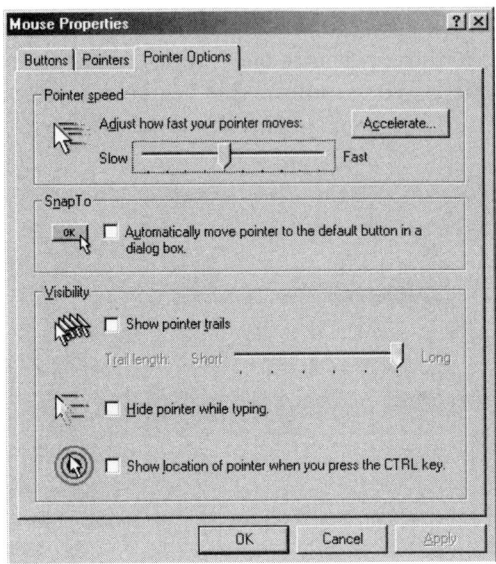

See also
Accessibility Options, Accessibility Wizard

Moving and Arranging Icons

In Windows, you can arrange icons in several different ways. In Explorer, Control Panel, and many other windows, you can move or arrange icons using the following selections in the View menu:

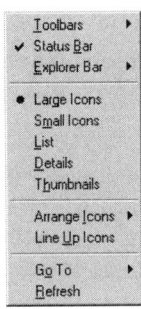

Large Icons   Displays the files and folders as larger-sized icons.

Small Icons   Displays the files and folders as smaller-sized icons.

List   Displays small icons alongside the names of the files and folders.

Details   Displays files and folders in the List style and adds columns for the size of file, date last modified, and type of file. To sort entries within these columns, simply click the column heading. Click once for an ascending sort (A to Z and zero to nine); click a second time for a descending sort.

Thumbnail   Displays the files and folders with previews of each graphics file. If a file is not a graphics file, its icon appears instead. Not all windows have this viewing option.

Arrange Icons   Opens a submenu you can use to sort the icons by name, type, size, or date. Auto Arrange places the icons on an invisible grid. In My Computer, you can arrange icons by drive letter, type, size, or free space. In Network Neighborhood, you can arrange icons by name or by comment.

Line Up Icons   Rearranges icons into straight vertical and horizontal lines.

TIP   To rearrange icons on the Desktop, simply drag them to their new location. To tidy up the Desktop quickly, right-click an area of free space and choose Arrange Icons.

 You can click the Views button on the Explorer toolbar to open a drop-down list of the view types and choose quickly among them.

Moving Files and Folders

When you move a file or folder, you move the original to another location—no duplicate is made. In Windows, you can move files and folders in three ways:

- By dragging and dropping
- By choosing Edit ➢ Cut or Edit ➢ Paste
- By clicking the right mouse button

MOVING FILES AND FOLDERS

Using Drag-and-Drop

To use drag-and-drop, both the source and the destination folders must be visible—for example, in Explorer or on the Desktop. Hold down the left mouse button and drag the file or folder from one location to the other. When the file or folder reaches the correct destination folder, release the mouse button. The source and destination folders must be on the same drive. If you drag a file or a folder to a different drive, it will be copied rather than moved. If you want to move a file or folder to a different drive, you must hold down the Shift key as you drag.

You can also right-drag (that is, drag with the right mouse button). When you drop, a shortcut menu appears, and you can choose Move from the shortcut menu.

TIP If you forget where you just moved a file to in the Explorer, use Edit ➤ Undo, or press Ctrl+Z.

Using the Edit Menu

The Edit menu in My Computer, Explorer, or any folder window provides a Cut and Paste feature. Here are the steps to follow:

1. Select the file or folder you want to move.
2. Choose Edit ➤ Cut, or press Ctrl+X.
3. Find the destination file or folder and open it.
4. Choose Edit ➤ Paste, or press Ctrl+V.

TIP You can select multiple contiguous files or folders to move by holding down Shift and clicking the first and last file or folder. To select noncontiguous files or folders, hold down Ctrl and click the files or folders you want.

Using the Right Mouse Button

Right-clicking a file or folder opens the shortcut menu, which you can use to perform a variety of functions, including moving. Follow these steps:

1. Right-click the file or folder you want to move, and select Cut from the pop-up menu.
2. Open the destination folder, right-click, and then select Paste.

TIP If you drag a folder or a file with the right mouse button, a pop-up menu opens when you release the button, allowing you to copy the object, move it, or create a shortcut.

See also   Copying Files and Folders

MS-DOS Mode

Earlier versions of Windows had a special operating mode in which you could run MS-DOS based programs. Windows Millennium does not have this feature, because there are so few MS-DOS based programs available today.

However, you should be able to run almost any MS-DOS program from within Windows by double-clicking its application icon in Explorer. Or, you can open an MS-DOS Prompt window and type the command for running the program there.

See also   MS-DOS Prompt

MS-DOS Prompt

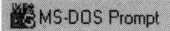   Opens an MS-DOS window in which you can load and run MS-DOS programs and execute commands from the MS-DOS prompt.

TIP To switch MS-DOS programs between a full screen and a window, press Alt+Enter (some MS-DOS programs cannot run in a window).

To open an MS-DOS window, choose Start ➤ Programs ➤ Accessories ➤ MS-DOS Prompt. To close the window and end the MS-DOS session, type **Exit** at the prompt, or click the Close button.

The small toolbar at the top of the MS-DOS window contains buttons you can use to set the font, mark, copy, paste, change to a full-screen display, open the Properties dialog box, run in the background, and open the Properties dialog box at the Font tab. You can also click the small MS-DOS icon in the top-left corner of the window to open the Control menu, which contains many of these same functions.

TIP When you are at the command prompt, you can get help with MS-DOS commands by typing the command name followed by **/?**. For example, to display a short Help screen on the directory command, type **dir /?**

See also Startup Menu

MSN Messenger Service

 A real-time instant messaging program, through which you can send and receive private messages with people who are online when you are.

Instant messaging is different from a chat program, in which there are public chatrooms where many people participate in the discussion at once.

Signing Up for MSN Messenger Service

The MSN Messenger Service is free, but you must sign up for it. You must also have a "Passport," which is a login to the system. If you have a Hotmail e-mail account, you can use that as your passport; otherwise you can sign up for one for free during the MSN Messenger Service sign-up.

To start the sign-up process:

MSN MESSENGER SERVICE

1. Choose Start ➢ Programs ➢ Accessories ➢ Communications ➢MSN Messenger Service.

2. Choose Next.

3. If you need a Passport, click the Get a Passport button and follow the prompts to enter the needed information. Otherwise click Next.

4. Enter your sign-in name and password to use. If you have a Hotmail account, enter that name and password here; if you signed up for a Passport, enter that name and password.

5 Click Finish. It logs you in to the MSN Messenger service.

After the initial sign-up, MSN Messenger Service loads automatically each time you start your PC. To disable it from loading, remove its shortcut from the Startup program group.

Adding a Contact to Your Contact List

If you know the sign-in name of a friend or coworker, you can add that name to your Contacts list so you can see when that person is online, as shown below.

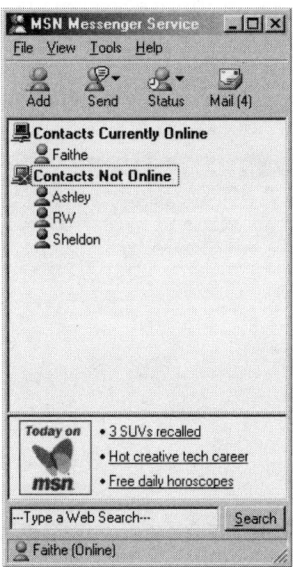

Follow these steps to add a contact.

147

MSN MESSENGER SERVICE

1. Click the Add button.
2. Choose how you want to add the person: by e-mail address (must be Hotmail), by Passport, or Search for a contact. Then click Next.
3. The next screen varies, depending on what you chose in step 2. Enter the information prompted for, and click Next.
4. Continue filling in the information as prompted, clicking Next until you come to the Finish screen.
5. Click Finish to add that person to your Contacts list and close the window.

Using Instant Messaging

You can have a real-time chat with any of your contacts who is online at the same time as you. A contact who is online appears on your Contacts list in the Contacts Currently Online section, as shown in the preceding figure.

To initiate a chat, do the following:

1. Double-click the person's name. An Instant Message window opens.

 TIP Instead of step 1 you can click the Send button on the MSN Messenger Service's main toolbar and then select the person's name from the menu that drops down.

2. Click in the bottom pane and type your greeting, as shown here.

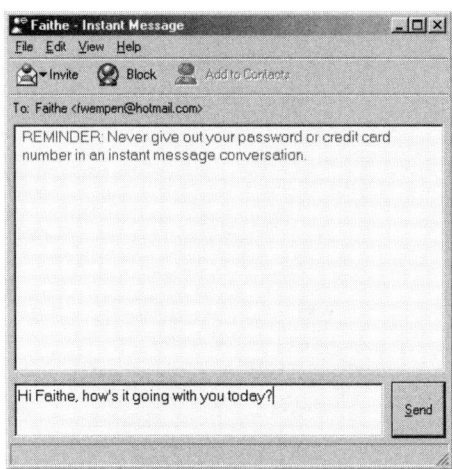

3. Click Send. The message is sent to the recipient.

A similar window appears on the recipient's PC, showing your greeting. He or she can respond by clicking in the bottom pane and typing a message.

Other MSN Messenger Service Activities

Instant messaging is the main purpose of MSN Messenger Service, but here are some other things you can do with it too:

- Check your Hotmail e-mail. Click the Mail icon to do so.
- Set your status. This changes how you appear to others. For example, perhaps you don't want to appear as online because you don't want to be bothered. Click the Status button and choose a status from the menu.
- Send an invitation to start NetMeeting. Use this if you need the more sophisticated chatting abilities of NetMeeting, primarily a business conferencing tool. Choose Tools ➤ Send an Invitation ➤ To Start NetMeeting {version number}. The version number depends on what's installed on your PC.
- Send e-mail. You can send e-mail to one of your contacts who is not online right now by double-clicking the name and choosing Yes. A mail composition window appears.

See also   NetMeeting, Outlook Express

My Briefcase

Synchronizes files between two computer systems. The feature is particularly useful if you work on two computers, perhaps a laptop on the road and a full-sized desktop system back in the office. How do you keep often-used files synchronized on the two systems?

TIP If you do not see the icon for My Briefcase on your Desktop, you may need to install it using the Add/Remove Programs applet in the Control Panel. Also the briefcase will not appear on the desktop if you have already been using the feature and the briefcase has been temporarily transferred to another PC.

The simplest way to think about My Briefcase is to consider it a folder that contains copies of all the files that you want to keep up to date. When you switch from your desktop computer to your laptop, you drag the Briefcase folder

MY BRIEFCASE

to a floppy disk icon and copy the contents of the floppy to the hard disk in your laptop. If your laptop is connected to a network, you can drag the Briefcase folder directly onto your laptop's hard disk. Now you can work on the files on your laptop all week, and when you return to the office, you reverse the process. My Briefcase takes care of details such as which copy of any given file has the latest changes in it and where they should be copied. You can create as many Briefcases as you need, and, of course, they can be used between any two computers—not just desktop and laptop systems.

WARNING The My Briefcase feature needs to be installed on both PCs that will be doing the briefcase-sharing; it is not installed by default. Use Add/Remove Programs in the Control Panel to add it as you would any optional Windows component.

My Briefcase Window

Double-click the My Briefcase icon on the Desktop to open the My Briefcase folder:

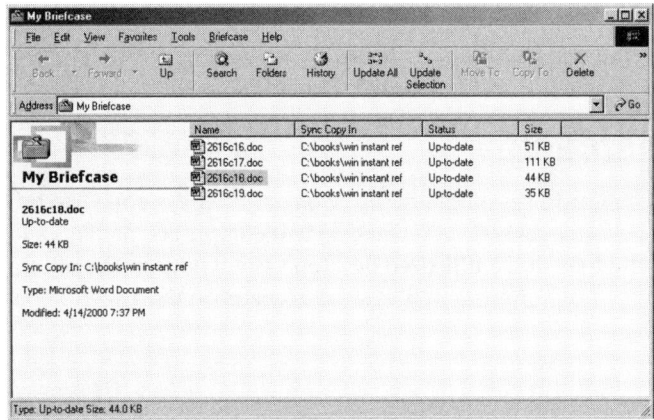

NOTE If you see an introductory box, click Finish to move past it.

MY BRIEFCASE

The My Briefcase folder contains several standard Window menus—File, Edit, View, Go, Favorites, and Help. The Briefcase menu, however, is unique to My Briefcase. It contains these options:

Update All   Updates all files in the Briefcase.

Update Selection   Updates only the files you select.

Split from Original   Splits a file from the Briefcase so that it is no longer updated when the original version changes.

The files in My Briefcase show the location of the synchronized copy, whether it has been updated, the size of file, the file type, and the date on which it was last modified. To display the specific properties of any file, click the filename and then choose File ≻ Properties, or right-click the filename and select Properties.

TIP   To create a new My Briefcase folder from Explorer, open the folder in which you want to create the new My Briefcase folder, and then choose File ≻ New ≻ Briefcase.

Copying a File to the Briefcase

To use the Briefcase, you must first copy files to be synchronized to the Briefcase. Follow these steps:

1. In Explorer, find the files you want to keep synchronized.

2. Drag the selected files (not their shortcuts) to the My Briefcase icon on the Desktop, or open the My Briefcase folder and drag the files into that.

3. Insert a floppy disk and use My Computer or Explorer to drag the My Briefcase icon to the floppy disk. You may be prompted to change disks if you have a really big Briefcase. Remove the floppy and insert it into the drive on your other system.

4. You can work on the files on the floppy, or you can copy them to the hard disk in the other system. If you do copy them to the hard disk, you will have to remember to copy them back into the Briefcase before going on to the next steps.

TIP   To check on the status of a file or folder in My Briefcase, select the file, choose File ≻ Properties, and click the Update Status tab.

MY COMPUTER

Synchronizing Files in the Briefcase

When you want to access the files on your original machine, follow these steps:

1. Insert the floppy disk or access the computer on your network containing My Briefcase with the files to be synchronized. (My Briefcase may remain on the network or be copied onto your hard disk.)

2. Open My Briefcase, and select the files to be synchronized.

3. Choose Briefcase ➤ Update All to update all files in My Briefcase, or choose Briefcase ➤ Update Selection to update only the selected files. The Update My Briefcase dialog box displays the status of files in the Briefcase on the left and the status of the source files on the right. An arrow between the two files shows the assumed direction of the update.

4. To change the update direction, right-click the direction arrow to open a pop-up menu from which you can choose the direction or choose to skip the update.

TIP Click the What's This? option to display an explanation of the dialog box.

5. Click the Update button in the Update My Briefcase dialog box to finish the file synchronization.

NOTE If the Briefcase detects that both copies of a file have changed, the Skip option is displayed instead of the Replace option. If you right-click, you can choose whether to skip the update or to replace one of the files. If you choose to replace one file with another, you will lose the updates in the replaced file.

See also Add/Remove Programs

My Computer

One of the file-management tools available with Windows. You can use My Computer to locate folders, files, disks, or printers on your computer or on mapped drives on other computers connected to the network.

My Computer Folder

Click the My Computer icon on the Desktop to open the My Computer folder, showing an icon for each drive and drive-level folder on your computer. Click an icon to display the contents of one of these folders or drives in a separate window.

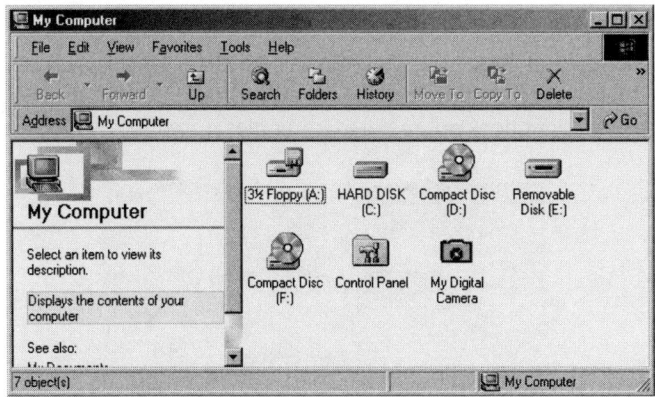

Finding a File or Folder with My Computer

When you open My Computer, the My Computer folder displays all the disks and folders on your computer. Follow these steps to find the file or folder you want:

1. Click the down arrow at the end of the Address toolbar to find the device or folder you want. You will see all the shared disks on your network, important folders such as Control Panel, Printers, and Dial-Up Networking, and other Windows elements, such as Internet Explorer, My Network Places, Recycle Bin, and My Briefcase. What you see depends, of course, on which Windows components you installed.

2. Click a disk or a folder to see its contents in the window.

3. Once you find the file or folder (which may be several levels down), click it to open it.

NOTE You can access a remote computer by opening the Dial-Up Networking folder in My Computer. This allows you to establish connections to a remote computer over phone lines, using a modem.

See also Dial-Up Networking

My Documents

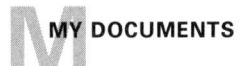

A Desktop folder that provides a convenient place to store graphics, documents, or any other files you might want to access quickly. When you save a file in programs such as Paint or WordPad, the file is automatically saved in My Documents unless you specify a different destination folder.

To specify a different destination folder, right-click My Documents and select Properties. Type the name of the new folder in the Target field and click OK. Changing to a different folder does not move existing files stored in My Documents.

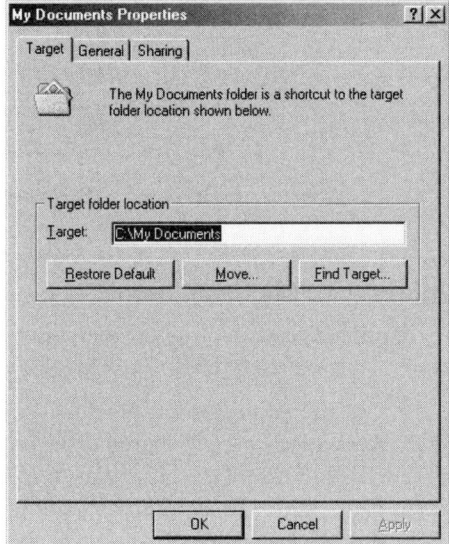

My Network Places

A viewer that presents system information from a purely network perspective. Like My Computer and Explorer, it allows you to access all computers on your network. However, the display of data in My Network Places is a little different in that you reach from one level of computer information to the next by first viewing the network components, then the computer contents, then the disk, then a folder, and finally files, rather than scrolling up and down a list.

See also Network

NAMING FILES AND FOLDERS

Naming Disks

You can give a hard or floppy disk a name that can be a maximum of 11 characters. To name or rename a disk, follow these steps:

1. Open My Computer or Explorer.

2. Right-click the disk you want to name, and select Properties to open the Properties dialog box.

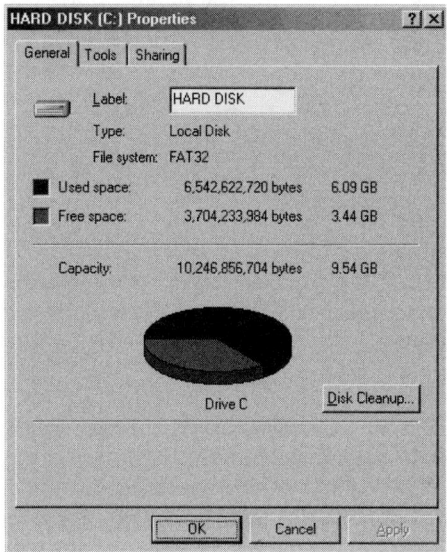

3. Select the General tab, and type the name you want to use for this disk in the Label field. Click OK.

Naming Files and Folders

The first time you save a file using the Save or Save As command, you are asked to provide a name for the file. When you create a new folder, it is always called New Folder until you change the name. A name for a file or folder can contain a maximum of 255 characters, including spaces, but cannot contain any of these special characters: /\?:*"<>|.

Renaming a File or Folder

You can rename both files and folders in Explorer or My Computer. Follow these steps:

1. Open Explorer or My Computer and find the file or folder you want to rename.

2. Click the name once, pause, then click it again. Or click the name once and press F2.

   A box will enclose the name, and the name will be selected. If you move the mouse inside the box, the pointer will become an I-beam.

blue2.jpg

Type the new name or edit the existing name and press Enter.

TIP If you discover you have renamed the wrong file in Explorer, use Edit ➤ Undo, or press Ctrl+Z.

Net Watcher

 Monitors who is currently using the shared resources on your network. System administrators can use Net Watcher to add shared folders to those resources being monitored and to disconnect users from your computer resources. You must be connected to a network before you can use Net Watcher.

Net Watcher Window

Choose Start ➤ Programs ➤ Accessories ➤ System Tools ➤ Net Watcher to open the Net Watcher window:

NET WATCHER

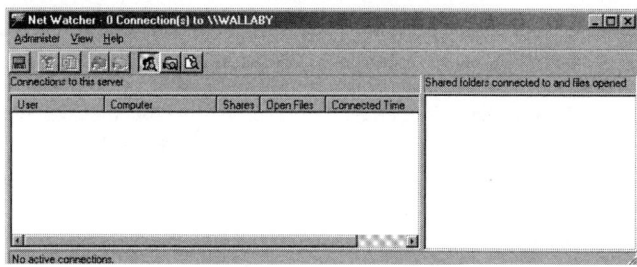

Net Watcher Toolbar

The Net Watcher toolbar contains the following buttons:

 Select Server   Allows you to select a computer so that you can monitor its shared resources.

 Disconnect User   Lets you disconnect a user from your computer. Any files open and being shared may lose data if you do this without notifying the user.

 Close File   Closes a shared file.

 Add Share   Allows you to specify a folder to be added to the shared resources.

 Stop Sharing   Removes a folder from the shared status. If someone is using it and is unaware of the change, that person could lose data.

 Show Users   Displays the users or computers connected to the network and the resources they are currently sharing.

 Shared Folders   Displays the devices and folders on the network currently available to be shared and the names of any folders and files currently being shared.

 Show Files   Displays the files that are currently open and being shared on the network.

Net Watcher Menus

These menus duplicate some of the toolbar functions and also contain some unique options, as Table N.1 shows.

157

NETMEETING

TABLE N.1: Unique Options on the Net Watcher Menus

Menu	Item	What It Does
Administer	Shared Folder Properties	Displays the Properties dialog box for a selected shared device or folder
View	Refresh	Renews the display of resources currently being shared

---

WARNING Always notify users before you disconnect them, close a file being shared, or stop sharing a folder. Users can lose information if you disconnect them without warning.

NetMeeting

 A conferencing application that allows people working in different locations to collaborate simultaneously on the same project, sharing Microsoft applications to edit documents. NetMeeting also supports audio- and videoconferencing over the Internet (as long as you have the appropriate hardware, such as a video camera or microphone attached to your computer system), as well as a file-transfer function. NetMeeting allows you to contact friends, relatives, and business colleagues all over the world for the cost of a local telephone call.

Choose Start ➢ Programs ➢ Accessories ➢ Internet Tools ➢ NetMeeting to open NetMeeting. The first time you run the program, a Wizard takes you through the initial configuration steps; you can always change these settings later if you wish.

Main NetMeeting Buttons

The primary NetMeeting functions are available as buttons in the main NetMeeting window:

 Place Call   Initiates a new call.

 End Call   Terminates the current call.

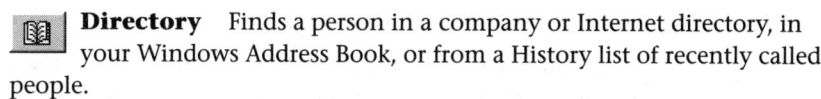

Directory Finds a person in a company or Internet directory, in your Windows Address Book, or from a History list of recently called people.

Start/Stop Video Starts or stops the video presentation.

Picture-in-a-Picture Displays the video image as a small video image within the main window.

Adjust Audio Volume/View Participant List Lets you turn the volume up or down and see a list of the people participating in the current call.

Share Program Allows other participants in the call to work with your shared application.

Chat Allows you to use the chat feature.

Whiteboard Opens the Whiteboard for use.

Transfer Files Opens the File Transfer window so you can send one or more files to the call participants.

File-Transfer Buttons

The file-transfer functions are available as buttons in the File Transfer window:

Add Files Adds a file to the list of files to be transferred.

Remove Files Deletes a file from the list of files to be transferred.

Send All Initiates a file transfer and sends the selected files to the appropriate recipients.

Stop Sending Aborts the file transfer.

View Received Files Opens a window on the folder that contains files received from a call participant.

Call Status Indicators

The last line of both the NetMeeting window and the File Transfer window is a status line, where you will see a text description of the current activity as well as one or more of the following status indicators:

In a Call   Indicates a call is in progress.

No Connections   Indicates no connections are available for a call.

Do Not Disturb   Indicates you are logged on to a directory server, but are unavailable for calls.

In a Secure Call   Indicates that all connections in the current conference are secure. You cannot mix secure and nonsecure calls in the same conference; your calls must be one or the other. In a secure call, you can use Chat and Whiteboard, share programs, and transfer files, but don't use the audio or video, as they are not encrypted.

Logged On   Indicates you are logged on to a directory server.

Not Logged On   Indicates you are not logged on to a directory server.

Making a Call and Chatting

To make a call using NetMeeting, both participants must be connected to the Internet and running NetMeeting. Follow these steps:

1. Choose Call ➤ New Call or click the Call button on the toolbar to open the Place a Call dialog box.

2. In the To box, enter the modem phone number, e-mail name, computer name, or network address of the person you want to call, or click the Directory button to see a list of the directories available from your computer. Make a selection and click Call.

3. When the person you are calling accepts the call, you'll see that person's name on your screen.

4. Click the Chat button to open the Chat window.

5. To send a message, type in the Message text box and press Enter. Any text you type in the Message box appears opposite your name on the other person's screen, and anything that person types appears on your screen opposite their name.

6. When you are done, close the Chat window and click End Call to terminate the call.

Joining a Meeting

You can also use NetMeeting to hold meetings involving more than two users. When you host a meeting, you are in charge of starting and ending it. Other people can join and leave the meeting as they see fit, but when you leave, the party's over.

Choose Call ➤ Host Meeting to start; other participants can now call you and join the meeting. You can also join a meeting by calling someone who is already participating in the meeting, but if that person disconnects, you will be disconnected too. To terminate a call at any time, click the End Call button.

Sharing Applications

Two or more people can work on the same document at the same time using NetMeeting, but only the original owner of the document is allowed to edit it. For example, you can open a Word document, let the other meeting participants look at the contents, and then make changes based on their opinions.

To share a document, set up a meeting as described in the previous section, and then follow these steps:

1. Open the document using the same application you used when you first created it; for example, if it's a Word document, open it in Word.

2. Arrange the Word window on your Desktop, then switch to NetMeeting.

3. Choose Tools ➤ Sharing, or click the Share Program button to display a small menu listing all the applications running on your system.

4. Choose the application that you want to share with the other meeting participants from those listed in this menu, and it will start on every meeting participant's Desktop, with the document open.

You can read the comments made by other meeting participants as they are displayed in the Chat window, or you can hear them if you are using NetMeeting's audio features. You can edit the document, and the other participants can watch the changes being made on their systems.

NETMEETING

Using the Whiteboard

The NetMeeting Whiteboard is an electronic version of the boards used in conference rooms, but the difference is that several people can draw on the NetMeeting Whiteboard at the same time, and they don't all have to be in the same physical location.

The Whiteboard window looks like many of the popular draw or paint applications, and you can draw shapes, add text, highlight areas, and even save the Whiteboard to disk so that you can use it in the future.

To start the Whiteboard, choose Tools ≻ Whiteboard or click the Whiteboard button. All participants in the call will see the same Whiteboard image on their screens, and they all have their own local pointers they can use to enter text and draw shapes.

Transferring Files

Once you finish collaborating on a document, you can send a copy of the final version of the file to all the meeting participants:

1. Choose Tools ≻ File Transfer to open the File Transfer window, then click Add Files to open the Select a File to Send dialog box.

2. Choose the file you want to send and click Send, or select several files and click Send All.

NetMeeting now transfers the file to the other meeting participants; a dialog box opens on their screens giving them the chance to accept or refuse the file transfer. You can also cancel the transfer if you discover you selected the wrong file by clicking Stop Sending in the File Transfer window. All the files received during a NetMeeting session are saved in the Received Files folder; to look at them, click View Received Files.

NetMeeting Options

To look at or change the NetMeeting settings, choose Tools ≻ Options to open the Options dialog box, which has the following tabs:

General   Details your personal information, including your name and e-mail address. Remember that this information will be seen by others during meetings and can be used in online directories. If you don't want your information displayed in directories, check the Do Not List My Name in the Directory option on this tab.

Security Lets you specify whether outgoing and incoming calls will be secure, and lets you choose the type of security and digital certificate to use.

Audio Lets you fine-tune audio settings, including microphone sensitivity.

Video Lets you customize settings used when sending and receiving video with NetMeeting.

See also Internet, Internet Explorer, MSN Messenger Service, Network, Winipcfg

Network

Displays the properties of the network components installed on your system. Choose Start ➤ Settings ➤ Control Panel ➤ Network to open the Network dialog box. It has three tabs.

Configuration Tab

Details the networking components that Windows detected during installation or that have been separately installed, and allows you to change, add, or delete components and specify system resource sharing.

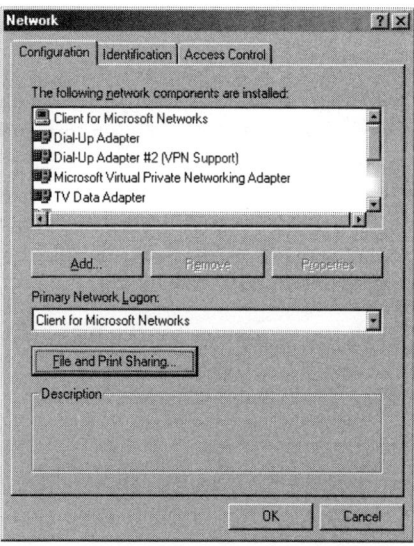

NETWORK

Add   Allows you to add components to your network configuration. Click Add to open the Select Network Component Type dialog box.

Network

When you select a type of component and click Add, additional dialog boxes will open, relating to the specific component. The four types of network components are as follows:

Client   Software that connects your computer to other computers so that you can access their disks, printers, and other resources. Examples include products from Banyan, Microsoft, and Novell. For a Windows-based network, you typically choose Client for Microsoft Networks from the Network Clients list.

Protocol   The formal specification that defines how computers transmit and receive data. Communications protocols define the format, timing, sequence, and error checking used on the network. Windows supports protocols from the major networking manufacturers such as Novell, Microsoft, Banyan, and IBM, as well as industry-standard protocols such as TCP/IP, which is used for Internet communications.

Service   Software that allows you to share the resources on your computer with other computers.

NOTE   New network adapters, such as network interface cards, are added through the Add New Hardware Wizard.

Remove   Deletes the selected component from the list and from your computer. No message is displayed asking for confirmation. If you mistakenly remove an item, you will have to reinstall it.

Properties   Displays the properties for the highlighted component. Depending on the component, the screen may have more than one tab. You can change the settings from these screens.

Primary Network Logon   Displays options for logging on to your computer. Select the Windows Logon option, for example, if you are not using the network, or select Client for Microsoft Networks or Client for NetWare Networks if you are using one of those networks.

File and Print Sharing   Displays a File and Print Sharing dialog box that allows you to select whether you want to give other users access to your files and printers. If you are undecided about whether to share your files and printers, consult your system administrator.

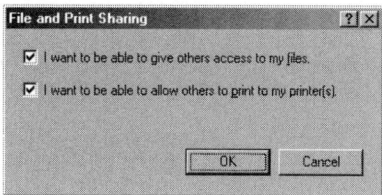

Identification Tab

Allows you to list and change the names by which you are known on the network. It contains the following options:

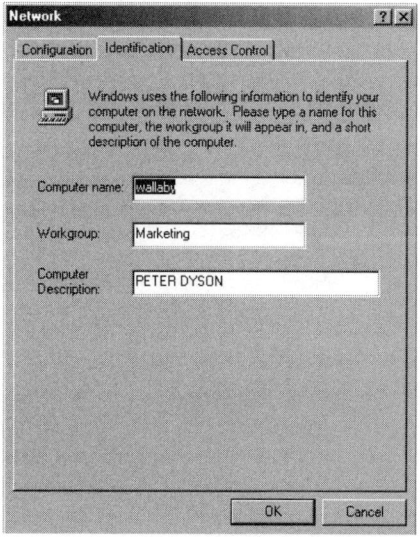

Computer Name   Identifies your computer to other users on the network. This name can contain a maximum of 15 characters, but no blanks.

Workgroup   Identifies the group of computers to which you belong. The name can be a maximum of 15 characters and is usually set by the system administrator.

Computer Description   Adds an optional comment that identifies you in more detail to others on the network. You can enter a maximum of 48 characters.

Access Control Tab

Lets you specify whether other users will require a password to use your resources. It contains these options:

Share-Level Access Control   Allows you to assign a password to shared resources. Others using the files or printers will need to know the password before they are allowed access.

User-Level Access Control   Allows you to list specific persons who can access your files and printers without a password.

Obtain List of Users and Groups From   This option is available only when User-Level Access Control is selected, and it allows you to enter the network domain name or computer containing the list of users allowed to share resources.

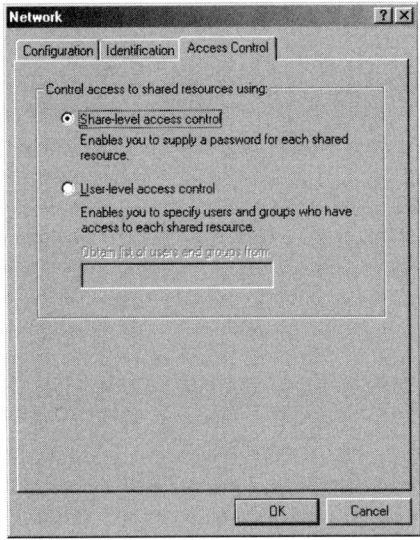

See also   My Network Places, Passwords, Sharing Resources

Notepad

 An editor used with small (less than 64K) unformatted text files. You can use it to look at the contents of the Clipboard and to display the contents of `Readme.txt` files.

Notepad Window

Choose Start ➤ Programs ➤ Accessories ➤ Notepad to open the Notepad window, containing the File, Edit, Search, and Help menus.

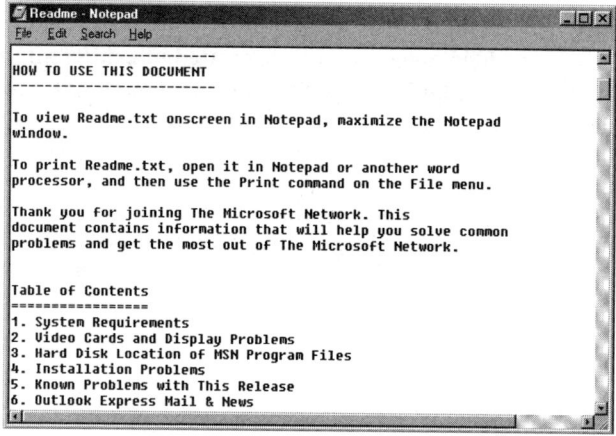

All these menus contain standard options. Of note, though, is the File menu's Open command, which will strip the opened file of any formatting, making it into an ASCII file. In addition, the Edit menu contains a Word Wrap option, which is a switch for turning Word Wrap on and off.

Retrieving Text

To view text in Notepad, you have three options:

- Type the text manually.

- Choose File ÿ Open to open a file. You can open or save a file only in ASCII format.

- Choose Edit ÿ Paste after copying or cutting data from another application to the Clipboard.

See also WordPad

ODBC Data Sources (32bit)

ODBC Data Sources (32bit)

An applet in the Control Panel that enables you to control how you connect to various database resources.

ODBC is a programming interface that enables applications to access data in database management systems. This is a specialty tool for database and server administrators, not something for the average user.

OLE

Stands for Object Linking and Embedding. Allows you to create documents containing linked or embedded objects that were created in a different program. For example, with OLE (Object Linking and Embedding), you might link or embed a graph created by Excel in a Word document, along with a logo from Paint.

NOTE To use OLE, both the object-creating program and the "container" program must be OLE-compatible. Objects to be linked or embedded must have an extension that is recognized as an OLE-compatible application, such as Word, Excel, and Paint.

See also Linking and Embedding

Online Services

Allows you to sign up for any of several popular online services such as AOL and Earthlink. Before you can use any of these services, you must first register with the service. You can do this using the items in the Online Services menu; each item connects you to a specific service. You can also use the Online Services folder on the Desktop.

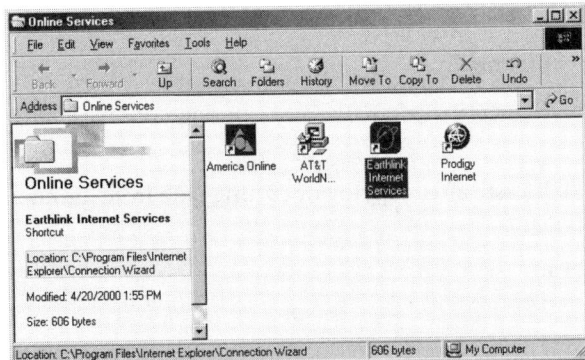

ON-SCREEN KEYBOARD

NOTE America Online (AOL) is an online service that also offers Internet. In contrast, the other services available in the Online Services folder are purely Internet Service Providers (ISPs), that use Windows's own built-in Web browser and e-mail program. AOL generally appeals to novices, while true ISPs are preferred by more experienced users.

Before you start, connect your modem to the phone line, and close any other open applications. Each service is a little different in its requirements, but in general, be ready to supply your name, address, phone number, credit card number and expiration date, username, and password during the registration process. Simply follow the instructions on the screen to complete your registration.

NOTE Many of these services use a toll-free 800 number to sign you up as a member. After that, you will use a different telephone number, usually a local number supplied to you when you register.

See also Internet Connection Wizard, Internet Explorer, Microsoft Network (MSN), Outlook Express

On-Screen Keyboard

On-Screen Keyboard A new Accessibility feature in Windows Millennium Edition that allows the mouse to be used with an on-screen keyboard to "type." To enable it, choose Start ➤ Programs ➤ Accessories ➤ Accessibility ➤ On-Screen Keyboard. Then type by clicking the letter buttons. Close the On-Screen Keyboard window when finished with it.

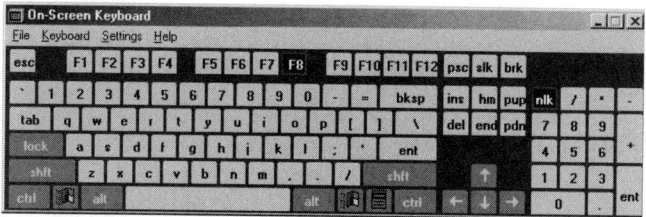

See also Accessibility, Accessibility Options, Accessibility Wizard

Outlook Express

 Windows application used to send and receive e-mail, and read and post messages to Internet newsgroups. To start Outlook Express, click the Outlook Express Desktop icon, or choose Start ➢ Programs ➢ Outlook Express. You can also click the Launch Outlook Express button on the Quick Launch toolbar, or use the Mail menu from within Internet Explorer.

Outlook Express Window

The main Outlook Express window contains the usual menu bar with a toolbar below and the Folders and Contacts areas along the left side of the window. The central portion of the window contains icons for common activities such as Read Mail, Set Up a Newsgroups Account, and Create a New Mail Message. These icons are arranged under the headings E-Mail, Newsgroups, and Contacts. There is also a Tip of the Day area to the right of the window.

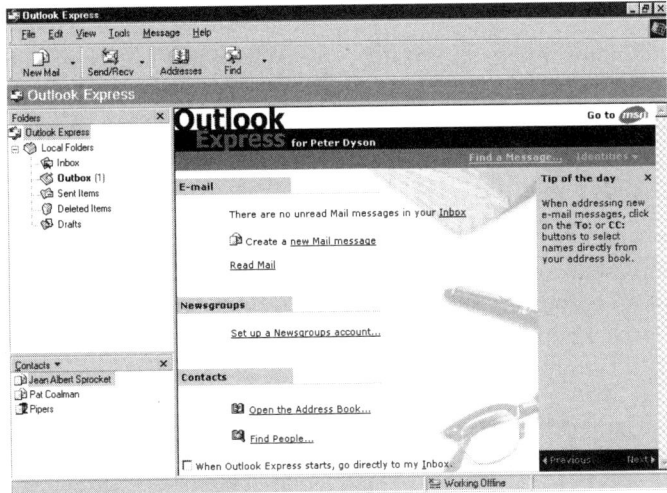

Outlook Express Toolbars

When you first open Outlook Express, the toolbar contains the following buttons:

 New Mail Allows you to create a new message. Click the arrow to the right to choose a stationery format for your message. To keep the message as small and compact as possible, choose No Stationery from this list.

OUTLOOK EXPRESS

 **Send/Recv** Sends all the messages in your Outbox and collects all messages waiting for you on your ISP's mail server. Click the arrow to the right to select Receive All or Send All options.

 Addresses Opens the Windows Address Book.

 Find Opens the Find Message dialog box so you can search through your existing messages by sender name, subject, or message content, or search for messages received before or after specific dates. Click the arrow to the right to select the People search option.

The Outlook Express toolbar is very flexible. Right-click an empty area and choose Customize if you want to add buttons to or remove buttons from the toolbar.

To add or remove whole toolbars, use View ➤ Layout to open the Layout dialog box. Check the boxes associated with the toolbars you want to use, and click Apply. If you check the Outlook Bar box, the Outlook Bar is displayed on the left of the Outlook Express window and contains these buttons:

 Inbox Contains your most recently received e-mail messages.

 Outbox Holds the e-mail messages that are waiting to be sent.

 Sent Items Contains messages that you have sent.

 Deleted Items Contains messages that you deleted after reading them.

 Drafts Contains messages in draft form that are not yet ready to be sent.

OUTLOOK EXPRESS

Outlook Express Menus

All the functions available on the Outlook Express toolbars are also available from the menus, as you would expect, but the menus add a significant number of additional features. Some of the menus, including the File and Edit menus, are dynamic, just like the toolbar, and they add or remove selections depending on where you are in Outlook Express and the nature of your current activity.

Reading Your Mail

Click the Inbox icon on the Outlook Bar or click Read Mail in the main Outlook Express window to look at your mail. A welcoming message from Microsoft will be waiting for you there. The Preview Pane is divided horizontally: message header information is in the upper pane, and the message itself is in the lower pane.

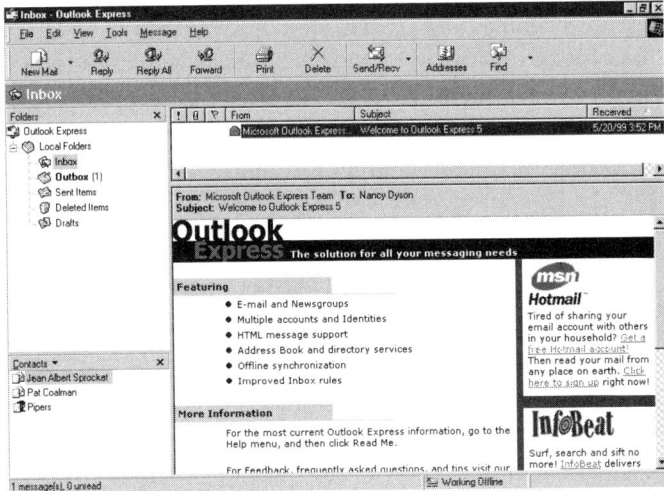

The other major Outlook Express functions all use this dual-pane window; so once you get the hang of it here, it is easy to use the other Outlook Express components.

TIP You can drag the boundary between these two panes to change the relative proportions if you wish.

OUTLOOK EXPRESS

Once you read a message, you can mark it as read or as unread, you can reply to the originator or forward the message to someone else, you can move it to a different folder on the Outlook Bar, or you can delete it. Right-click any message to open the pop-up menu containing selections for all these functions.

You can retrieve your e-mail in several ways:

- Click the Send/Recv button on the toolbar in the main Outlook Express window. This also sends any mail waiting in your Outbox.

- Choose Tools ➤ Send and Receive. This option works the same way as clicking the Send/Recv button on the toolbar.

Creating and Sending a Message

To create a new message, click the New Mail button on the toolbar or choose Message ➤ New Message to open the New Message window, and follow these steps:

TIP You can also simply double-click a name in the Contacts area of the main Outlook Express window to open a new message already addressed to that person.

1. Enter the e-mail address of the recipient in the To field. If you have previously entered addresses in your Address Book, Outlook Express will use Auto-Complete to fill in the rest of the entry once you type the first few letters.

2. Enter e-mail addresses in the Cc (carbon copy) field if you wish.

3. Enter a subject line for your message. The subject is automatically copied into the title bar of this message dialog box.

4. Type the text of your message in the lower part of the dialog box. You can create messages in several formats, including Plain Text and Rich Text (HTML). The default is Rich Text (HTML), which may cause duplicate messages to appear if your correspondent uses an online service such as CompuServe, which does not understand this format.

TIP In the New Message dialog box, use the selections available in the Insert menu to add other elements to your message, including a signature, business card, horizontal line, picture, or hyperlink to a Web site. Outlook Express allows you to have several different signatures, and each one can be associated with a different mail or news account.

173

OUTLOOK EXPRESS

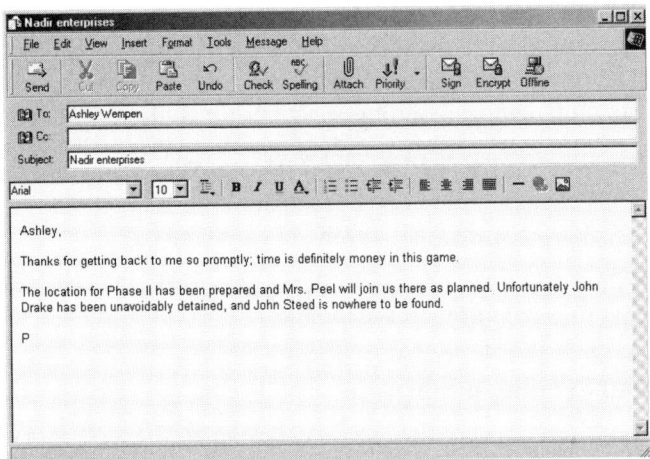

The New Message window toolbar contains the following buttons to help you compose your message:

 Send Puts the message in your Outbox.

 Cut Cuts the selected text to the Windows Clipboard.

 Copy Copies the selected text to the Windows Clipboard.

 Paste Pastes the current contents of the Windows Clipboard into the message at the insertion point.

 Undo Undoes the last change.

 Check Checks the name used in the e-mail against current entries in your Address Book.

 Spelling Checks the spelling.

 Attach Lets you select a file to attach to this e-mail.

OUTLOOK EXPRESS

Priority   Lets you select a priority for this e-mail message. Many e-mail protocols do not allow messages to be prioritized.

Sign   Allows you to add a digital signature to your message.

Encrypt   Allows you to encrypt the contents of this e-mail.

Offline (or Online)   Toggles between Online and Offline, indicating the current status of your Internet connection.

Once your message is complete, you can send it to the Outbox in several ways:

- Click the Send/Recv button on the toolbar in the main Outlook Express window. This also retrieves any mail waiting for you and places it in your Inbox.
- Click the Send icon on the New Message window toolbar.
- Choose File ➤ Send Message.
- Choose File ➤ Send Later.

If you don't have a full-time Internet connection, it makes sense to collect several messages in your Outbox until you are ready to connect to the Internet, rather than sending them one at a time—unless they are urgent, of course. Click the Send/Recv button on the Outlook Express toolbar to connect to the Internet, to send out all the mail from your Outbox, and to pick up all the mail waiting for you and store it in your Inbox.

Attaching a File

To attach a file to an e-mail message, follow these steps:

1. In the New Message window, choose Insert ➤ File Attachment. Or click the Attach button.
2. In the Insert Attachment dialog box, select the file you want to attach, and then click Attach.
3. Your e-mail message now contains an additional header line indicating that a file is attached, the name of the file, and its size. You can repeat this process to attach additional files as you see fit.

175

Reading the News

Outlook Express is also a newsreader that you can use to access the tens of thousands of specific-subject newsgroups on the Internet.

WARNING Anything goes in many of these Internet newsgroups. There is absolutely no censorship, and if you are easily offended (or even if you are not), you might want to stay with the more mainstream groups.

In the same way that you set up an e-mail account with an ISP, you must also set up a newsgroup account, complete with password, before you can use Outlook Express as a newsreader. Your ISP will provide all the configuration information you need for this.

You can use Outlook Express to download a complete list of all the newsgroups available to your ISP and then search for newsgroups that might interest you. Once you select a newsgroup, you can read the articles posted to the newsgroup by others, and you can post your own articles using the Outlook Express e-mail functions. You can even download newsgroup posts and read them later offline to save on connection charges.

Configuring Outlook Express

Configuration options for Outlook Express are quite extensive. You can customize the toolbar and add buttons for the tasks you perform most often, and you can define the rules you want Outlook Express to follow when you are creating, sending, and receiving e-mail. Choose Tools ➢ Options to open the Options dialog box. It has the following tabs:

General Contains general-purpose settings for Outlook Express. The long text description beside each of the checkboxes on this tab make the entries self-explanatory.

Read Specifies options used when displaying articles from newsgroups.

Receipts Specifies whether, and in what situations, to request a read receipt—that is, a confirmation that a recipient has opened the message.

Send Specifies the format for sending mail and for posting articles to newsgroups, as well as several other mail-related options, such as whether to include the text of the original message in any reply.

OUTLOOK EXPRESS

Compose   Lets you choose the font to use, the stationery for your message, and whether to include your business card in the message.

Signatures   Controls the signature settings for outgoing messages. You can use multiple signatures if you wish. Click New to create a new signature.

Spelling   Lets you configure the spell checker.

Security   Establishes security zones and specifies how Outlook Express manages digital certificates (also known as digital IDs) and message encryption.

Connection   Specifies the options used when connecting to your ISP by dial-up connection.

Maintenance   Specifies housekeeping options as well as several troubleshooting options of interest only to system administrators.

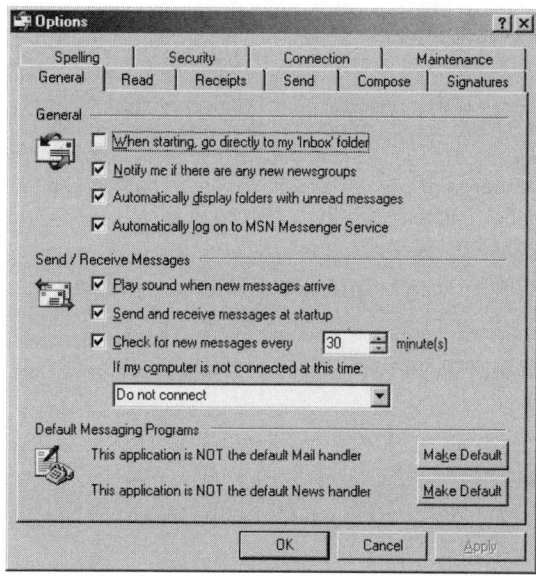

You can also choose View ➤ Layout to open the Layout Properties dialog box. Check the boxes associated with the Outlook Express function you want to enable or clear the checkbox to disable a function. Click Customize Toolbar if you want to create your own toolbar or edit the existing toolbar.

OUTLOOK EXPRESS

TIP You can establish a set of rules for Outlook Express to use when managing your e-mail or newsgroups. Choose Tools ➤ Message Rules, and then either Mail to set up rules for use with e-mail, News to set up rules for use with newsgroups, or Blocked Senders List to automatically route e-mail from specified sources straight to your Deleted Items folder.

Using Identity Manager

You can use Identity Manager to create profiles for different users of Outlook Express. In this way, different people can use Outlook Express without having to log off and log on again. These profiles are shared with the Windows Address Book and are protected by a password. Use File ➤ Identities ➤ Add New Identity to open the New Identity dialog box and enter a name to associate with this new identity.

Once you have created two or more identities, use File ➤ Switch Identity to change from one to the other.

WARNING Setting up separate identities does not allow multiple users to share a single e-mail address with privacy for each. For multiple-user privacy, you must sign up for separate e-mail addresses for each person and then configure them in Outlook Express with Tools ➤ Accounts.

See also Address Book, Search, Internet Connection Wizard, Internet Explorer, Modems

Paint

Paint A program with which you can create lines and shapes, with or without color, and place text within graphics. You can also use it to create backgrounds for the Desktop. Choose Start ➤ Programs ➤ Accessories ➤ Paint to open the main Paint window.

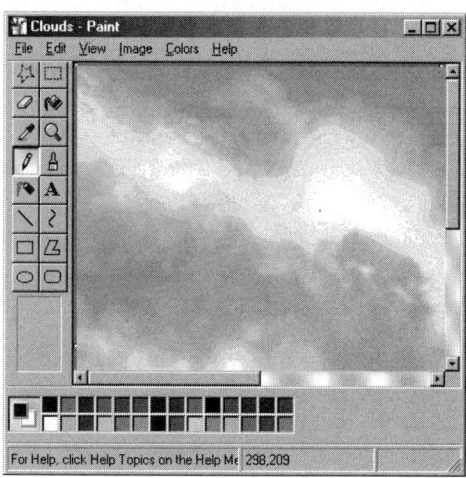

Paint Toolbar

Arranged down the left side of the main window, the Paint toolbar provides the following tools for drawing lines and shapes and working with color and text:

Free-Form Select Selects an irregularly shaped area of the image to move, copy, or edit.

Select Selects a rectangular area of the image to move, copy, or edit.

Eraser/Color Eraser Erases an area of the image as you move the eraser tool over it.

Fill with Color Fills an enclosed area with the currently selected color.

Pick Color Selects the color of any object you click. It is for use with the tool that you chose immediately before you selected Pick Color.

PAINT

Magnifier   Enlarges the selected area.

Pencil   Draws a freehand line one pixel wide.

Brush   Draws lines of different shapes and widths.

Airbrush   Draws using an airbrush of the selected size.

Text   Inserts text onto the drawing. Click Text, click the color you want for the text, and then drag a text box to the location where you want to insert the text. In the font window that appears, click the font, size, and style (Bold, Italic, Underline) you want. Click inside the text box, and begin typing your text.

Line   Draws a straight line. After dragging the tool to create a line segment, click once to anchor the line before continuing in a different direction, or click twice to end the line.

Curve   Draws a curved line where one segment ends and another begins. After dragging the tool to create a line segment, click once to anchor the line before continuing. To create a curve, click anywhere on the line and then drag it. Click twice to end the line.

Rectangle   Creates a rectangle. Select the fill style from the Color Palette below the main Paint window.

Polygon   Creates a polygon (a figure consisting of straight lines connecting at any angle). After dragging the first line segment, release the mouse, place the pointer where the second line segment is to end, click the mouse button, and repeat until the drawing is complete. Click twice to end the drawing.

Ellipse   Draws an ellipse. Select the fill style from the Color Palette below the main Paint window.

Rounded Rectangle   Creates a rectangle with curved corners. Select the fill style from the Color Palette below the main Paint window.

Below the toolbar, there is an area containing additional choices depending on the type of tool you choose. For example, if you choose the Brush tool, a selection of brush edges is displayed. If you choose Magnifier, a selection of magnifying strengths is displayed. At the bottom of the main window, the Color Palette displays a series of colored squares.

When you create an image in Paint, first select the tool, then select the tool shape, if applicable, and then click the color you want to use from the Color Palette at the bottom of the Paint window. The currently active color is displayed in the top square on the left of the palette. To change the background color, click Pick Color, and then click the color you want. The next image you create will use the new background color.

Paint Menus

Contain many of the standard Windows options. Table P.1 shows the menus and their unique options.

TABLE P.1: Unique Options in the Paint Menus

Menu	Item	What It Does
File	Set As Wallpaper (Tiled)	Places the Paint object (when saved) as the background wallpaper, with the design repeated in a tiled design.
	Set As Wallpaper (Centered)	Places the Paint object (when saved) as the background wallpaper, with the design centered.
View	Zoom	Displays a submenu of options for viewing objects.
	Normal Size	Displays an image.
	Large Size	Enlarges an object.
	Custom	Sets specific zoom percentages.
	Show Grid	Displays a grid against the object.
	Show Thumbnail	Displays a thumbnail of the selected part of an object.
	View Bitmap	Displays an image in full-screen view. Pressing any key returns you to the Paint window.
Image	Flip/Rotate	Flips the image horizontally or vertically, and rotates the image 90, 180, or 270 degrees.
	Stretch/Skew	Stretches or skews the object in a horizontal or vertical direction by precise percentages or degrees.
	Invert Colors	Reverses colors or changes them to their complement.

Continued on next page

TABLE P.1: Unique Options in the Paint Menus (*cont.*)

Menu	Item	What It Does
	Attributes	Changes the width and height of the object. You can specify its measurement in inches, centimeters, or pixels, and you can specify colors or black and white.
	Clear Image	Removes the image from the screen. If you have not saved it, it is lost.
	Draw Opaque	Switches between opaque and transparent drawing. An opaque drawing covers the existing picture; a transparent object allows the underlying picture to show through.
Colors	Edit Colors	Defines custom colors.

See also Imaging

Passwords

Allows you to specify a Windows logon password. Windows maintains a set of user profiles, each containing a different username and password, Desktop preferences, and Accessibility options. When you log on to Windows, your profile ensures that your Desktop settings, including elements such as your own Desktop icons, background image, and other preferences, are automatically available to you.

Enabling User Profiles

To enable user profiles, follow these steps:

1. Choose Start ➤ Settings ➤ Control Panel ➤ Passwords to open the Passwords Properties dialog box, and click the User Profiles tab.

2. Select Users Can Customize Their Preferences and Desktop Settings.

3. In the User Profile Settings box, you can select one or both of the following options:

    - Include Desktop icons and Network Neighborhood contents in user settings.

    - Include Start menu and Program groups in user settings.

4. You'll have to use Shut Down to restart your computer for these changes to be applied.

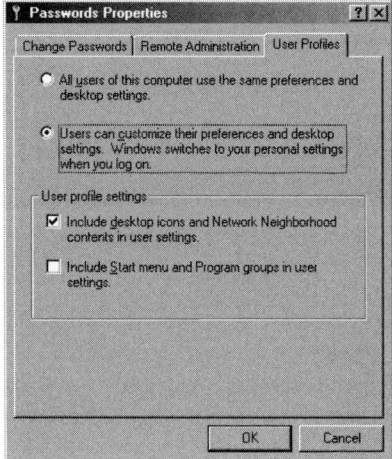

Specifying a Windows Password

When you start Windows for the first time after installing it, you are prompted to enter a username and password, and then to confirm that password. If you don't enter anything for the password, Windows will not prompt you to log in again unless you have user profiles set up (described in the preceding section).

NOTE Note that a Windows login is different from a network login. If you are connected to a network, you may also be asked to enter a network password.

After the first time, you are not asked to confirm the password; you merely enter it along with your user name to log in.

WARNING Windows Millennium Edition is not a password-secure operating system. If you don't remember your password, you can simply enter a different user name and create a new user login to access the PC. A network password, on the other hand, is set up on your network server, so a person who does not know the network login password cannot connect to the network.

183

PASSWORDS

Changing the Windows Password

To change a password, follow these steps:

NOTE You must know the current password to change it.

1. Choose Start ➤ Settings ➤ Control Panel ➤ Passwords to open the Passwords Properties dialog box.

2. Select the Change Passwords tab, and then click the Change Windows Password button to open the Change Windows Password dialog box.

3. Type the old password (asterisks will appear as you type) and enter the new password. You will have to retype the new password to confirm it. Click OK to close the Change Windows Password dialog box.

4. Click OK to close the Passwords Properties dialog box and finalize your new password.

TIP Next time you log on to Windows, remember to use your new password.

In addition to your logon password, you can establish a password for the following resources, using other parts of Windows (provided that file and printer sharing is installed):

Dial-Up Connections To change passwords, choose Start ➤ Settings ➤ Dial Up Networking ➤ Select Connections ➤ Dial-Up Server. Click Allow Caller Access to enable the Change Password button.

NOTE If the Dial-Up Server selection is not available in your Connections menu, it was not installed along with the other Windows components. Use the Add/Remove Programs applet in Control Panel to complete your installation. Under the Communications category in Add/Remove Programs, be sure that both Dial-Up Networking and Dial-Up Server are selected for installation; you need them both to set up a Dial-Up Networking server.

PASSWORDS

Disks To set and change sharing access passwords, right-click the disk in the Explorer window and select Sharing from the pop-up menu.

Folders To change the password or sharing status, open Explorer or My Computer, select the folder, choose File ➤ Properties, and then click the Sharing tab.

Printers To change the password or sharing status, open the Printers folder from Explorer, My Computer, or Control Panel. Right-click the printer and select Sharing from the pop-up menu. You can also select the printer, choose File ➤ Properties, and then click the Sharing tab.

Network Administration Set password access to shared devices from the Access Control tab in the Network applet in the Control Panel.

Screen Savers You can use a password to prevent others from gaining access to your files when a screen saver is active. To change a password, choose Start ➤ Settings ➤ Control Panel ➤ Display to open the Display Properties dialog box. Select the Screen Saver tab and click Password Protected, and then click the Change button.

WARNING Screen saver passwords do not offer very strong protection. Restarting the PC resets the screen saver, allowing access.

Shared Resources To change the password or sharing status, open Explorer or My Computer, select the resource, choose File ➤ Properties to open the Properties dialog box, and select the Sharing tab. If the resource is shared, you can change the password. You can also change the sharing status from the Access Control tab in the Network applet in the Control Panel.

You may also be able to click the Change Other Passwords button in the Passwords Properties dialog box to work with these other passwords. If other passwords can be changed from there, the Change Other Passwords button will be available—if the button is not available they cannot be changed from there.

Allowing Remote Administration

You can specify whether a system administrator can create shared folders and shared printers on your computer, and you can see the username of anyone who connects to them by using the options on the Remote Administration tab in the Passwords Properties dialog box. To use this you must, of course, have your PC set up for networking and for file and printer sharing.

See also Log Off, Log On, Profiles, Users

Paste Command

Copies the contents of the Clipboard into the current document. It is available from the Edit menu and from some pop-up menus that are displayed when you right-click a file or folder.

See also   Copying Files and Folders

Path

Defines the information needed to locate a specific file and includes disk drive, folder, subfolder, and filename. For example, the path for the FreeCell game might be `C:\Windows\Freecell.exe`; `C:` is the disk drive, `\Windows` is the folder, and `\Freecell.exe` is the filename. The backslash (\) separates the different parts of the address.

If the name of a file is more than eight characters or includes blanks or spaces, enclose the full path in quotation marks, as "`C:\FinanceTechnologyStocksQuotes.xls`".

To specify a path to a folder or a file on the disk drive of another computer that is not mapped to a drive name on your computer, precede the computer name with two backslashes, as `\\Marty\Doc\Budget.doc`. `Marty` is the name of the other computer.

To specify a path to a file or folder on another computer that *is* mapped to a drive name on your own computer, type the path as you would for your own disk drive.

See also   Map Network Drive

Personalized Menus

A new feature in Windows Millennium Edition adapts to your usage of the Start menu, so that commands you have used before appear on a shorter, abridged list at first. You can click the down arrow button at the bottom of the menu to view the complete menu if you don't see the command you want. The next time you use that command, Windows will have remembered it and placed it on the initially appearing menu.

When you open the full menu, you'll notice that the initially hidden commands appear pressed in, while the ones that appeared from the start don't.

PERSONALIZED MENUS

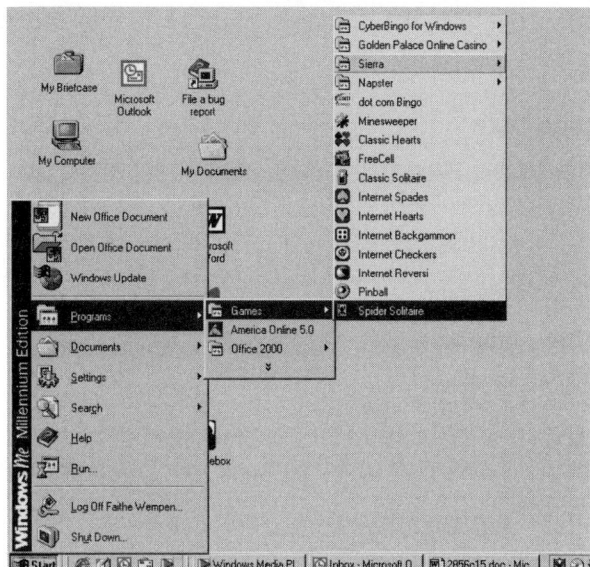

Turning Off Personalized Menus

Some people prefer not to use personalized menus. To turn them off, follow these steps:

1. Right-click the Taskbar and choose Properties.
2. Deselect the Use personalized menus checkbox.
3. Click OK.

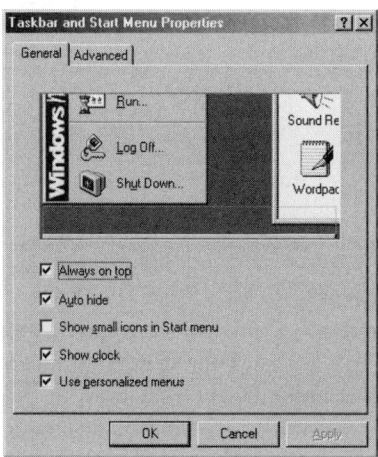

Do the same thing, selecting the checkbox this time, to turn the feature back on again.

Resetting Usage Data

To reset the usage tracking that Windows stores, starting again with a default set of initially appearing commands, do the following:

1. Right-click the Taskbar and choose Properties.
2. Click the Advanced tab.
3. Click the Clear button.
4. Click OK.

This not only clears the usage data for personalized menus, but also clears the Documents menu's list of recently used documents and your Web browser's history list.

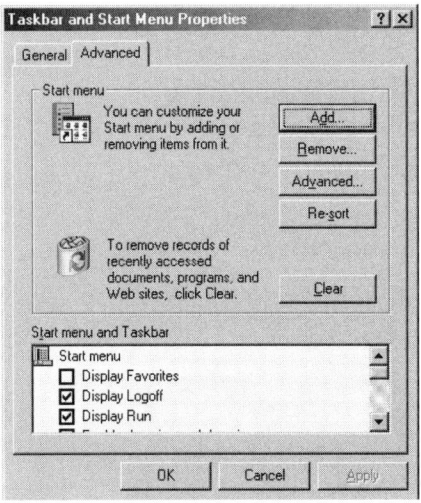

See also Start, Taskbar and Start Menu Properties

Phone Dialer

Dials phone calls from your computer using your modem. To open the Phone Dialer dialog box, choose Start ➤ Programs ➤ Accessories ➤ Communications ➤ Phone Dialer.

PHONE DIALER

Phone Dialer Dialog Box

The menus in the Phone Dialer dialog box all contain standard Windows options, except for the Edit and Tools menus.

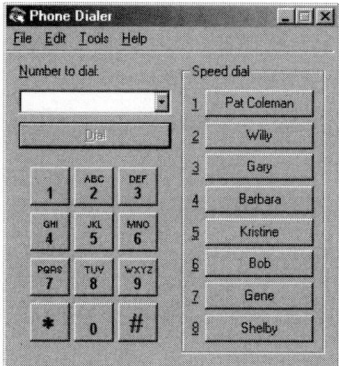

Edit Menu

The Edit menu contains only one unique command, Speed Dial. This option displays the Edit Speed Dial dialog box, in which you can enter a name and a phone number to assign to a speed dial button. It also lists previously entered phone numbers that you can dial immediately by clicking the appropriate button.

Tools Menu

The Tools menu contains three unique commands:

Connect Using   Allows you to specify which modem or telephone line you want to use when you have more than one. Click Line Properties to open the Modem Properties dialog box where you can look at or change modem properties. If you want the Phone Dialer to be used for all voice call requests even if another program initiates them, click Use Phone Dialer to handle voice call requests from other programs.

Dialing Properties   Displays the Dialing Properties dialog box in which you can set options such as area code, country, calling card, call waiting disabling, tone or pulse dialing, and other details.

Show Log   Displays a list of calls that you have dialed.

Setting Up a Speed Dial Number

To set up a Speed Dial number, you can either click a blank button in the Speed Dial box or choose Edit ➢ Speed Dial to open the Edit Speed Dial dialog box.

PLUG AND PLAY

Choose a button, and then enter the name and phone number you want to associate with that button. Click Save when you are done.

Dialing a Number with Phone Dialer

You can dial a number in three ways:

Click the numbers in the phone pad and then click Dial.

Type a number in the Number to Dial box and then click Dial.

Click a Speed Dial button. The appropriate phone number is entered in the Number to Dial box and is automatically dialed.

See also Dial-Up Networking, Modems

Plug and Play

A Windows feature that automatically detects hardware installed in your computer system. Today, most hardware is specifically designed with Plug and Play in mind. You just install the hardware, and Windows takes care of the details, loading the appropriate device drivers and other related software automatically.

Plug-and-Play adapters contain configuration information stored in permanent memory on the board, including vendor information, serial number, and other configuration data. The Plug-and-Play hardware allows each adapter to be isolated, one at a time, until Windows identifies all the cards installed in your computer. Once this task is complete, Windows can load and configure the appropriate device drivers. After installing a new Plug-and-Play adapter in your computer system, Windows will often ask you to restart the system. This is so the new device drivers can be loaded into the correct part of system memory.

See also Add New Hardware, Device Manager, Shut Down

Power Options

Manages the way your computer uses power. The extent to which you can take advantage of power-management features depends entirely on your computer hardware. Some laptop computers have a fully implemented power-saving scheme designed to optimize battery life, and some desktop systems can power down the hard disk and the monitor if they have been inactive for a while.

POWER OPTIONS

Choose Start ➤ Settings ➤ Control Panel ➤ Power Options to open the Power Options Properties dialog box. It has two tabs.

Power Schemes Tab

You can set the length of idle time after which you want Windows to turn off your monitor and your hard disk; time periods extend from After 1 Minute to Never, which effectively disables the power-management features on your computer.

NOTE You may also be able to select the Hibernate tab to specify that your laptop goes into hibernation when you close the lid. If the Hibernate tab is not available, your computer does not support this feature. When you put your computer into hibernation, everything in memory is saved to the hard disk so that when you turn your computer on again, all the applications and documents that were open when you closed the lid are reloaded.

Once you have chosen the appropriate settings for your system, you can save them as a named Power Scheme or, in other words, as a group of preset options. Click the Save As button in the top part of the Power Options Properties dialog box to perform this task.

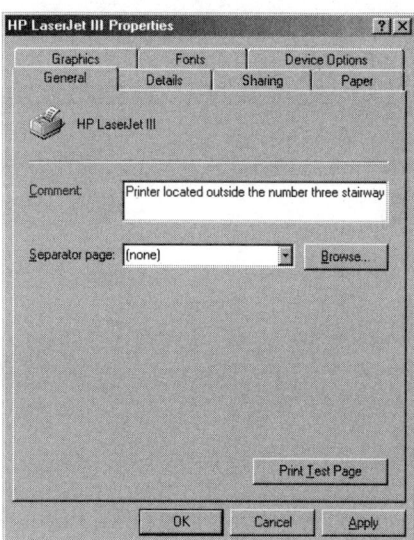

Advanced Tab

This tab contains only a single checkbox: Always show icon on the taskbar. This turns on/off the Power icon in your system tray.

When the Power icon appears in the system tray, you can double-click it for quick access to the Power Options Properties dialog box. On laptops, this checkbox is on by default; on desktops it's off by default.

See also   Display, Screen Saver

Printers

Manages all functions related to printers and printing. From here you can add a new printer, check on a job in the print queue, change the active printer, or modify a printer's properties.

Printers Folder

To access the Printers folder, choose Start ➤ Settings ➤ Printers. You can also open the Printers applet in the Control Panel.

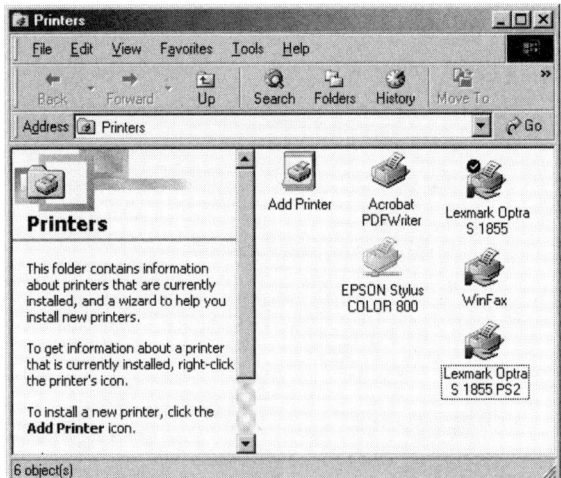

The Printers folder lists all the printers connected to your computer or available to you on the network. Click the Add Printer icon to start the Add Printer Wizard, which guides you through the process of adding a new printer to your system.

Note the differences in the printer icons shown in the above graphic:

- Printers with a hand under them are local printers you are sharing on the network.

- Printers with a cable under them are network printers that are not physically connected to your PC.

- Printers that appear dimmed are not currently available, perhaps because the network connection is not established.

- The default printer has a checkmark in a black circle in the top-left corner of its icon.

Printing a Document

Unless you specify otherwise, Windows applications pass your documents to the underlying operating system for printing. If you don't specify a printer, Windows automatically sends your document to the default printer (the one with the checkmark in the Printers folder).

TIP When you print a document in Windows, the document is first sent to a temporary disk file rather than directly to the printer. Windows then spools the file to the specified printer. Because Windows is in overall charge of this operation, different print jobs can be queued up, rearranged, deleted, and so on.

You can print a document in three ways:

- Within your application, choose File ➤ Print, and fill in whatever information you are asked to provide. Some applications have elaborate dialog boxes for choosing a printer, scaling options, or other graphical options, and others simply ask for basic information such as the name of the printer to use, the number of copies you want, and the page range you want to print.

- If you arrange your Desktop so that you can see both the document you want to print and the printer icon, you can then simply drag the file to the printer. The original copy of your document is not moved from its folder; it is simply passed to the Windows print spooler for printing. You can also place a shortcut on your desktop for the printer, and drag files to that shortcut to print them.

- Right-click a document and note whether the menu contains a Print selection. If it does, you can use the command to print the file; if there is no such option, press Esc.

PRINTERS

Print Queue

If you print a large number of files at the same time, or if you allow printer sharing by other network users, you may have to check on the status of a print job.

Double-click the appropriate printer icon in the Printers folder to open the printer's own dialog box, which lists the name of the document being printed or waiting to be printed, the status of the document, the owner of the document, its progress, and when it entered the print queue. The status bar at the bottom of the dialog box displays the number of jobs in the queue.

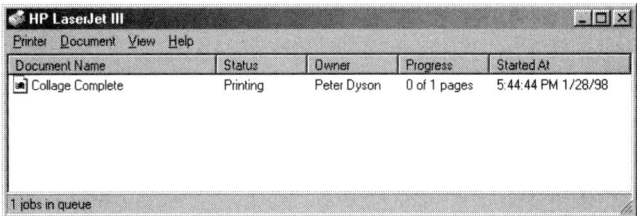

TIP The printer queue dialog box is also displayed when you double-click the printer icon on the Taskbar when a print job is initiated.

The Printer menu contains these specialized options:

Pause Printing   Temporarily interrupts the print job.

Set As Default   Specifies this printer as the default printer.

Purge Print Documents   Deletes all print jobs from the print queue.

Properties   Displays the Properties dialog box for the specified printer.

The Document menu contains the options for starting and stopping printing:

Pause Printing   Temporarily interrupts the print job.

Cancel Printing   Removes a document from the print queue.

NOTE To change the order of documents in a print queue, click the document and drag it to the desired position in the list. You cannot change the order of documents in a network printer queue (except if it is your own local printer shared on the network).

PRINTERS

Interrupting Printing

Occasionally, you may need to interrupt a print job. You can do so in three ways:

- Click the printer icon on the Taskbar to open the printer queue dialog box. Choose Document ➤ Pause Printing or Document ➤ Cancel Printing.

- Choose Start ➤ Settings ➤ Printers. Click the icon for the printer you want to interrupt to display the printer queue dialog box. Choose Document ➤ Pause Printing or Document ➤ Cancel Printing.

- Using either the printer icon or the Printers folder, go to the printer queue dialog box, right-click the document you want to interrupt, and select Pause Printing or Cancel Printing.

To continue printing the document, repeat the process described above, only this time remove the check mark next to Pause Printing.

Printing to a Disk File

Most Print dialog boxes contain an option you can check to print your document to a file rather than to a printer. The file created this way is not a simple copy of your document, but is fully formatted with the codes that control your printer, including font information, page breaks, and even bold and underline attributes.

Once your application creates the file, you can send it to a coworker as an e-mail attachment or copy it to a floppy. The file can then be printed on any compatible printer.

Printer Properties

Every printer has a collection of associated settings you can look at or change with the Properties dialog box. Because of the huge number of printers of many types now supported by Windows, each with its own individual features, generalizing about what you might see in the Properties dialog box for your printer is difficult.

> **TIP** To see a quick explanation of what each option in a dialog box does, click the Help question-mark icon and then click the option. A small text box explains the option and how to use it.

PRINTERS

Choose File ➢ Properties or right-click a printer icon and choose Properties to display that printer's Properties dialog box. You can also press Alt+Enter to open the Properties dialog box.

NOTE The Properties controls are determined by the printer's driver. The Properties box shown below is typical of a laser printer; different printers will have other tabs and other controls on each tab.

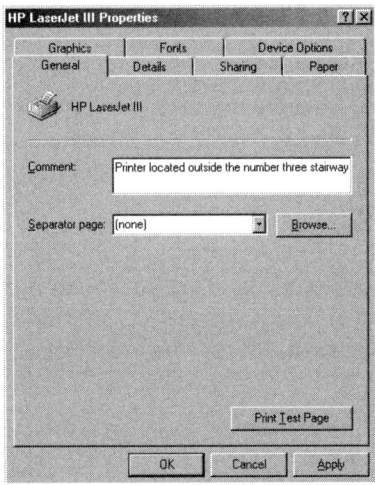

The number of tabs in this dialog box and the options they contain depend on the specific printer attached to your system. Here are some common tabs and options:

General   Contains options that allow you to enter comments, specify a separator page to be used between print jobs, and print a test page.

Details   Contains options to establish and manage printer ports and drivers. You can also set time-out limits for how long Windows is to wait for a printer to be online before Windows displays an error message. From this tab, you can also set options for the print spooler.

Sharing   Allows you to indicate whether a printer is to be shared and to specify the shared name and password.

Paper   Contains settings relating to the size and orientation of the paper. It may contain layout options, page source, and the default number of copies.

Graphics Allows you to specify graphics quality. Settings include graphic image resolution, dithering (blending of colors into patterns) or halftoning, and intensity of image (how light or dark it is).

Fonts Manages fonts, including identifying the font cartridge you want to use, specifying how TrueType fonts are printed, and installing additional fonts.

Device Options Contains options such as the amount of printer memory available, and lets you adjust printer memory tracking.

Depending on the type of printer you have, you might also see a PostScript tab or a Color Management tab.

Adding a New Printer

Click the Add Printer icon in the Printers folder to start the Add Printer Wizard, which guides you through installing a new printer on your system. The Wizard can be used to set up either a local printer (one connected directly to your PC) or one you will access through the network.

Adding a Network Printer

1. Double-click Add Printer in the Printers folder. When the Wizard opens, click Next.

2. Choose Network printer, and then click Next.

3. Fill in the Network path or queue name. Click the Browse button to search for the printer if you are not sure of the path.

4. If you will be using any MS-DOS programs, click Yes for Do You Print from MS-DOS Based Programs. If you clicked Yes, you may have to identify a printer port for MS-DOS printing.

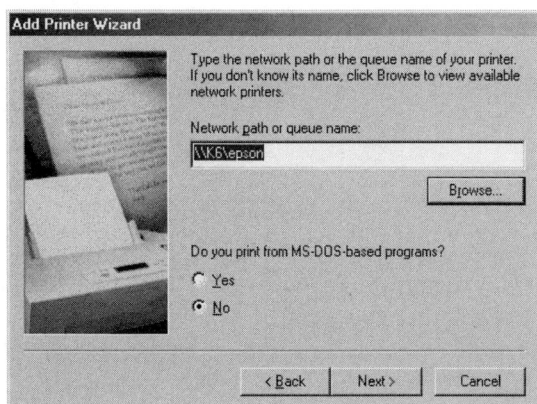

PRINTERS

5. Click Next.

6. Enter a name for the printer (choose one that you are sure to remember), and then select whether you want to set this printer as your default printer. Click Next.

7. To print a test page, turn on the printer, load paper if necessary, and click Yes. Otherwise click No, and then click Finish. The printer icon will be added to the Printers folder.

Adding a Local Printer

1. Double-click Add Printer in the Printers folder. When the Wizard opens, click Next.

2. Choose Local printer, and then click Next.

3. Select the name of the maker from the Manufacturers list and the model from the Printers list.

   If you have a disk that came with the printer, place it in the PC and click Have Disk, then navigate to the drive containing the files.

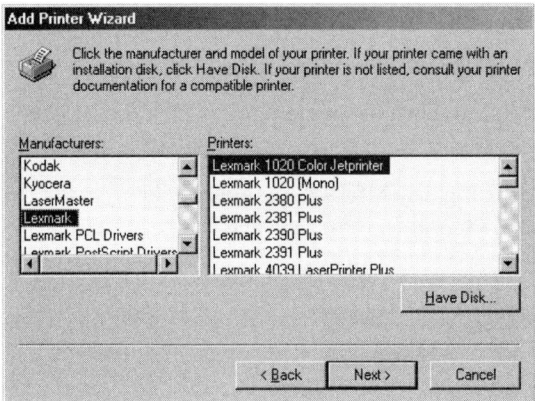

4. Click Next.

5. Click the port you want to use with the printer, normally LPT1. Click Configure Port to verify that the settings are appropriate and then click Next.

6. Enter a name for the printer (choose one that you are sure to remember), and then select whether you want to set this printer as your default printer. Click Next.

PROFILES

7. To print a test page, turn on the printer, load paper if necessary, and click Yes. Otherwise click No, and then click Finish. The printer icon will be added to the Printers folder.

Sharing a Printer

The easiest way to set up printer sharing is to run the Home Networking Wizard. You can rerun it at any time, even if you have run it before.

You can also set up the sharing manually. First make sure File and Printer sharing is enabled by doing the following:

1. Start ➤ Settings ➤ Control Panel, and double-click Network.
2. Click the File and Printer Sharing button.
3. Make sure the checkbox for printer sharing is marked.
4. Click OK.

You may be prompted to restart your PC after doing the above. After restarting, share the individual printer by doing the following:

1. Right-click the printer's icon in the Printers folder and choose Sharing.
2. Choose Shared As.
3. Enter the name by which the printer should be known on the network in the Share Name box.
4. (Optional) To assign a password for using the printer, enter one in the Password box.
5. Click OK.

See also   Home Networking Wizard, Passwords, Network

Profiles

Contain the characteristics of the object or user and relevant defaults. Windows maintains both *hardware* and *user* profiles.

Hardware Profiles

When you specify the hardware profile you want to use when you start Windows, Windows loads only the device drivers needed to support the hardware

PROFILES

enabled in that profile. This can come in handy, for example, if you have a laptop with a built-in network card, but you are not always connected to the network. It takes several seconds for the network connection to time out when you restart the PC unconnected. By creating a separate hardware profile for non-network operation, you can prevent Windows from trying to establish the network connection when no network is available.

You can create additional profiles to enable or disable certain hardware devices on your system. If you do so, you will be prompted when Windows starts to choose which profile to use in the current session.

Follow these steps to create a new hardware profile:

1. Choose Start ➤ Settings ➤ Control Panel ➤ System to open the System Properties dialog box.

2. Click the Hardware Profiles tab.

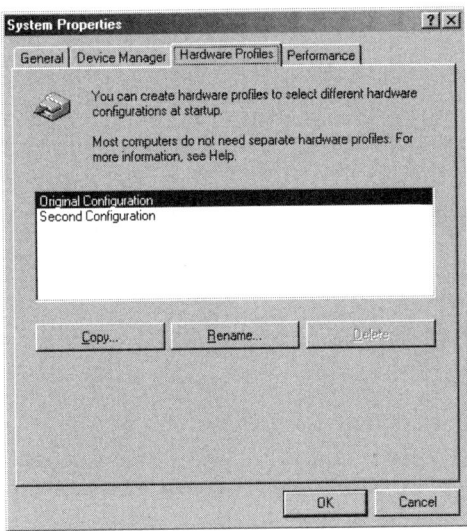

3. Select the profile you want to use as the basis for the new profile, and then click Copy to open the Copy Profile dialog box and create a duplicate.

4. Enter a name for the copy and click OK. A new hardware profile appears in the Hardware Profiles list.

5. Restart the PC and, when prompted, select the new profile.

6. To enable or disable individual hardware drivers for this new profile, choose Start ➤ Settings ➤ Control Panel ➤ System again and select the Device Manager tab.

7. Click the plus sign next to a device type to see all the devices under it.

8. Double-click the hardware device you want to change. A Properties dialog box opens.

9. Select or deselect the Disable in This Hardware Profile checkbox.

10. Click OK.

11. Click Close on the Device Manager tab.

User Profiles

Windows is installed as a single-profile system: users get the same settings every time they log on regardless of the username and password they use. User Profiles allow people to customize their Desktop settings and passwords. When you log on after establishing a user profile, Windows uses your settings until another user logs on. Follow these steps to set up user profiles:

1. Choose Start ➤ Settings ➤ Control Panel ➤ Passwords to open the Passwords Properties dialog box:

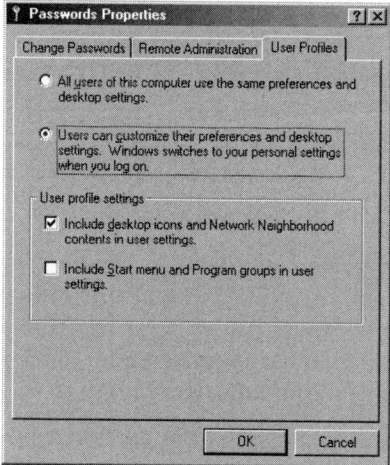

2. Select the User Profiles tab, which has the following options:

All Users of This Computer Use the Same Preferences and Desktop Settings. Select this option if you do not want to establish a customized user profile.

Users Can Customize Their Preferences and Desktop Settings. Windows Switches to Your Personal Settings When You Log On. Use this option if you want to set up customized Desktop settings for multiple users.

When you select this second option, two other options become available:

Include Desktop Icons and Network Neighborhood Contents in User Settings. Specifies that Desktop icons and Network Neighborhood contents be customized for an individual user. This can include Desktop colors, fonts, and passwords.

Include Start Menu and Program Groups in User Settings. Specifies that the contents of the Start menu and the options in the Program menu can be customized for a user.

3. Once you select the options you want—you can check either or both—click OK.

After configuring Windows to use multiple user profiles, you can then set up the user profiles through the Users icon in the Control Panel. The first time you select it, the Add User Wizard runs to help you configure your first user. After that, revisiting the Users icon in the Control Panel opens a box that lets you add and manage users.

See also Log Off, Log On, Passwords, Shut Down, System, Users

Programs

Lists the programs available in Windows, either as stand-alone applications or as collections of applications located in submenus or program groups. Any selection that has an arrow pointer to the right of the name is not a single program but a program group. Choosing one of these groups opens another menu listing the items in the group.

Follow these steps to start a program from the Programs menu:

1. Choose Start ➤ Programs to display the current list of program groups.

2. Select a program group to display a list of the programs it contains.

3. Click an application name to start it.

Adding a New Submenu to the Programs Menu

Most Windows programs are added to the Programs menu automatically as they are installed—you are generally asked to verify in which folder or program group any new program should be placed—and the Setup program takes care of the rest. However, you can create a new submenu manually if you wish. Follow these steps:

1. Right-click the Start button and choose Open to open the Start Menu folder.

2. Double-click the Programs folder, and then choose File ➤ New ➤ Folder. This creates an empty folder in the Program group with the name New Folder.

3. Type the name you want to use for the submenu as the name of this new folder, press Enter, and then open the folder you just created.

4. Choose File ➤ New ➤ Shortcut to start the Create Shortcut Wizard, which guides you through the process of adding applications to your new folder.

5. Enter the path and filename for the application in the Command Line box, or click the Browse button to locate the file.

6. Type a shortcut name for the program and click Finish.

The next time you open the Programs menu, you will see the entry you just created, and when you select that entry, you will see the list of items that it contains.

See also   Add/Remove Programs, Browse, Start, Taskbar and Start Menu

Properties

Characteristics of something in Windows—a computer, a peripheral such as a printer or modem, a file, or a folder—are displayed in the Properties dialog box. The properties for any item depend on what it is. To open any Properties dialog box, follow these steps:

1. Select the item in Explorer.

2. Choose File ➤ Properties.

You can also open the Properties dialog box by right-clicking an object and then selecting Properties from the pop-up menu.

Radio

See Windows Radio, Windows Media Player

Recycle Bin

A folder that stores deleted files until they are finally removed from your hard disk. The Recycle Bin is represented on the Desktop by a wastebasket icon. Files are copied to the Recycle Bin both directly and indirectly: you can simply drag a file there, or you can send a file to the Recycle Bin by choosing Delete from a pop-up menu. When you empty the Recycle Bin, the files it contains are permanently removed from your hard disk; once you empty the bin, anything it contained is gone for good.

TIP If the Recycle Bin contains deleted files, you will see paper protruding from the top of the wastebasket icon.

Recycle Bin Folder

Click the Recycle Bin icon to open the Recycle Bin folder, listing all the files it contains. Choose View ➤ Details to display the original location of the file, the date deleted, the type of file, and its size.

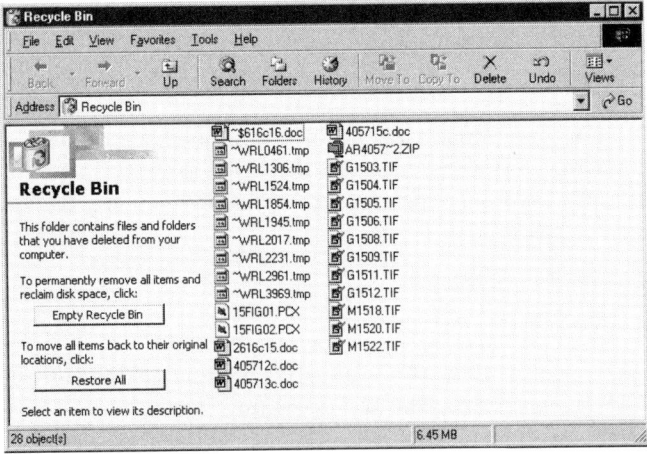

RECYCLE BIN

The Recycle Bin menus contain standard Windows options, with the following exceptions in the File menu:

Restore   Becomes available when a file is selected, and moves it back to its original directory or folder.

Empty Recycle Bin   Deletes files from the Recycle Bin folder and from your hard disk.

Emptying the Recycle Bin

Periodically you'll want to empty the Recycle Bin to free up the space the Recycle Bin files are taking on your hard disk. Follow these steps:

1. Double-click the Recycle Bin icon on the Desktop to open the Recycle Bin folder.

2. To empty the whole bin, choose File ➤ Empty Recycle Bin. To remove selected files, hold down Ctrl and click the files you want to remove. Then press the Delete key or choose File ➤ Delete.

3. Click Yes to verify that you want to delete the files.

TIP   You can also empty the Recycle Bin by right-clicking the icon on the Desktop and choosing Empty Recycle Bin from the pop-up menu.

Changing the Size of the Recycle Bin

The initial maximum size of the Recycle Bin is set at 10 percent of total disk space, but you can change that in the Properties dialog box. If you have more than one hard disk, each hard disk contains its own Recycle Bin. You can allocate the same amount of space for the Recycle Bin on all your disks, or you can configure each hard disk individually. Follow these steps to change the configuration and size:

1. Right-click the Recycle Bin icon and select Properties to open the Recycle Bin Properties dialog box.

205

RECYCLE BIN

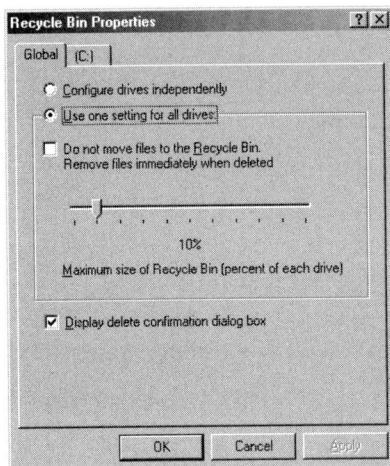

2. To use the same amount of hard-disk space for the Recycle Bin on all your hard disks, select Use One Setting for All Drives and then drag the slider to the percentage of disk space you want to allocate for the Recycle Bin.

3. To specify different sizes for the Recycle Bin for each of the disks on your system, select Configure Drives Independently. Then click the tab for each disk and drag the slider to the percentage you want to allocate to the Recycle Bin on that disk.

4. Click OK.

NOTE The Disk Cleanup feature in Windows can automatically delete the contents of the Recycle Bin as part of its effort to free up disk space. You can schedule Disk Cleanup to happen on a regular schedule with the Maintenance Wizard.

Recovering Files from the Recycle Bin

To recover files from the Recycle Bin and move them back to their original folders, follow these steps:

1. Double-click the Recycle Bin icon to open the Recycle Bin.

2. Select the files you want to restore, holding down Ctrl to select multiple files.

3. Choose File ➤ Restore. If you delete a folder and the files it contains, only the files appear in the Recycle Bin. If you restore a file that was originally located in that deleted folder, Windows first re-creates the folder and then restores the file into it.

You can also simply drag a file out of the Recycle Bin or undo the delete operation by choosing Edit ➤ Undo Delete in any folder or Explorer window.

WARNING If you delete more files than can be held in the disk space allocated for the Recycle Bin, your earliest deleted files will disappear without warning.

Bypassing the Recycle Bin

If hard-disk space is at a premium, and you decide to conserve as much space as possible for applications, you can configure Windows to delete files immediately and not copy them into the Recycle Bin. Open the Recycle Bin Properties dialog box and select the Global tab. Select Do Not Move Files to the Recycle Bin/Remove Files Immediately on Delete.

You can also delete individual files or groups of files without sending them to the Recycle Bin by holding down the Shift key as you press Delete to delete them.

See also   Disk Cleanup, Maintenance Wizard, Undeleting Files

Regional Settings

Sets the system-wide defaults for country (and therefore language), number, currency, time, and date formatting. If you are using English in the United States, you will probably never need Regional Settings. If you want to use a different language, this is the place to start. Choose Start ➤ Settings ➤ Control Panel ➤ Regional Settings to open the Regional Settings Properties dialog box.

Regional Settings Tab

On the Regional Settings tab, use the Language and Country/Region drop-down lists to choose your current location and language.

REGIONAL SETTINGS

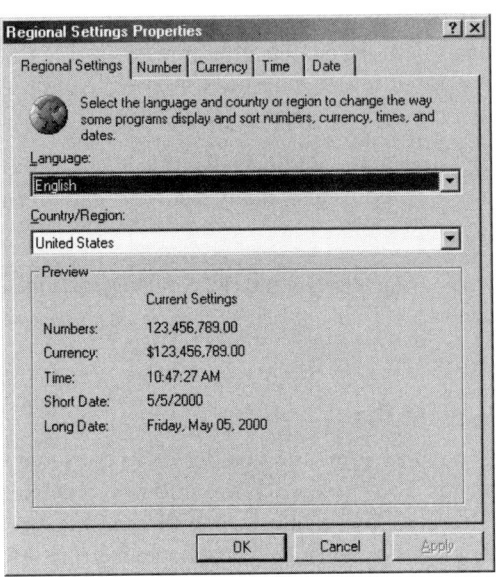

 TIP The Regional Settings tab also shows previews of the values set on the other tabs, such as Number, Currency, and Time.

Number Tab

Sets the defaults for how positive and negative numbers are displayed, the number of decimal places, the separator between groups of numbers, and so on. This tab contains the following options:

Decimal Symbol Establishes which symbol will be used as a decimal point. The default in the United States is a period.

No. of Digits after Decimal Specifies how many numbers will be placed to the right of the decimal point. The default is 2.

Digit Grouping Symbol Determines the symbol that will group digits into a larger number, such as the comma in 999,999. The default is a comma.

No. of Digits in Group Specifies how many numbers will be grouped together into larger numbers. The default is 3, as in 9,999,999.

REGIONAL SETTINGS

Negative Sign Symbol   Establishes which symbol is used to show a negative number. The default is a minus sign.

Negative Number Format   Establishes how a negative number will be displayed. The default is to display the negative sign in front of the number, such as –24.5.

Display Leading Zeroes   Determines whether a zero is shown in front of a decimal number. The default is yes, as in 0.952.

Measurement System   Determines whether the system of measurement will be U.S. or metric.

List Separator   Specifies which symbol will separate items in a list or series. The default is a comma.

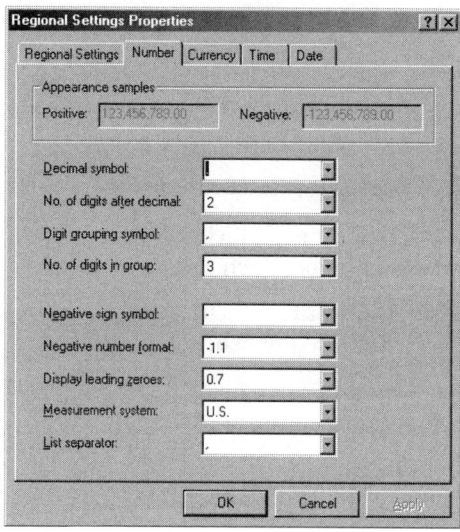

Currency Tab

Determines the format for displaying currency. For example, you might want to vary the number of decimal points or the presentation of negative numbers. This tab contains the following options:

REGIONAL SETTINGS

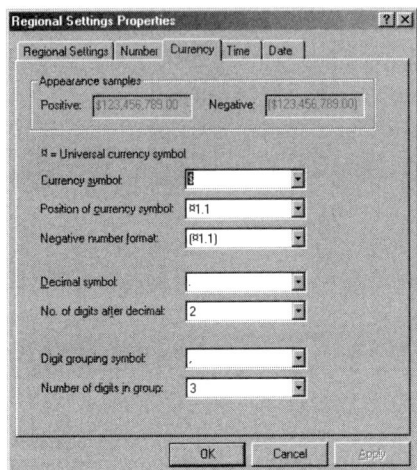

Currency Symbol   Displays the symbol of the currency, such as the dollar sign.

Position of Currency Symbol   Shows where the currency symbol is displayed in the number—usually in front of a number.

Negative Number Format   Specifies how negative numbers are displayed.

Decimal Symbol   Determines which symbol separates the whole from the fractional parts of a number, such as a period or a comma.

No. of Digits after Decimal   Specifies how many digits are shown by default after the decimal—usually two.

Digit Grouping Symbol   Shows which symbol—usually a comma—separates the number groups, such as thousands, millions, and so on.

Number of Digits in Group   Specifies how many digits determine a number group, such as 3 for thousands, millions, and so on.

Time Tab

Establishes the default formatting for the time. The Time tab has the following options:

Time Style   Determines how the time will be formatted.

Time Separator   Determines which symbol separates the hours from the minutes and seconds. The default is a colon.

REGIONAL SETTINGS

AM Symbol Specifies the default for the morning symbol.

PM Symbol Specifies the default for the afternoon symbol.

Click OK to activate any changes you make.

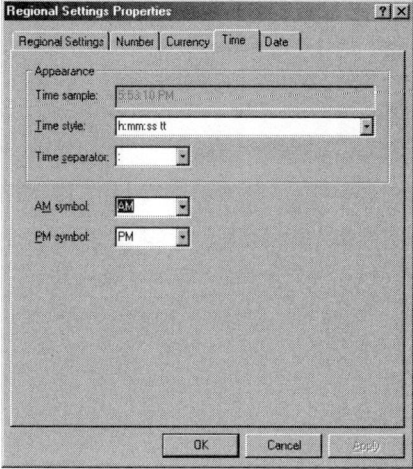

Date Tab

Establishes the default formatting for the date. The Date tab has the following options:

Calendar Type Displays the types of calendars from which you can choose. Think carefully before changing to a different calendar type, as any change will affect the naming and calculation of days, months, and years. You cannot change the calendar from the Gregorian Calendar setting unless you first alter the country and language settings in the Regional Settings tab.

When a Two-Digit Date Is Entered, Interpret as a Year Between Specifies how some programs interpret a two-digit date over a 100-year time span. Four-digit dates are not affected by this option. By default, the beginning date is January 1, 1930, and the ending date is December 31, 2029.

Short Date Style Lists the formats available for displaying the date.

Date Separator Lists the symbols that can be used to separate the month, day, and year.

Long Date Style Lists the formats available for displaying a formal date notation.

See also Date/Time

Registry

Location of all the system defaults and properties for all devices, files, folders, users and user preferences, communications protocols, and other resources in Windows. It is the central source of information for both users and computers; everything from passwords to color settings is stored in the Registry database.

Users do not normally interact directly with the Registry, but any changes you make using the Windows Control Panel applets will be stored in the Registry.

If you install a program or edit the registry and your computer doesn't work right afterward, you can restore the registry to an earlier, working configuration with the System Restore utility.

See also Registry Checker, System Restore

Registry Checker

A system utility that you can use to find and fix problems in the Windows Registry database. Registry Checker creates a backup copy of the Registry every day and can store a maximum of five compressed copies of these backups.

Each time you start your system, Registry Checker runs a check on your Registry, looking for problems and inconsistent entries. The Windows Setup program also invokes Registry Checker automatically whenever you upgrade the Windows operating system.

To run Registry Checker, choose Start ➤ Run, type **scanreg** into the Open box, and then click OK. Program operation is automatic, and user interaction is limited to preparing another backup of the Registry.

If Windows detects a registry error at startup, it may run the Registry Checker automatically for you to restore an earlier, working copy of the registry. When that happens, there is no need for you to interact with the program; simply allow it to do its business.

If you suspect a registry problem, you can restore an earlier copy of the registry yourself with the System Restore utility.

See also   Help, Registry, System Restore

Remote Access

See   Dial-Up Networking, NetMeeting

Resource Meter

 Measures the resource load on your computer as you open and use applications. It measures the use of memory each time a function is performed, such as a program being loaded, a dialog box being displayed, or a menu item being selected. Follow these steps to use the Resource Meter:

1. Choose Start ➤ Programs ➤ Accessories ➤ System Tools ➤ Resource Meter.

2. An introductory message tells you what the Resource Meter is all about. Click OK to close this message, and an icon appears on your Taskbar next to the time.

3. Double-click the icon to display the usage of resources on your system.

NOTE   The Registry Checker might not be installed by default; you may need to add it with Add/Remove Programs.

TIP You can also display the Resource Meter readout by right-clicking the icon in the Taskbar and selecting Details from the pop-up menu.

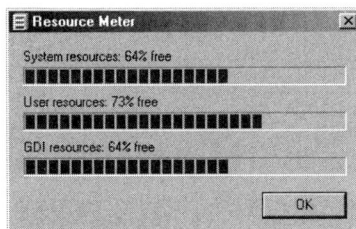

Horizontal bars represent three areas in your computer's memory where specialized processing information is stored:

- System resources
- User resources
- GDI (Graphic Device Interface) resources

Various programs use these areas in varying amounts. As you use your system with different application loads, you'll see the percentages of use in these areas change slightly.

4. When you finish with the Resource Meter, click OK.

5. To remove the Resource Meter from the system tray, right-click the icon in the Taskbar and choose Exit to close the program.

See also Add/Remove Programs, System, System Information, System Monitor

Run

 Starts a program or opens a folder when you type its path and name. You often use Run with a Setup program or installation programs, or to run a program such as Sysedit or Scanreg that does not have a Windows shortcut. Follow these steps:

1. Choose Start ➤ Run to open the Run dialog box.

 RUN

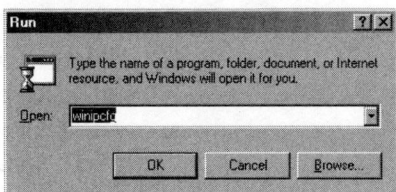

2. If you have run this program recently, you may find its name already entered in the Open list box. Click the down arrow, select it by name, and then click OK.

3. If you have not run this program recently or if the Open box is blank, type the full path and program name, such as **C:\Folder\Program**.

4. If you are not sure of the path or program name, click Browse to find and select the program. Then click OK to load and run the program.

See also   Path, Start, Startup, Taskbar and Start Menu

ScanDisk

 Checks a disk for certain common errors. Once ScanDisk detects these errors, it can fix them and recover any data in corrupted areas. If Windows is shut down improperly, as might happen during a power outage, ScanDisk runs automatically upon restart.

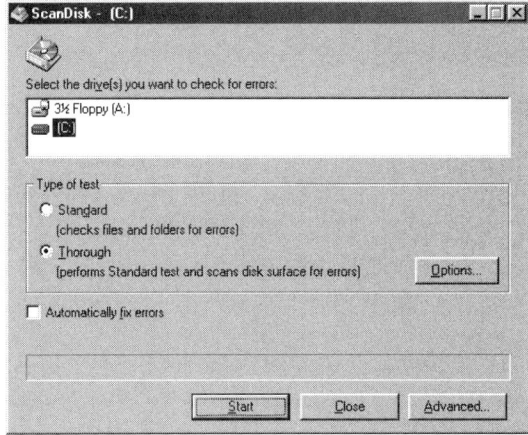

Choose Start ➢ Programs ➢ Accessories ➢ System Tools ➢ ScanDisk to open the ScanDisk dialog box. First, select the drive you want to check for errors and then select the type of test you want to run:

Standard Tests the selected disk for simple file and folder errors.

Thorough Runs the standard tests and also scans the disk surface for errors. If you opt for the Thorough test, you can click the Options button to specify which areas of the disk you want to scan and how they should be tested:

System and Data Areas Checks the entire disk for errors. This is the most commonly used option.

System Area Only Checks that portion of the disk occupied by the Windows system files. Much of the information stored in this part of the disk is location-specific and cannot be moved to another area of the disk. Thus, ScanDisk cannot repair any problems in the system area.

Data Area Only Checks that portion of the disk occupied by your applications and the data files they create. In many cases, ScanDisk can repair errors in this part of the disk and can relocate any data recovered to a known safe part of the disk. The damaged area is then marked so that it will not be used in the future. If the problem is not found early enough, however, data in the damaged area may actually be unreadable. In this case, ScanDisk marks the area of the hard disk as bad.

Do Not Perform Write-Testing Restricts ScanDisk to performing read tests, which may be less rigorous in unearthing errors and damaged data. Clear this box if you want ScanDisk to perform more rigorous write-testing.

Do Not Repair Bad Sectors in Hidden and System Files Prevents ScanDisk from repairing and moving hidden or system files. In certain cases, moving a hidden or system file to a new location may cause an application to not work properly. Some forms of copy protection require that certain files stay in the same location on disk, and some system files are location-specific and cannot be moved to a new location.

Check the Automatically Fix Errors checkbox if you want ScanDisk to attempt to fix any errors found. If you don't check this box, a dialog box opens when ScanDisk finds an error, and you can choose whether to repair the error, delete the file, or ignore the error and continue the test scan.

TIP If you suspect that something serious has happened to your hard disk, try running ScanDisk more than once. You may find that ScanDisk can locate and fix additional errors on a second scan. If it finds no errors, an additional test will probably not turn up any.

Click the Advanced button to open the ScanDisk Advanced Options dialog box. Here you specify how any errors found during testing will be handled:

Display Summary Displays information about the drive being scanned and any errors discovered and repaired once the scan is complete.

Log File Records the results of a scan in a file named `Scandisk.log`.

Cross-Linked Files Deletes, ignores, or copies two or more files pointing to the same data on a disk.

Lost File Fragments Deletes or converts fragments that cannot be linked to existing files so you can verify that they are no longer useful.

Check Files For Looks for invalid and duplicate names and invalid dates and times, which can cause a file to be unreadable or improperly displayed in sorted data.

Prompt Before Fixing Errors on Improper Shutdown Chooses whether ScanDisk will run with Automatically Fix Errors turned on when it runs automatically after an improper shutdown.

Report MS-DOS Mode Name Length Errors Reports any errors found in filenames.

After setting the options you want, click Start to begin scanning the disk. A status bar across the bottom of the ScanDisk dialog box indicates which area of the disk is being tested and shows the progress of the tests.

When ScanDisk is finished, it displays a brief summary of any problems found and fixed on your system, as well as a summary of how the space on the disk is divided among hidden and user files, folders, and free space. Click the Close button to close this report. You can then choose another disk to test from those listed in the main ScanDisk dialog box or click the Close button to close ScanDisk.

See also Disk Cleanup, Disk Defragmenter, Maintenance Wizard, System File Checker

Scanners and Cameras

Scanners and Cameras

Provides a central point in the Control Panel for managing the digital cameras and scanners used with the computer. You can add new scanners and cameras using the Add Device feature, or manage the settings on an existing one.

Adding a Scanner or Digital Camera

Most new devices will be automatically detected by Plug and Play, so you do not have to go through any special procedure to add them to the system. However, if Windows does not detect a new scanner or camera, you can use the following steps:

1. Choose Start ➢ Settings ➢ Control Panel.
2. Double-click the Scanners and Cameras icon.
3. Double-click the Add Device icon. The Scanner and Camera Installation Wizard runs.

SCANNERS AND CAMERAS

4. Click Next.

5. Select the manufacturer and model of the device, or click Have Disk and choose the location of the driver disk that came with the device.

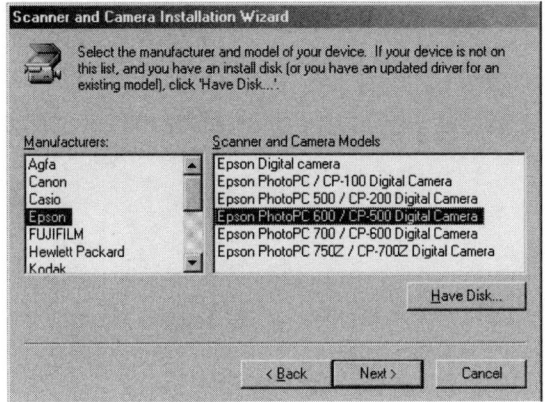

6. Click Next.

7. Choose the port you want to use with the device, or choose Automatic Port Select. Then click Next.

8. Change the device name if desired, and then click Next.

9. Click Finish.

You may be prompted for the Windows CD or a driver disk, and you may be prompted to restart your PC. Follow the prompts to complete the installation.

Setting Scanner or Digital Camera Properties

You can set a device's properties to control the way it operates. To do so for an installed scanner or digital camera, do the following:

1. Right-click the device in the Scanners and Cameras window and choose Properties.

2. (Optional) If desired, click the Test Scanner or Camera button on the General tab to make sure the device is correctly installed. Then click OK when you see the test results.

SCHEDULED TASKS

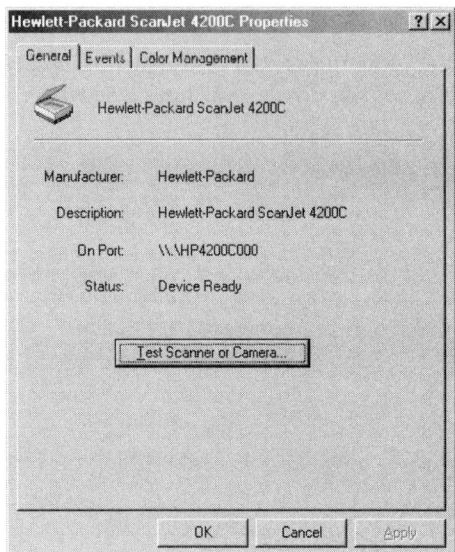

3. Change the device's settings in the box that appears. The options available depend on the device.

4. Click OK to close the properties when finished.

Transferring Images from a Digital Camera

Some digital cameras, when connected to your PC, show up as an icon in My Computer. If you see an icon for your camera there, you can double-click it to browse the camera's stored images. Then you can transfer them to your hard disk the same as you would transfer any other files.

See also Add New Hardware, My Computer

Scheduled Tasks

Scheduled Tasks Also called the Task Scheduler. A utility you can use to run selected applications at specific times—daily, weekly, or even monthly—without any input or involvement on your part. Scheduled Tasks starts running in the background every time you start Windows. The utility just sits there until it is time to run one of your selected tasks, and then it moves into action.

SCHEDULED TASKS

Certain tasks, such as running the hard-disk utilities ScanDisk and Disk Defragmenter, are well-suited to unattended automatic operation. You can run these programs while you work, but often it makes more sense to run them when your system is turned on but not too busy, such as at lunch time, when you are attending a regularly scheduled company meeting, or during the night. The Maintenance Wizard feature in Windows sets up ScanDisk, Disk Defragmenter, and Disk Cleanup to run as scheduled tasks, but you can schedule other programs to run too.

To open the Scheduled Tasks folder, choose Start ➢ Programs ➢ Accessories ➢ System Tools ➢ Scheduled Tasks. You can also open it from the Scheduled Tasks icon in the Control Panel.

Any currently scheduled tasks are listed in the main window along with information about when they will next run and when they last ran.

Adding a New Scheduled Task

To add a new scheduled task, follow these steps:

1. Open the Scheduled Tasks folder.

2. Double-click Add Scheduled Task to open the Scheduled Task Wizard.

3. Click Next.

4. Choose the program to schedule and then click Next.

5. Choose an interval at which to perform the task (Daily, Weekly, etc.) and then click Next.

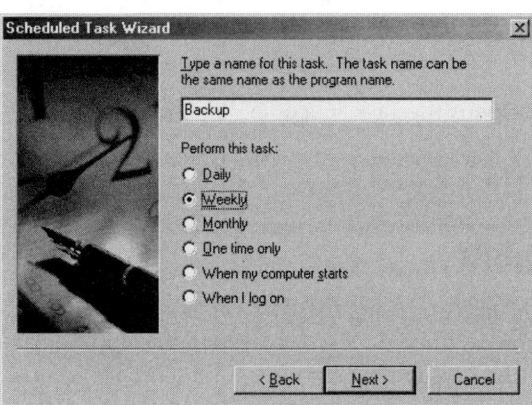

SCREEN SAVER

6. Specify a time and date to run the program next and then click Next.

7. Click Finish. The task appears in the Scheduled Task window.

To modify an existing task, right-click the task and then choose Properties from the pop-up menu:

Task   Changes the name of the program you want to schedule.

Schedule   Changes when the program is run.

Settings   Customizes the task configuration.

To halt a scheduled task that is currently executing, right-click to open the pop-up menu and then select End Task; to resume the task, right-click and choose Run. To remove a task, right-click it and select Delete from the pop-up menu.

Using the Advanced Menu

The Task Scheduler Advanced menu includes the following options:

Stop Using Task Scheduler   Turns the Task Scheduler application off and halts all scheduled tasks. Task Scheduler will not start automatically the next time you start Windows. This menu selection changes into Start Using Task Scheduler so that you can use it to restart operations.

Pause Task Scheduler   Temporarily stops the Task Scheduler. This menu item changes into Continue Task Scheduler so that you can restart operations. Any tasks that were due to run during the time Task Scheduler was paused will not run until their next scheduled time.

Notify Me of Missed Tasks   Informs you of any scheduled tasks that did not run.

View Log   Opens the Task Scheduler log file in a Notepad window.

See also   ScanDisk, Disk Defragmenter, Disk Cleanup, Maintenance Wizard

Screen Saver

Displays an image on the screen after a fixed period of inactivity. The screen saver hides the normal information displayed by the application you are using and replaces it with another image.

You can change or select a screen saver using the Display applet in the Control Panel. You can set the speed, shape, density, and color of the screen saver, and

SEARCH

you can set a password to get back to your work and other settings. You can also use certain active channels as screen savers.

See also   Channels, Display, Internet Explorer

Search

Settings   Windows includes options for finding files and folders, a computer, information on the Internet, or people. Choose Start ➤ Search and select an option, or choose the Search button on the toolbar in Explorer.

This feature replaces the Find feature in earlier versions of Windows.

Searching for Files or Folders

To locate a file or folder, you can use either My Computer or Explorer to scan the disks yourself, or you can use the Search command to have Windows conduct the search for you.

There are two ways to access the Search command. You can open a Search pane by clicking the Search button on the toolbar in Explorer, or by choosing Start ➤ Search ➤ For Files or Folders. Either way, Windows Explorer opens (if it was not open already) with the Search pane to the left of the main window.

Enter the file name to search for in the Search for Files or Folders Named box, and/or enter text contained in the file in the Containing Text box. Then click Search Now. A list of files matching the criteria appears.

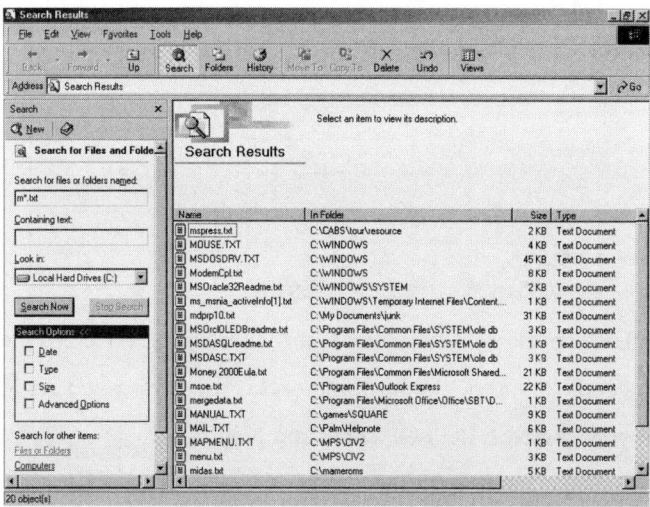

SEARCH

The Search utility in Windows has many options and is a powerful tool for finding the files and folders you want. Click the Search Options hyperlink to open a list of checkboxes: Date, Type, Size, and Advanced Options. Mark the checkbox for the criteria you want to search by, and additional controls appear for entering your specifications.

Searching on the Internet

The Search menu's On the Internet option uses Internet Explorer to connect to the Microsoft Web site. This single Web site gives you access to some of the most powerful and popular search engines on the Internet, including Infoseek, AOL NetFind, Lycos, Excite, and Yahoo! Each works slightly differently, and each has strengths and weaknesses.

And if that isn't enough, you can also use one of the other sites in the categories of General Search, Guides, White Pages, Newsgroups, Chat Guides, Specialty, or International. If you can't find what you are looking for using one of these search engines, what you are looking for doesn't want to be found.

Searching for People

The Search menu's People option lets you search public LDAP (Lightweight Directory Access Protocol) directories on the Internet, such as Bigfoot Internet Directory Service, Yahoo! People Search, and WhoWhere Internet Directory Service, for particular information. Here are the steps:

1. Choose Start ➢ Search ➢ People.

2. In the Look In list, select the name of the directory service you want to use.

3. In the People tab, type the information on the person you are looking for.

4. When your search is defined, click Find Now.

SETTINGS

The results of a search may vary depending on which of the services you use, but you will normally see a long list of names with different e-mail addresses. It is then up to you to decide which of those names is actually the person you want to contact.

See also Explorer, Internet Explorer

Send To

Sends items, such as floppy disk drives, a fax, an e-mail, or My Briefcase, to common destinations. You can quickly send a file to a destination by following these steps:

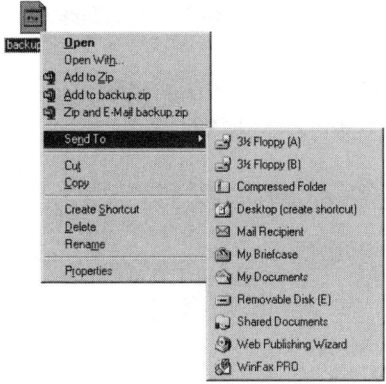

1. Right-click the file or folder to open the pop-up menu.
2. Select Send To. A submenu appears.
3. Click the appropriate destination.

Settings

Choose Start ➢ Settings to access all the Windows configuration tools, including the Control Panel, Dial-Up Networking, Printers, and Taskbar and Start Menu.

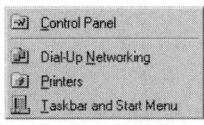

See also Control Panel, Printers, Taskbar and Start Menu, Dial-Up Networking

Sharing Resources

Make network resources available to other network users. If you are connected to a network and want to allow others to access your files, folders, printers, and other resources, you must specify this in the Network applet in the Control Panel by setting certain sharing options. You can also specify whether you want the sharing to be restricted by password or to a specific list of users.

Setting Global Sharing

To share files and printer resources, follow these steps:

1. Choose Start ➢ Settings ➢ Control Panel ➢ Network to open the Network Properties dialog box.

2. Select the Configuration tab, and then click File and Print Sharing to open the File and Print Sharing dialog box:

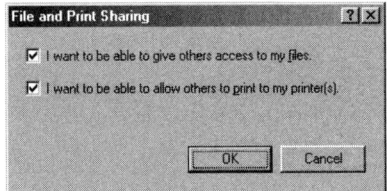

3. Click the type of access you want to give others, and then click OK. Click OK to close the Network Properties dialog box.

TIP You can limit access either by requiring a password to access your resources or by creating a list of users that have permission to use the resources. Set these options on the Access Control tab in the Network applet.

Setting Individual Sharing Properties

You can determine whether a particular disk, file, folder, printer, or other resource is to be shared and, if it is, the type of access permitted. Follow these steps:

1. Find and select the resource you want to share (for example, your hard disk, a file or folder, or the printer) in Explorer or My Computer.

SHARING RESOURCES

2. Choose File ➤ Sharing.

3. Click Shared As if you want to share the resource with others, and then make these additional selections:

   Share Name   Specifies the name of the resource. Other users will use this name when they want to access this resource.

   Comment   Contains notes about the resource that will be available to others in the Details view of your computer.

   Access Type   Specify Read-Only to restrict others to reading the file or folder only, Full to allow others to read and write to the resource, and Depends on Password to allow variations of accessibility.

   Passwords   Restricts users to Read-Only Password or to Full Access Password.

4. Complete choosing the options you want and click OK to close the dialog box.

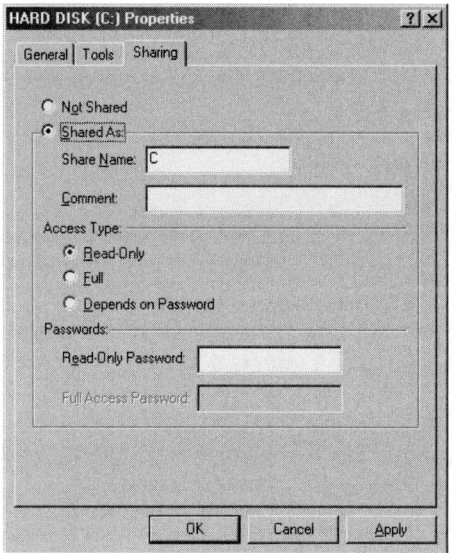

See also   Network

SHORTCUTS

Shortcuts

Quick ways to open an application or to access a disk, file, folder, printer, or computer without going to its permanent location using the Windows Explorer. Shortcuts are useful for applications that you use frequently: when you access a shortcut, the file, folder, printer, computer, or program is opened for you. You can create a shortcut using the File menu, pop-up menus, or drag-and-copy.

Creating Shortcuts

To create a shortcut, follow these steps:

1. Find and select the item for which you want to create a shortcut using My Computer or Explorer. (In Explorer, be sure that the object is displayed in the pane on the right.)

2. Choose File ➢ Create Shortcut. The shortcut is created and appears in the pane on the right.

3. Drag the shortcut where you want it.

TIP An even quicker way to create a shortcut—in My Computer or Explorer, or on the Desktop—is to right-click the item and then choose Create Shortcut from the pop-up menu.

You can also create a shortcut by dragging the item for which you want a shortcut to its destination, such as another folder or the Desktop, while pressing Ctrl+Shift. (Pressing Shift moves a file, Ctrl copies a file, and Ctrl+Shift creates a shortcut for it.) You can also drag the item with the right mouse button. When you finish dragging, Windows displays a pop-up menu from which you can choose Create Shortcut.

TIP To change the properties of a shortcut, such as what sort of window it starts in, right-click the shortcut and choose Properties.

Adding a Submenu to the Programs Menu

You can also add a shortcut to the Programs menu by creating a new submenu. Follow these steps:

1. Right-click the Start button, and then choose Open.

2. Select the Programs folder.

SHUT DOWN

3. Choose File ➤ New ➤ Folder.

4. Enter the name you want to use for the new submenu.

5. Press Enter and then open the folder you just created.

6. Choose File ➤ New ➤ Shortcut.

7. Follow the directions given by the Create Shortcut Wizard to add new items to the submenu.

 NOTE Deleting a shortcut does not delete the original item; it still remains on the disk. To delete a shortcut, simply drag it to the Recycle Bin.

See also Taskbar and Start Menu, Toolbar

Shut Down

The procedure for closing Windows. You must always follow the Shut Down procedure before turning your computer off or restarting your system. If you don't, you run the risk of losing data. Follow these steps to shut down:

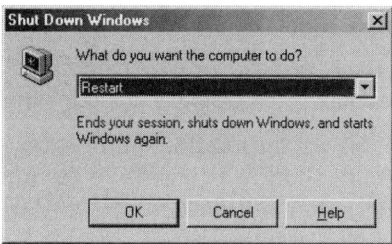

1. When you are ready to turn off your computer, choose Start ➤ Shut Down to open the Shut Down Windows dialog box.

2. Open the drop-down list and choose which shutdown type you want:

   Shut Down Prepares the computer to be turned off (or, on some machines, actually turns the PC off).

   Restart Restarts the PC.

229

2. Click OK.

3. Respond to any other questions that Windows displays. If you need to save your work in an open program, for example, you might be prompted to do so.

When Windows has finished saving data to your hard disk, it displays a final message telling you that it is now safe to turn off your computer. Or, on computers with the ability to turn themselves off, the PC turns off at that point.

Sound Recorder

Records sounds from an audio input device such as a CD-ROM player or a sound card with a microphone installed on your computer. To hear playback, you need speakers attached to the sound card.

Choose Start ➤ Programs ➤ Accessories ➤ Entertainment ➤ Sound Recorder to open the Sound Recorder dialog box.

Sound Recorder Dialog Box

While creating a sound track, you use the information and buttons in this dialog box. The Sound Recorder dialog box displays the following information:

 Position   Gives the location on the sound track. It is coordinated with the slider, which gives you a visual impression of where the sound track is positioned.

 **Track Visual Display**   Gives a visual image of the quality of the sound.

 Length   Shows the current length of the sound track.

The Sound Recorder dialog box also contains the following buttons:

 **Slider**   Shows the current relative position within the sound track. As the sound records or plays, the slider moves to the right.

Seek to Start Repositions the sound track at the beginning.

Seek to End Repositions the sound track at the end.

Play Plays the sound track from the current position forward.

Stop Interrupts the playback or recording.

Record Activates the recording function.

Sound Recorder Menus

Provide special options that aid in the creation of a sound track. The File menu contains the standard options, plus three special options:

New Creates or records a new sound file. When you click New, the Record button becomes available.

Properties Displays the Properties dialog box for the current sound file.

Revert Removes the changes made to the sound file since the last time it was saved.

The Edit menu contains these special options:

Copy Copies a portion of the file. Position the file where the copy is to begin, choose Edit ➤ Copy, and then click Stop when you want the copy to stop.

Paste Insert Inserts the copied sound, beginning at the current position. It overlays the current sound.

Paste Mix Mixes the copied sound with the sound on the file, beginning at the current position.

Insert File Inserts a .WAV file into the sound track, beginning at the current position.

Mix with File Combines a sound, beginning in the current location, with those already on the sound track.

Delete before Current Position Deletes the contents of the sound file from the current position to the beginning of the file.

Delete after Current Position Deletes the contents of the sound file from the current position to the end of the file.

Audio Properties Displays the audio properties of the file, such as information on playback and recordings.

SOUNDS AND MULTIMEDIA

 TIP If you don't see the green line in the visual display, the sound file is compressed, and you cannot modify it.

The Effects menu contains the following options for producing special effects with the sound file: Increase Volume (by 25%), Decrease Volume, Increase Speed (by 100%), Decrease Speed, Add Echo, and Reverse.

Sounds and Multimedia

Controls the sounds assigned to system events and the settings for multimedia playback such as sound and video.

To open the Sounds and Multimedia Properties box, double-click the Sounds and Multimedia icon in the Control Panel. The dialog box that appears contains four tabs: Sounds, Audio, Voice, and Devices.

Sounds Tab

Assigns sounds to certain system events, such as warning dialog boxes, and to more common events, such as opening or closing windows or receiving an e-mail message.

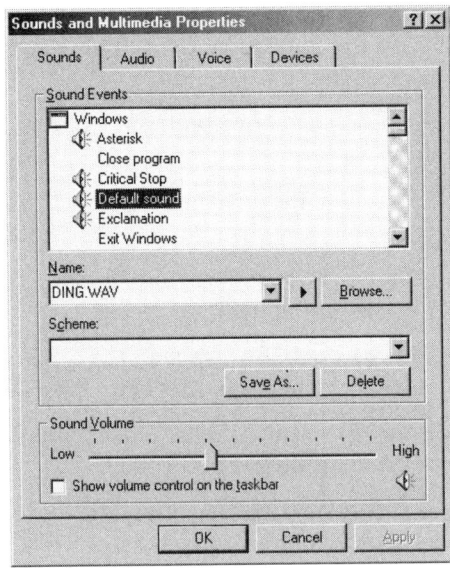

SOUNDS AND MULTIMEDIA

It contains the following options:

Sound Events   Lists the Windows events to which you can assign sounds. If an event has a loudspeaker icon to its left, a sound is assigned to it that you can change.

Name   Selects the name of the sound that you want to assign to an event. This option becomes available when you click an event.

Browse   Searches through the available sounds. Sounds are usually contained in a .WAV file.

Play   Plays the sound if you have a sound card and speakers. When a Sound Name is selected, the Play button becomes available.

Scheme   Lists sets of events with particular sounds assigned to the listed events. Windows Default is the name of the default scheme. The set of associated sounds is displayed under Events. You can change the sounds associated with the schemes and then save them under a different name, if you want. Choose None from the Schemes list to silence all these sounds when you use your system in the library.

Sound Volume   A slider you can drag from side to side to set the master volume for your system.

Show Volume Control on the Taskbar   Mark this checkbox to add a Speaker icon to your system tray. You can then double-click it at any time to open a Volume Control box to control volume for various sound types.

Follow these steps to assign a sound to an event:

1. Choose Start ≻ Settings ≻ Control Panel ≻ Sounds and Multimedia to open the Sounds Properties dialog box.

2. Click an event to which you want to assign a sound or a new default sound setting.

3. Assign a sound from the selections in the Name drop-down list box. If you don't know the sound you want, click Browse to see a list of available sounds.

4. Click a sound and then click the Play arrow to hear it. Continue to select sounds and preview them until you have the sound you want. Click OK twice.

233

SOUNDS AND MULTIMEDIA

5. If desired, save the set of sounds in a new sound scheme by clicking Save As and typing a new name. Click OK.

You can always go back to the original Windows sounds by selecting Windows Default from the Schemes list box.

Audio Tab

Establishes the default settings for multimedia devices connected to your computer. Its contents depend on which multimedia devices you have installed.

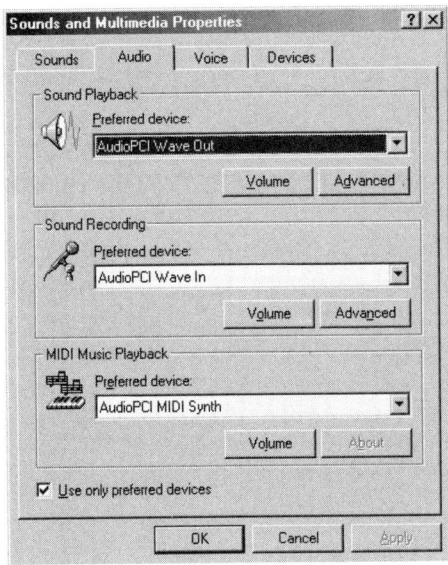

For the first two categories—Sound Playback and Sound Recording—there are three controls:

Preferred Device A drop-down list of the available devices on your system for that type of audio.

Volume Opens the Volume control box.

Advanced Opens an Advanced Audio Properties box in which you can set specifics for that type of device. For example, you might specify what type of speakers you have for Sound Playback, or what type of microphone for Sound Recording.

A third category, MIDI Music Playback, has the Preferred Device and Volume controls only.

Voice Tab

The same controls as on the Audio tab, but for voice recording and playback devices. Most people will not have separate multimedia equipment for voice, and so will not use these controls.

Device

Lists all the multimedia recording and playback devices on the system and enables you to set properties for them. Much like Device Manager, but focused specifically on sound and video equipment.

See also Accessibility Options, Add New Hardware, CD Player, Device Manager, Media Player, Sound Recorder, Volume Control, Windows Media Player

Start

The primary way to access files, folders, and programs on your computer. Initially, the Start button is on the bottom left of your screen at the left end of the Taskbar. Click Start to display the Start menu. Some of the options on this menu are standard with Windows, but you can add others to give you fast access to your favorite applications.

STARTUP

The Start menu contains the following options:

Shut Down   Prepares the computer to be shut down or restarted.

Log Off   Logs off the system quickly so that you can log back on with a different user profile or so that another user can log on.

Run   Opens the Run dialog box so that you can run a program or open a folder by typing its path and name.

Help   Opens the extensive Windows Help system.

Search   Searches for a file, folder, device, or computer. You can also search the Internet and look for personal contact information.

Settings   Accesses the Control Panel, Printers, Taskbar and Start Menu, Folder Options, and Active Desktop controls so that you can configure the way Windows operates.

Documents   Gives you access to the last 15 documents you opened.

Programs   Gives you access to the program groups and files on your computer.

Windows Update   Automatically connects to the Microsoft Web site to check for updates to the Windows operating system.

You may have other items listed on the Start menu as well; many programs add themselves to it. For example, America Online, Microsoft Office, and WinZip all add themselves to the top of the Start menu.

TIP   To add a program or a shortcut to the Start menu, simply drag its icon to the Start button.

See also   StartUp, Task Scheduler, Taskbar and Start Menu

StartUp

  A submenu on the Start menu in which shortcuts appear for programs that start automatically when you start Windows. Many programs place shortcuts for themselves here when you install them.

236

Placing a Program on the StartUp Menu

To place a program on the StartUp menu so that it starts automatically when Windows starts, do the following:

1. Create a shortcut to the program on the desktop. (See Shortcuts earlier in this book.)

2. Drag the shortcut onto the Start button, but do not release the mouse button. The Start menu opens.

3. Still holding down the mouse button, point to Programs, and then to Startup.

4. Release the mouse button, dropping the shortcut onto the StartUp menu.

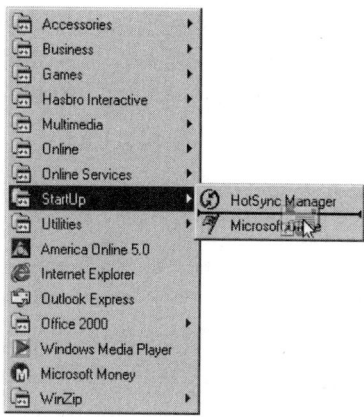

Another way to add a shortcut to the StartUp menu is to browse the Start menu's content by right-clicking it and choosing Explore. Then drag the shortcut from the desktop into the folder.

Removing a Shortcut from the StartUp Menu

To prevent a program from starting automatically when Windows starts, remove its shortcut from the StartUp submenu by doing the following:

1. Choose Start ➤ Programs ➤ StartUp. The StartUp submenu's contents appear.

2. Right-click the shortcut you want to remove. A shortcut menu appears.

STARTUP MENU

3. Choose Delete. A confirmation box appears.

4. Choose Yes.

See also Start, Taskbar and Start Menu, Startup Menu

Startup Menu

Presents several choices for loading parts of Windows so that you can attempt to identify and isolate a serious system problem. Follow these steps to get to this menu:

1. Restart the computer by selecting Start ➤ Shut Down ➤ Restart, and then click OK.

2. Once Windows begins to reload, but before the blue Windows screen appears (you may also hear a short beep), press and hold down the Ctrl key to open a menu containing the following options:

   Normal Starts Windows in the usual way.

   Logged Creates a system log while rebooting, documenting each step of the boot process into a file.

   Safe Mode Starts Windows by bypassing the usual startup files (such as the Registry) and loading only the basic drivers (mouse, keyboard, and standard VGA device).

   Step-by-Step Confirmation Starts Windows by requiring you to confirm each step of the startup files, line by line.

3. Make a selection from the menu. If you don't make any selection within a certain period of time, Windows automatically executes the first option in the menu and starts up in the usual configuration.

WARNING You should not run your computer in anything except Normal mode for regular operation. Use these other modes only for troubleshooting purposes. When finished troubleshooting, restart the computer and let it boot normally.

See also Safe Mode

Synchronize

Synchronize Allows you to use Synchronization Manager to refresh and update certain items automatically each time you log on to your computer. This makes sure that you always have the latest information from the Internet or from your company network when you disconnect.

You can use Synchronization Manager with any program that supports its use, including Web pages, e-mail folders, and Microsoft SQL 7 databases. Click Start ➤ Programs ➤ Accessories ➤ Synchronize to open the Items to Synchronize dialog box. You can also start Synchronization Manager from within the Windows Help system.

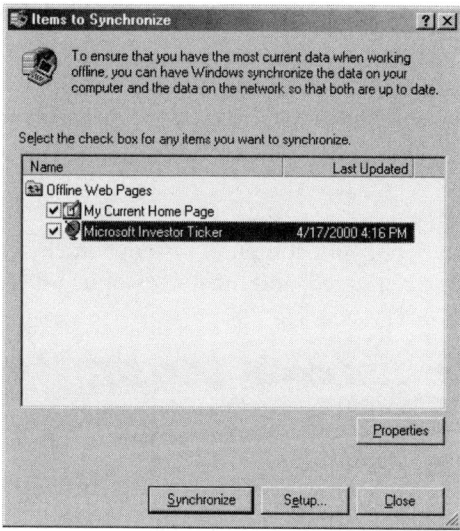

Check the appropriate boxes for the items you want to synchronize, then click Synchronize. Synchronization Manager updates the checked items as needed.

Click the Setup button to look at or change the Synchronization Manager configuration options. The Synchronization Settings dialog box contains tabs you can use to specify when synchronization takes place:

Logon Lets you specify that items are synchronized when you log on to your computer or to the network.

On Idle Lets you specify that items are synchronized after your computer has been idle for a specific period of time. Click the Advanced button on this tab to select the time period. You can also specify that synchronization not be performed when your laptop computer is running on battery power.

Scheduled Lets you specify that items are synchronized at a specific time. Click Add to open the Scheduled Synchronization Wizard, and follow the instructions on the screen.

See also My Briefcase, Active Desktop, Internet Explorer

System

Provides information and allows you to optimize system performance. Use the System applet with care, however, because changing some settings without detailed technical knowledge can actually degrade the performance of your system.

Choose Start ➢ Settings ➢ Control Panel ➢ System to open the System Properties dialog box. It has four tabs: General, Device Manager, Hardware Profiles, and Performance.

General Tab

Contains information about your computer system: which version of Windows you have, to whom it is registered, and the processor board type and amount of memory installed in your system.

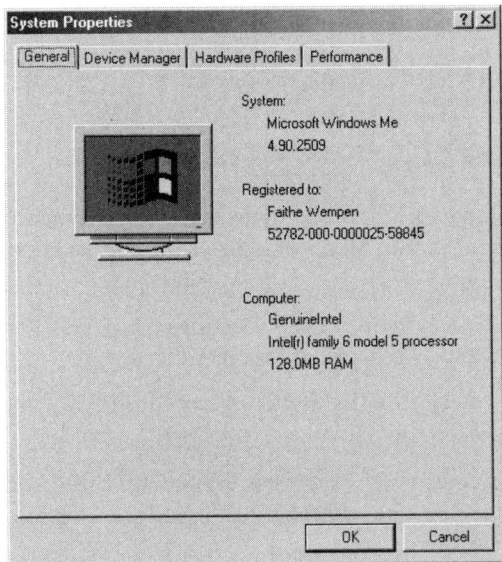

SYSTEM

Device Manager Tab

Lists all the devices installed in or attached to your computer, both shared and directly connected. It contains various options for managing these devices.

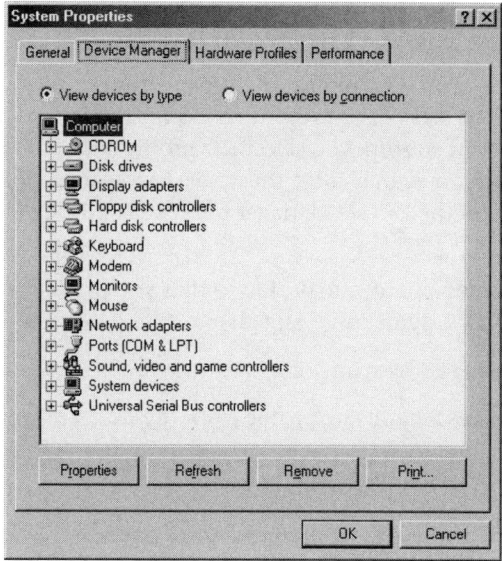

View Devices by Type Lists such devices as disk drives or keyboard by type, in alphabetic order. Click the plus sign next to a device name to display more detail. An X through an icon means that the device is disabled.

View Devices by Connection Shows how devices are connected to the computer.

Properties Displays the Properties dialog box for the selected device as well as a summary of its current status. You can also display this information by double-clicking the item name. Some devices have three or four Properties dialog boxes; the options depend on the device type.

Refresh Examines the devices on the system and redisplays the list.

Remove Deletes a device from the list and from the computer. If you remove a device from this dialog box, it really is deleted from your computer, and you will have to use Add New Hardware to reinstall it if you decide to use it in the future.

SYSTEM

Print Prints a summary, or a detailed report, of hardware resources on your computer. You can use this report to locate hardware problems: it shows you which devices are connected to which ports.

Hardware Profiles Tab

Allows you to create hardware profiles containing different devices or resources for your computer system. You might use this to establish specific hardware configurations for various users or to prevent access to certain resources, although this is not common. At startup, you select the profile containing the configuration you want to use. You can change the active hardware profile (the profile selected at startup) on the Device Manager tab. The Hardware Profiles tab contains three buttons:

Copy Duplicates a hardware profile so that you make changes to a copy while keeping the original unchanged.

Rename Changes the name of a hardware profile.

Delete Removes a hardware profile from the list.

Performance Tab

Displays information about your computer's use of memory, system resources, file system, disk compression, and so on. This tab has three Advanced Settings buttons:

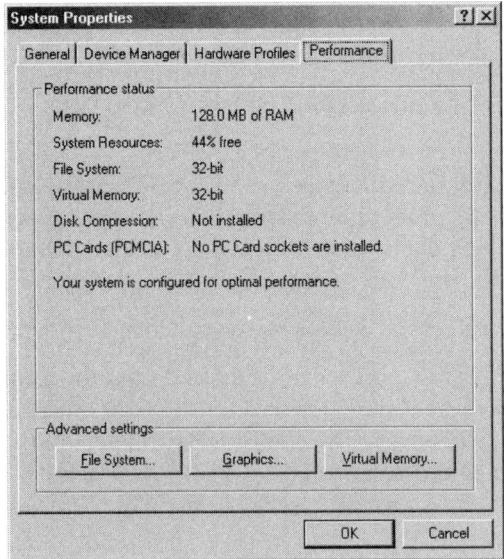

SYSTEM

File System Opens the File System Properties dialog box, which contains tabs for the disk-related hardware on your computer. You may see the following Advanced Settings tabs:

Hard Disk Provides options for optimizing hard-disk usage. When you specify the Typical Role for This Machine (desktop computer, mobile or docking system as in a portable computer, or network server), Windows tries to optimize for that use. You can also indicate the Read-Ahead Optimization when an application requests sequentially stored data. This controls whether Windows reads ahead increments of the data, varying from 0 to 64 kilobytes depending on the position of the slider.

Floppy Disk Lets you specify that Windows searches for new floppy disk drives each time your system starts running.

CD-ROM Helps Windows optimize the use of the CD-ROM drive. By moving the slider from Small to Large, you change the Supplemental Cache Size for the CD-ROM. As you move the slider, a message tells you how much physical memory will be used. To optimize Access Pattern for the CD-ROM, select from No-Read-Ahead, Single-Speed Drives, Double-Speed Drives, Triple-Speed Drives, or Quad-Speed or Higher. Based on this setting, Windows determines how much memory to set aside for this function.

Removable Disk Lets Windows optimize the settings for removable disks installed on your system.

Troubleshooting Provides settings that only advanced users and system administrators should change; this tab is primarily a diagnostic tool. It allows you to disable several options, such as 32-bit protect-mode disk drivers and synchronous buffer commits, so that you can test certain conditions without them.

Graphics Opens the Advanced Graphics Settings dialog box, in which you can set the acceleration functions of your display adapters. If your computer has no problems, set the slider on Full, the fastest speed. If your computer has severe problems, such as response degradation or unexpected errors in programs, and you suspect that graphic speed acceleration might be the cause, set the slider first to None, and then set it at increasing increments until the problem recurs. Then turn the setting back down to the last usable setting.

Virtual Memory Opens the Virtual Memory dialog box, in which you can specify your own virtual memory settings—the amount of hard-disk

SYSTEM CONFIGURATION EDITOR (SYSEDIT)

space used as extra memory—rather than having Windows control it. Attempt this only if you are an experienced user.

See also   Add New Hardware, Profiles, System Information, System Monitor

System Configuration Editor (Sysedit)

A utility that opens several important text-based configuration files for editing, all in one convenient window. This utility is not accessible through the Start menu; you must run it using the Run command, like so:

1. Choose Start ➢ Run. The Run dialog box opens.

2. Type **sysedit** and press Enter.

The System Configuration Editor opens `Autoexec.bat`, `Config.sys`, `Win.ini`, `System.ini`, and `Protocol.ini` for editing. Use System Configuration Editor just as you would Notepad to edit the files and save the changes to them.

WARNING   You should not make changes to these files unless you know what you are doing, because you can cause system problems.

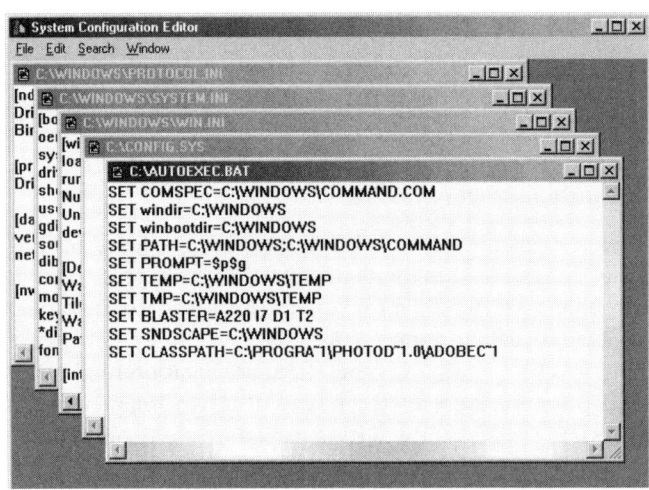

See also   Notepad, Run

244

System Configuration Utility

A Windows utility for controlling your PC's startup routine and overall configuration.

WARNING This is a rather advanced tool, and should be used only by experienced users who know what changes need to be made. Otherwise, you can cause problems in your Windows installation.

Starting the System Configuration Utility

The System Configuration Utility is available through the Tools menu in System Information. Do the following to open it:

1. Choose Start ➢ Programs ➢ Accessories ➢ System Tools ➢ System Information.
2. Choose Tools ➢ System Configuration Utility.

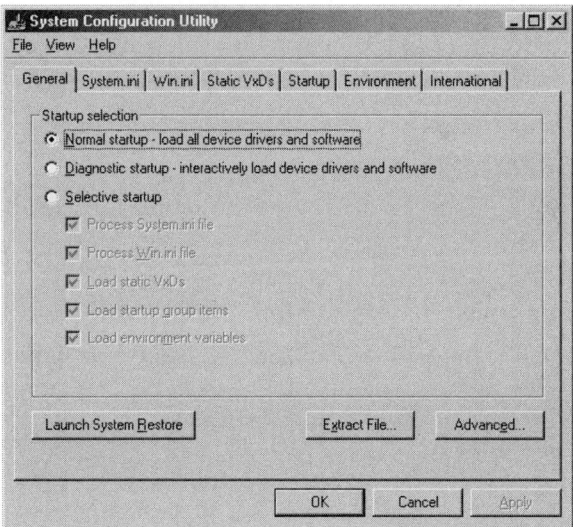

SYSTEM CONFIGURATION UTILITY

NOTE Like the System Configuration Editor, the System Configuration Utility is capable of effecting some significant changes to the way Windows operates. Do not make any changes unless you are an experienced Windows user who knows exactly why a certain change is being made.

System Configuration Utility Tabs

The System Configuration Utility box has seven tabs:

General   Select Normal, Diagnostic, or Selective Startup mode for the PC to start in. You can also extract a file from the Windows CD from here, and set advanced startup properties.

System.ini   Each line of the file appears, and you can disable a line by removing the checkmark next to it. Useful for troubleshooting.

Win.ini   Same as for System.ini.

Static VXDs   Lists the .vxd files that load at startup. You can disable one by removing its checkmark.

Startup   Lists all the programs that load automatically when Windows starts. To disable one, remove its checkmark.

Environment   Lists environment variables set for Windows startup. Disable one by removing its checkmark.

International   Lets you specify settings for non-USA Windows installation and usage.

Extracting Files from Your Installation Disk

On the General tab of the System Configuration Utility you'll find an Extract File button. You can use this to replace a certain system file that may have become corrupted with a fresh copy from your Windows CD.

NOTE In Windows 98 this capability was accomplished through the System File Checker utility, which is no longer part of the program in Windows Me.

1. Start in the System Configuration Utility, on the General tab.
2. Click Extract File.

SYSTEM INFORMATION

3. Place your original Windows installation CD in your CD-ROM drive.

4. Enter the name of the file you are looking for in the File to Extract field, or click the Browse button to find the file.

5. Click the Start button.

6. In the Restore From field, enter the name of the folder where the compressed .CAB files are located on your installation disk, and then click the OK button.

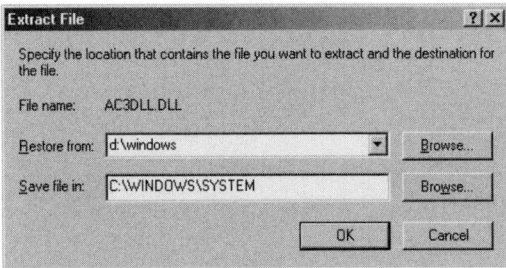

7. A prompt for a backup folder appears. Click OK to accept the default. If prompted to create the folder, click Yes.

8. A message appears that the file has been extracted. Click OK.

9. Restart your PC to see whether the new file solves your problem.

System Information

 An advanced reporting tool that collects a wealth of technical data about the hardware and software on your system into one convenient location. You can look at this information on the screen, send it to a printer, or send it to a text file so that you can add it to an e-mail message or fax. You can also access a variety of configuration and troubleshooting tools from its Tools menu.

NOTE Much of the data that System Information collects and displays is very technical and usually of interest only to technical support personnel trying to track down a particularly vexing system problem.

SYSTEM INFORMATION

Choose Start ➤ Programs ➤ Accessories ➤ System Tools ➤ System Information to open the System Information dialog box.

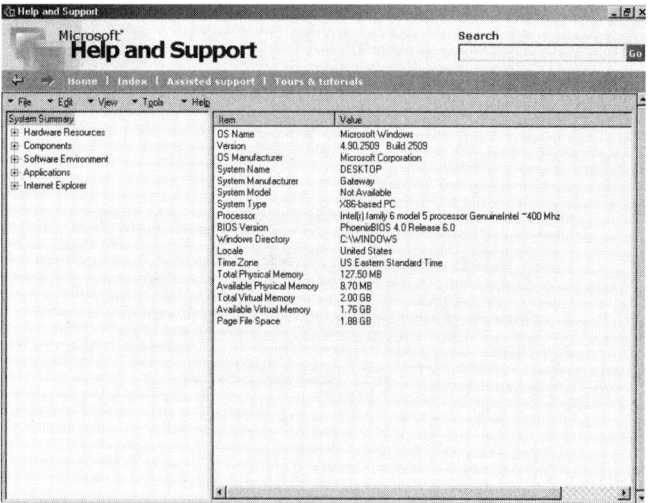

To display additional system data, click one of the plus signs opposite the System Information categories in the left pane:

Hardware Resources Contains hardware-specific settings, including memory address information and information on interrupts.

Components Displays information about your Windows system configuration, including currently installed device drivers and changes made to device drivers over time.

Software Environment Details the system and application software currently loaded into memory.

Applications Provides information about certain compliant application programs installed on the PC.

Internet Explorer Provides information about the version and configuration of Internet Explorer on the PC.

The information displayed in the right pane of the System Information dialog box depends on the category you choose.

SYSTEM MONITOR

Also, you may be able to look at basic or advanced data. To switch, open the View menu and select either Basic or Advanced. Much of this information is technical and very detailed, and is of only minor interest until something goes wrong with your system; then the information can be of vital importance in tracking down and fixing the problem.

TIP To print a copy of your system information summary, use Edit ➤ Print.

You can choose items from the Tools menu to run the diagnostic and support tools used by technical support personnel, but don't run them until you are asked to do so by a member of the technical support staff.

See also System, System Monitor, System Configuration Utility, System Restore

System Monitor

  Tracks the activity of your computer's processor by taking a snapshot of the processor's activity every 5 seconds and presenting it in graphic or numeric form.

TIP Use System Monitor when you are monitoring network activity or looking for heavy system resource use at specific times of the day or night.

Choose Start ➤ Programs ➤ Accessories ➤ System Tools ➤ System Monitor to open the System Monitor dialog box.

The System Monitor might not be installed by default. Use Add/Remove Programs to add it if needed.

System Monitor Toolbar

Contains tools for changing the presentation of the snapshot data and for adding additional resources to monitor.

Add Displays a list of system resources that you can monitor. Clicking a category displays a list of items within that category. Choosing an item to be monitored displays a separate monitoring graph. By selecting several system resources, you can build a complex picture of how your system responds under changing loads.

SYSTEM MONITOR

Remove   Deletes individual items from the list being monitored.

Edit   Lists monitoring charts that are currently displayed. Select the one you want to change and then click OK to open the Chart Options dialog box. Here you can change the color and the scale in use.

Line Charts   Displays the monitoring data in line-chart form.

Bar Charts   Displays the data in bar-chart form.

Numeric Charts   Displays the data in numeric form.

Start Logging   Allows you to store System Monitor information in a file.

Stop Logging   Halts the storing of System Monitor information into a file.

System Monitor Dialog Box

Displays an area chart of the activity on your computer as it is actually occurring, as a percentage. Occasional peaks up to 100 percent are normal and nothing to worry about, but prolonged high values indicate that your system is probably in need of attention.

The default chart shown is Kernel Usage, a good indication of overall system usage.

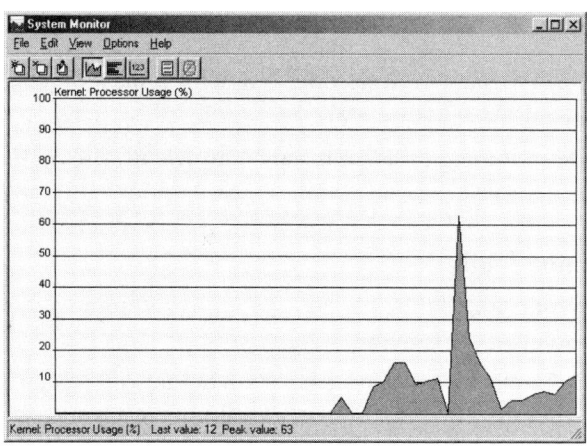

You can control the rate at which System Monitor updates the information that it displays. To change the frequency, choose Options ➢ Chart and adjust the slider to the new rate.

SYSTEM RESTORE

You can add other graphs to the System Monitor display by choosing from a range of items in several main categories, including Dial-Up Adapter, Disk Cache, File System, Internet Connection Sharing, Kernel, and Memory Manager. Depending on which Windows components you installed, you may see additional categories.

To display a new item, click the Add button on the toolbar or choose Edit ➤ Add Item. Choose a Category from the left side of the Add Item dialog box, and then choose one of the related items from the right side. Click OK to return to the System Monitor dialog box, where you will see that a new graph for your selected item is added to the display.

TIP Because System Monitor has items for your Dial-Up Networking connection, including Bytes Received/Second and Bytes Transmitted/Second, you can monitor your Internet connection very closely.

You can control some aspects of the graphical display used for each item by choosing Edit ➤ Edit Item. You can change the chart color and the value used for the vertical scale. To specify a different type of display for all items in the window, use the toolbar buttons or the options in the View menu. To delete an item from the System Monitor display, choose Edit ➤ Remove Item.

See also   System, System Information, Resource Meter

System Restore

A new utility in Windows Millennium Edition that allows you to return your system to an earlier configuration if you start having problems because of system changes you have made or programs you have installed.

System Restore makes a copy of your configuration files, including the Windows Registry, every day. It also makes additional copies whenever you specifically request it. That way, if you install a program that makes your PC malfunction, edit a configuration file incorrectly, or do anything else that causes problems, you can return to any of the saved configurations.

To start System Restore, choose Start ➤ Programs ➤ Accessories ➤ System Tools ➤ System Restore.

Saving a Configuration Snapshot

In addition to the automatic daily saves, you can at any time tell System Restore to save your current configuration as a "snapshot," a collection of copies of the system files. This might be useful immediately before installing a program you

SYSTEM RESTORE

are not sure about, for example, so you can easily remove all traces of that program from your system files later if needed.

From within System Restore, do the following:

1. Choose Create a Restore Point.
2. Click Next.
3. Type a description of the configuration (such as Before Installing Doom, for example). You do not have to include the date and time in your description; that will be recorded automatically.
4. Click Next.
5. Click OK.

Restoring a Configuration

When you want to return to an earlier configuration, use System Restore to do so. The process is completely reversible, so if you realize you don't want the restored configuration, you can go back to your present one later.

From within System Restore, do the following:

1. Choose Restore My Computer to an Earlier Time, and then click Next.
2. On the calendar, click the date that you want to restore your computer to.
3. If there are multiple snapshots for that day, choose the one you want from the list.

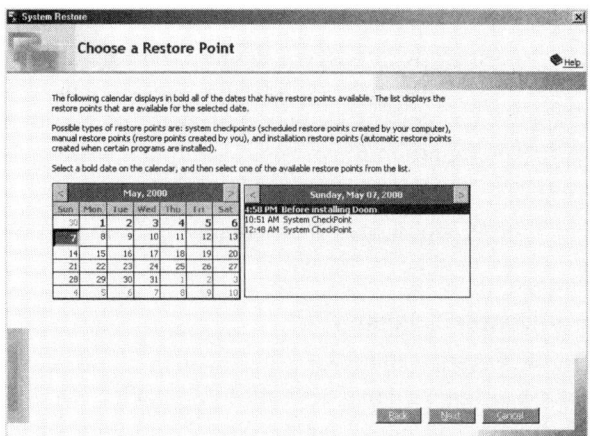

4. Click Next. A confirmation appears.

5. Click Next. Another confirmation appears.

6. Click Restore. The system files are modified and Windows restarts.

7. After the PC restarts, the System Restore dialog box reappears. Click Close to close it.

To undo a restoration, choose Undo my last restoration from within System Restore, click Next, and then follow the prompts.

System Tray

The area at the right end of the taskbar, to the immediate left of the clock. The system tray holds icons for programs running in the background in Windows, such as virus protection, a firewall, or the Task Scheduler.

To open a program in the system tray, double-click its icon. To control its properties, right-click it and choose Properties from the shortcut menu. Programs vary; not all of them may have a Properties command. Some might have an Options or Configure command instead.

To close a program from the system tray, right-click it and choose Exit. Again, not all programs may have an Exit command; some might have a Close or Disable command instead.

See also   Taskbar

Task Scheduler

See Scheduled Tasks

Taskbar

Launches programs and is the primary tool for switching from one application to another. The Taskbar contains several types of icons:

- The Start button at the left end of the Taskbar is responsible for launching applications, opening documents, and adjusting settings.

- The Quick Launch toolbar contains buttons you can use to

  - Open Internet Explorer

  - Bring the Desktop to the front

  - Open Outlook Express

  - Open Windows Media Player

- Rectangular buttons to the right of the Quick Launch toolbar represent the applications currently active in memory or open folders. You can use these icons to switch between the running applications.

- The system tray appears at the right end of the taskbar, showing icons for programs running in the background and a clock with the current time.

The Taskbar may also show other icons from time to time, indicating that an e-mail message is waiting, showing that you are printing a document, or providing the battery condition on a laptop computer.

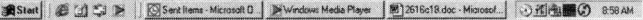

Working with the Quick Launch Toolbar

The four default buttons on the Quick Launch toolbar are shortcuts for four common activities:

 Starts Internet Explorer, the Web browser that comes with Windows.

 Minimizes all open windows so the desktop is fully visible. A great shortcut.

TASKBAR AND START MENU PROPERTIES

Opens Outlook Express, the e-mail program that comes with Windows.

Opens Windows Media Player, the multimedia player that comes with Windows (for playing CDs, MP3s, and so on).

You can also add your own buttons to the Quick Launch toolbar. Simply drag and drop any shortcut to the toolbar to place it there.

To remove a shortcut from the Quick Launch toolbar, right-click it and choose Delete from the Shortcut menu.

Switching Windows with the Taskbar

When you open a new application, the Taskbar gets another rectangular button, and by clicking that button, you can switch to the new application or folder. For the first few programs, the buttons on the Taskbar are long enough so that you can read the complete names of your open applications.

Working with the System Tray

The System Tray area contains icons for programs running "in the background." Such programs might include an antivirus or a utility that protects against system crashes. It is covered fully under "System Tray" in this book.

See also   Desktop, Internet Explorer, Outlook Express, Start, System Tray, Taskbar and Start Menu Properties, Windows Media Player

Taskbar and Start Menu Properties

There are several different ways to customize how the Taskbar and Start menu operate. You can

- Adjust the size and position of the Taskbar
- Use the Taskbar and Start Menu Properties dialog box to change the properties
- Add or rearrange items on the Start menu
- Display different toolbars, instead of or in addition to the Quick Launch toolbar

TASKBAR AND START MENU PROPERTIES

Changing the Taskbar Size and Position

As you open more programs and add more buttons to the Taskbar, the buttons have to get smaller and smaller to fit, so the names are truncated. If you really want to see the complete application names, you can resize the Taskbar and give it an additional line of buttons: simply drag the top edge of the Taskbar upward. The downside of this is that you reduce the effective size of your Desktop.

You can also place the Taskbar at the top of or at either side of the screen, not just at the bottom. Simply drag it to the edge of the screen where you want it.

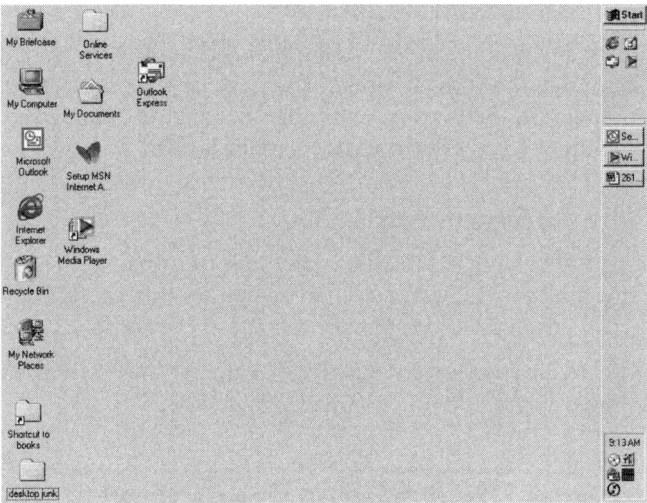

Changing Taskbar and Start Menu Properties

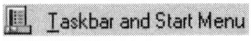 To adjust the settings for the Taskbar and/or the Start menu, open the Taskbar and Start Menu Properties dialog box by doing the following:

1. Choose Start ➤ Settings ➤ Taskbar and Start Menu to open the Taskbar and Start Menu Properties dialog box. You can also simply right-click an empty spot on the Taskbar and select Properties from the pop-up menu.

2. Place a check mark in the checkbox next to the options you want:

TASKBAR AND START MENU PROPERTIES

Always on Top Forces the Taskbar to remain on top of other windows, ensuring that it is always visible to you.

Auto Hide Displays the Taskbar as a small thin line on the bottom of the screen. To also display the thin line when a full-screen window is displayed, select both Always on Top and Auto Hide.

Show Small Icons in Start Menu Displays a small Start menu with smaller icons.

Show Clock Displays the time on the right end of the Taskbar. By double-clicking the clock you can reset the time or date.

3. Click Apply to make the changes final, and then click OK.

TIP Instead of using Auto Hide, you can shrink the Taskbar by dragging its top edge downward. To redisplay the Taskbar, simply drag its visible edge upward.

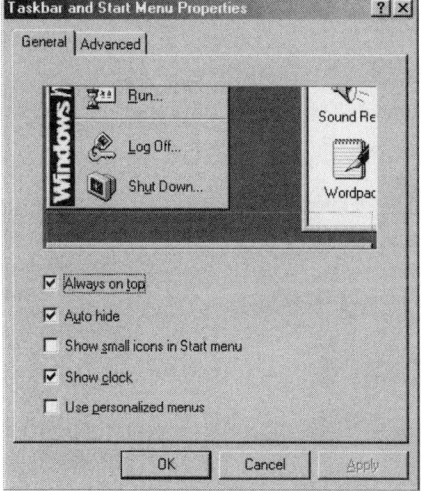

TIP To redisplay the Taskbar when Auto Hide is selected, place the pointer on the thin line on the bottom of the screen. The Taskbar will automatically reappear.

TASKBAR AND START MENU PROPERTIES

Adding Programs to the Start Menu

One easy way to add a program to the Start menu is by dragging, as follows:

1. Create a shortcut on your desktop for the program to be added to the Start menu.

2. Drag the shortcut onto the Start button, but do not release the mouse button. The Start menu opens.

3. Point to Programs, still holding down the mouse button. The Programs menu opens.

4. Point to submenus until the spot where you want the program to appear is visible. Then position the mouse pointer over the spot where the program should go.

5. Release the mouse button. The shortcut appears on the Start menu.

You can also add programs to the Start menu more formally, using a Wizard, as in the following steps:

1. Right-click the Taskbar and choose Properties.

2. Choose the Advanced tab.

3. Click the Add button. The Create Shortcut wizard appears.

4. Enter the path to the program, or click Browse and locate it.

5. Click Next. A folder structure appears, representing the submenus on the Start menu.

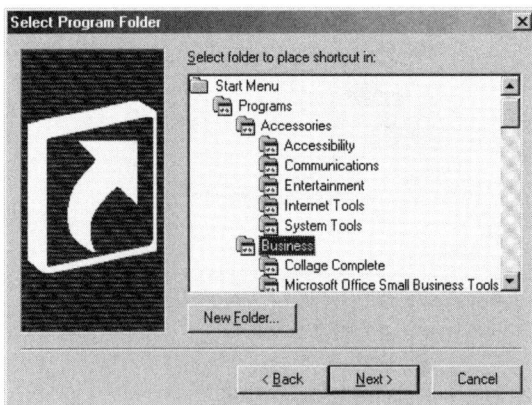

TASKBAR AND START MENU PROPERTIES

6. Select the folder into which the shortcut should be placed. (You can click New Folder to create a new submenu if desired.)

7. Click Next.

8. Type a name for the shortcut. This name will be the wording that appears on the menu. Then click Finish.

9. Choose OK to close the Taskbar and Start Menu Properties box.

Adding Toolbars

Windows Millennium Edition includes a default set of toolbars that you can add to your Taskbar if you wish:

Address Allows you to open an Internet address without first opening Internet Explorer.

Links Contains a set of Internet addresses.

Desktop Adds all your Desktop icons to the Taskbar. Because this toolbar is longer than the screen is wide, you can use the small arrows to see the other icons.

Quick Launch Contains buttons you can use to do the following:

- Open Internet Explorer
- Bring the Desktop to the front
- Open Outlook Express
- Open Windows Media Player

To add one of these toolbars to your Taskbar, right-click an empty spot on the Taskbar, choose Toolbars from the pop-up menu, and then select the toolbar you want to add to your Taskbar.

TIP You can also add your own shortcuts to the Quick Launch toolbar. Open My Computer or Explorer, select the application you want to add, and drag it to the Quick Launch part of the Windows Taskbar. You will see that program's icon appear next to the other icons on the Quick Launch toolbar. To remove an icon from the Quick Launch toolbar, right-click it and choose Delete.

Creating a Custom Toolbar

If the default toolbars don't meet your needs, you can always create your own. Follow these steps:

1. Right-click an empty part of the Taskbar to open the pop-up menu.
2. Choose Toolbars ➢ New Toolbar to open the New Toolbar dialog box.
3. Select a folder from the list or type an Internet address that you want to appear as a toolbar.

Another way to build a custom toolbar is to create a new folder, add all your favorite shortcuts to it, and then choose Toolbars ➢ New Toolbar to turn it into a toolbar.

This can obviously get out of hand in a hurry, with custom toolbars appearing all over the place, so be careful to create them only as you need them, and then it's probably best if you confine them to the Taskbar.

TIP To move a toolbar to the Desktop, simply drag it to the new location and then size it as you see fit.

See also   Internet Explorer, Shortcuts, Start, StartUp, Taskbar

Telephony

An applet you can use to establish dialing configurations and to set up telephony device drivers. In Windows, telephony services manage the interaction between your computer system and any telephone equipment that you connect it to, such as your modem and phone line, allowing your computer to control your telephone. Choose Start ➢ Settings ➢ Control Panel ➢ Telephony to open the Telephony dialog box, which has two tabs—My Locations and Telephony Drivers.

My Locations Tab

Selecting this tab opens the same dialog box you see when you click the Dialing Properties button in the Modems applet in the Windows Control Panel, or when you choose Tools ➢ Dialing Properties in the Phone Dialer. The changes you make in any one of these applications are always immediately available to the others.

TV VIEWER

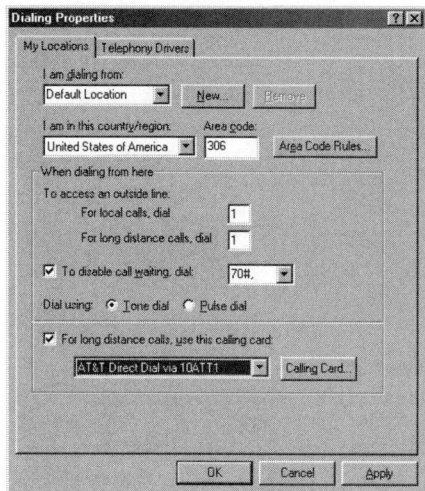

Select the My Locations tab to set up the dialing configuration you want to use. Click Area Code Rules to specify how local toll and long-distance calls should be dialed, and click the Calling Card button to enter information about any calling cards you want to use.

Telephony Drivers Tab

Use this tab to look at, change, or configure the telephony device drivers installed on your system. Click Add to install another device driver, Remove to delete an existing driver, or Configure to look at or change the device driver's settings. Some device drivers do not allow separate configuration; when that is the case, a message box tells you that the device driver does not support this function.

See also   Modem, Phone Dialer

Toolbars

See also   Taskbar, Taskbar and Start Menu

TV Viewer

See   WebTV for Windows

Undeleting Files

 When you delete a file or a folder, it is stored in the Recycle Bin, but until you actually empty the Recycle Bin, you can still retrieve any files you deleted. To recover a file from the Recycle Bin and return it to its original location, follow these steps:

1. Double-click the Recycle Bin on the Desktop.

2. Select the file or files you want to restore.

3. Right-click and choose Restore, or choose File ➢ Restore.

TIP To select multiple files, hold down Ctrl while you click.

You can also click the Restore All button to the left of the file listing to return multiple files to their original locations. (If one or more files are selected, the Restore All button becomes a Restore button and restores only the selected files.)

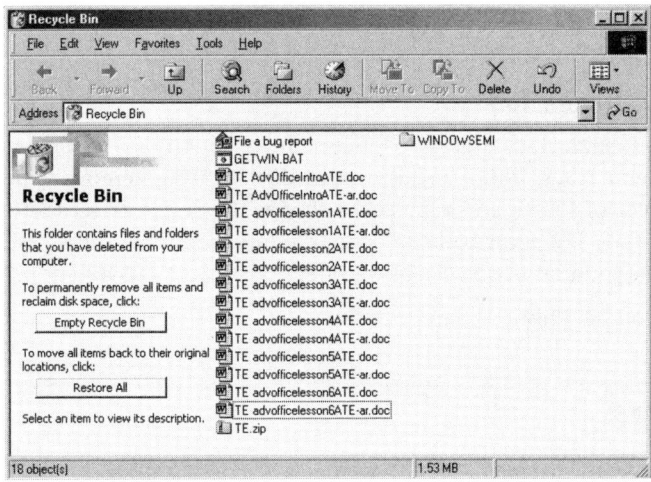

See also Recycle Bin

USER PROFILES

Uninstalling Applications

Add/Remove Programs — The Uninstall program removes an installed program from your system. It removes all references to the program from the Windows directories and subdirectories and from the Windows Registry, and therefore is preferable to simply deleting a program's files through Explorer.

The Uninstall feature is found in the Add/Remove Program Properties dialog box. Follow these steps to uninstall a program:

1. Choose Start ➤ Settings ➤ Control Panel ➤ Add/Remove Programs to open the Add/Remove Programs Properties dialog box.

2. If necessary, select the Install/Uninstall tab.

3. Select the software you want to remove from the list and click Add/Remove.

4. Follow the prompts that appear in order to remove the program from your system. The Uninstall routine varies, depending on the program's manufacturer.

See also Add/Remove Programs

Unmapping Network Drives

See Map Network Drive

USB

A technology (Universal Serial Bus) for connecting peripheral devices such as scanners, printers, digital cameras, and so on to your PC. Like a parallel or serial port, a USB port enables you to plug in a cable and then connect that cable to a device. However, USB offers many benefits over traditional ports such as parallel or serial, including the ability to plug and unplug devices while the PC is running (known as *hot swapping*) and the ability to connect multiple devices to the same USB port without taking up separate system resources for each.

To use USB, your PC must have one or more USB ports built in, or you must install a USB card in the PC.

User Profiles

See Profiles

263

Users

Windows maintains a set of user profiles, each containing a different username and password, and different Desktop preferences and Accessibility options. When you log on to Windows, your profile ensures that your Desktop settings—including elements such as your own Desktop icons, background image, and other settings—are automatically available to you.

To set up a new user profile, see the User Profiles section under the topic "Profiles" earlier in the book.

See also Accessibility Options, Log On, Passwords, Profiles, Shut Down, System

Volume Control

Volume Control An accessory you can use to control the volume of your sound card and speakers. If you have more than one multimedia capability installed—for example, MIDI or Wave-handling—you can control the volume and balance separately for each device. Follow these steps to access the Volume Control:

1. Choose Start ➤ Programs ➤ Accessories ➤ Entertainment ➤ Volume Control to open the Volume Control dialog box. It contains separate features to balance volume for the devices on your computer. Depending on the hardware installed on your computer, the following features may or may not appear:

   Volume Control Controls volume and balance for sounds coming out of your computer. This is the "master" control.

   CD Controls the volume and balance for audio CDs played through the system's CD-ROM drive.

   Wave Controls the volume and balance for playing .WAV files as they come into the computer.

   Synthesizer Controls the volume and balance for musical synthesizer devices plugged into the system.

   Microphone Controls the volume and balance for sound coming in via a microphone.

   Line Controls the volume and balance for an external device such as an audio tape or for an FM tuner that feeds sound into your computer.

   Modem Controls the volume and balance for the speaker in your modem, if you have one.

2. To control the volume of the components, move the vertical slider labeled Volume up or down to increase or decrease volume.

3. To control the balance between two speakers, move the horizontal slider labeled Balance to the left or right to move the emphasis to the left or right speaker.

4. Click Mute All or Mute to silence all components', or one component's, contribution to the sound.

Varying the Recording Volume

To vary the volume and balance when you are recording, follow these steps:

VOLUME CONTROL

1. From the Volume Control dialog box, choose Options ➤ Properties to open the Properties dialog box.
2. Select Recording to display a list of devices that apply to the recording task.
3. If it is not already checked, click the checkbox to select the device you want.
4. Click OK to open the Recording Control dialog box for the selected devices.
5. Move the Volume and Balance sliders to adjust the volume and balance of the sound.

Adjusting Playback Sound Quality

The Volume Control dialog box displays all the devices it knows about that relate to playback or the output of sound. If the device you want to adjust is not on the list, follow these steps to select the device:

1. From the Volume Control dialog box, choose Options ➤ Properties to open the Properties dialog box.
2. Select Playback to display a list of applicable devices.
3. If it is not already selected, click the device you want.
4. Click OK to open the Volume Control dialog box, which displays the selected devices.
5. Adjust the volume and balance as needed.

TIP To control the volume and balance for voice-command devices, select Other from the Properties dialog box and then select Voice Commands from the drop-down list box. A list of voice-command devices installed on your computer displays in the text box. The Other option will not be available if you don't have any compatible devices.

See also CD Player, Multimedia, Sound Recorder, Sounds

Web Publishing Wizard

Web Publishing Wizard — Manages the process of posting new Web content to a Web site. You simply enter the Web site configuration information the first time you use the Wizard, and it remembers this information and uses it in subsequent sessions. To use the Web Publishing Wizard, you must

- Have a connection to the Web server, either through the Internet or your company network, and permission to copy files to it. (Usually a server requires a valid username and password to connect.)

- Know the URL (the Web address) for the Web server. Ask your ISP or Web administrator if you aren't sure.

- Know the name of the folder on the server in which you should place your files. Your ISP or Web administrator can tell you this.

After you collect all this information, follow these steps to publish your files to the server:

1. Choose Start ➢ Programs ➢ Accessories ➢ Internet Tools ➢ Web Publishing Wizard to get things going. When the Wizard Welcome dialog box opens, click Next.

2. In the Select a File or Folder dialog box , enter the path and name of a single file or the name of the folder that contains the content you want to upload to the Web server. If you select a folder, all the files in the folder will be sent to the server. Choose the Include Subfolders option if you also want to copy the contents of any subfolders. Click Next.

3. In the Name the Web Server dialog box, enter a descriptive name for the Web server to which you are copying files. You can use this name during future uploads. Click Next.

4. In the next screen, specify the URL you use to access the Web server and the name of the folder on your system that you want to associate with this URL. Click Next. You may be asked to enter or confirm authentication information.

5. If a box appears for your username and password, enter them and click OK.

6. Click Next. Once the Wizard has all the information it needs, you can click Finish to actually start the file upload. To change information, click Back until you arrive at the appropriate screen.

The Wizard now copies the file or folders you selected to the destination Web server; a progress bar tells you how much still remains to be copied. When the Wizard is finished, it will close automatically.

See also Internet, Internet Connection Wizard, Internet Explorer

WebTV for Windows

Allows your computer to receive and display standard TV broadcasts. You must have a TV tuner adapter installed in your computer along with the appropriate antenna or cable hookup to receive television broadcasts. If you connect to the Internet, you can retrieve program listings as well as Internet broadcasts.

To start WebTV for Windows, click the WebTV for Windows icon on the Quick Launch toolbar, or choose Start ➤ Programs ➤ Accessories ➤ Entertainment ➤ WebTV for Windows. If the program is not there, use Add/Remove Programs in the Control Panel to install it from the Windows CD-ROM.

Once WebTV starts, it takes over the whole screen, and the normal Windows controls are no longer available. Press F10 to open the Viewer toolbar at the top of the screen. To close WebTV for Windows, click the Close button in the top-right corner of the window.

What's This?

Provides context-sensitive Help in some dialog boxes. If you right-click an item in a dialog box, a small menu opens, containing the single selection What's This. Click What's This to display Help text for that specific item.

Other dialog boxes have a Help button in the upper-right corner (look for the button with a question mark on it) next to the Close button. When you click this Help button, the question mark jumps onto the cursor; move the cursor to the entry on the dialog box that you want help with and click again. A small window containing the Help text opens. Click the mouse to close this window when you are done.

See also Help

Windows Media Player

▶ Windows Media Player Allows you to play multimedia files such as audio CDs, video, animation, and sound clips (including MP3s), depending on the hardware installed on your computer system.

Starting Windows Media Player

▶ Choose Start ➤ Programs ➤ Accessories ➤ Entertainment ➤ Windows Media Player to open the Windows Media Player dialog box, or click the Windows Media Player icon in the Quick Launch toolbar.

Windows Media Player has several tabs along the left side of the screen. The default tab, Media Guide, displays current content from the Internet. You can click one of the many hyperlinks shown there to download and play free content from Microsoft's Web site and the Web sites of other companies that Microsoft partners with.

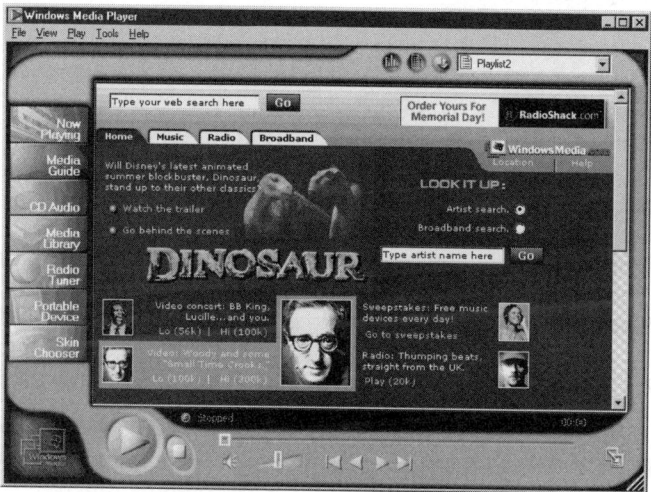

Playing an Audio CD

When you insert an audio CD-ROM in your CD-ROM drive, Windows Media Player launches automatically and starts playing the CD.

WINDOWS MEDIA PLAYER

If the CD does not start playing automatically, start up Windows Media Player as described in the preceding section. Then you can do either of the following:

- Click the CD Audio button. A list of tracks on the CD appears. Double-click the first track you want to play.
- Click the Now Playing button, and use the buttons that appear on that tab to control the CD play.

Here are the buttons you can use on the Now Playing tab to control the music:

 **Play**   Starts playing the clip.

 **Pause**   Pauses the playback.

 Stop   Stops the playback.

Skip Back   Repositions the clip to the previous marked position.

Rewind   Repositions the clip at the beginning.

Fast Forward   Advances the clip.

Skip Forward   Positions the clip at the next marked position.

Show Playlist   Displays or hides the track list for the CD.

Show Equalizer and Settings   Displays or hides the equalizer and other fine-tuning sound controls.

Shuffle   Turns the random play feature on or off; when selected, this feature plays tracks from the play list in a random order.

Mute   Toggles the sound on/off.

Volume Control   Lets you adjust the audio playback level of the clip.

The slider, located just to the right of the Play button, indicates your position within the clip or sound file. When a clip is loaded, a scale is displayed beneath the slider. As you drag the slider to the right, the clip advances accordingly. Below this, there is an information area that lists details of the clip, including the clip name, author, and copyright.

Playing Music Clips Stored on Your Hard Disk

Use the Media Library tab to organize and play stored clips such as MP3 files on your hard drive.

To search your hard disk for clips to include in your library, choose Tools ➤Search Computer for Media and then click Start Search. All the clips in compatible formats appear in a list on the Media Library tab.

Then simply double-click a clip to play it. To control the clip play, use the controls at the bottom of the screen described in the preceding section.

Listening to Internet Radio

There are hundreds of radio stations available on the Internet. When you choose a station, its content feeds in real time through the Internet to your PC, buffering as needed to compensate for any delays or slow connections. Some of these stations are Internet versions of real radio stations all over the world; others are produced specifically for Internet broadcast.

WINDOWS MEDIA PLAYER

To find and play a station, choose the Radio Tuner tab. Then find a station (open the drop-down lists under Station Finder to narrow the choices) and double-click it to tune in to the broadcast.

If you want to remember a station for later use, select it and click Add to add it to the Presets pane.

Other Windows Media Player Features

In addition to the features already described here, you can do the following with the Windows Media Player:

- Create your own playlists on the Media Library tab, organizing groups of stored clips as desired.
- Copy a CD audio clip to your hard disk with the Copy Music button on the CD Audio tab.
- Connect with a portable audio device such as an MP3 player, and transfer music from your PC to the portable player, using the controls on the Portable Audio tab.
- Change the look of the Windows Media Player program and controls on the Skin Chooser tab.

See also Sound Recorder, Volume Control

Windows Movie Maker

A utility program that enables you to copy video footage from a video camera or VCR to your hard disk, and then edit that video footage into your own movies with narrative voice-over, musical soundtracks, fade-out transitions, and other special effects. You can also make slide shows with still photos and narration or music.

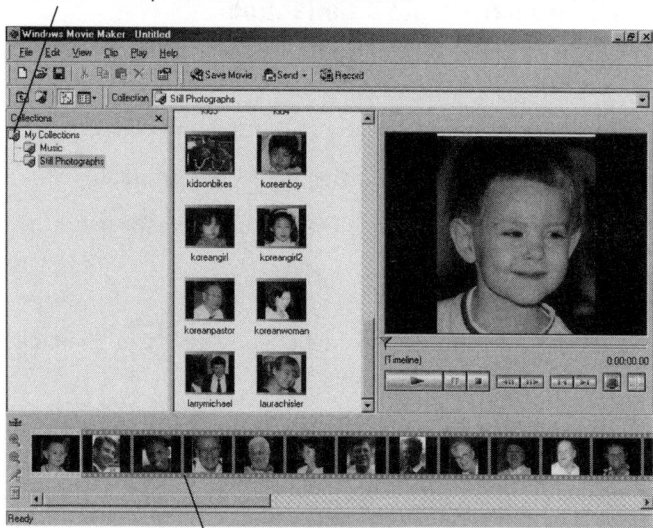

Collections of clips available for use in the movie

Storyboard of the movie

In order to import video from a video camera or VCR, you must have a Windows-compatible videocapture device that converts analog video into digital. (If you have a digital video camera, all you need is a way to connect it to your PC, such as a FireWire port.) You can still use the Windows Movie Maker with existing video, audio, and/or graphic content already on your hard disk, though, even if you don't have video input capability.

The basic process is this:

1. First, import your content into Collections. Collections are folders you create and use to organize clips of various kinds on various topics. For example, you might create a collection called Music for audio clips and another called Still Photos for scanned images.

2. Next, start a new Project, and place content from the collections into the project as you want it to appear in the movie.

3. Finally, preview your movie and then save it to your hard disk. You can then distribute it to others via e-mail or disk.

Movies can be played through Windows Media Player (described in the preceding section). Windows Media Player is available for free from the Microsoft Web site, so users need not have Windows Millennium Edition to play movies.

Importing a File from Disk into a Collection

If the clip already exists on disk, you can import it into Windows Movie Maker for use in a movie by doing the following:

1. Select the collection into which the clip should be placed.

2. Choose File ➤ Import. The Select the File to Import dialog box opens.

3. Choose the clip, and then choose Open. The clip appears in the collection.

Recording a Clip

If you have an input device, such as a videocapture device or a microphone, you can record a sound or video clip by doing the following:

1 Select the collection into which the clip should be placed.

2. Click the Record button on the toolbar or choose File ➤ Record. The Record dialog box opens.

3. If the correct video or audio recording device does not appear next to Video Device or Audio Device, click Change Device and choose it.

4. Prepare the recording device. If recording from a camera, point the camera at the source. If recording from a VCR or stereo, pause the tape or other media at the desired beginning point.

5. Click Record, and then quickly press Play on the VCR or stereo, or activate the recording feature on the video camera.

6. When finished recording, click Stop. The Save Windows Media File dialog box appears.

7. Enter a name for the clip, and click Save.

Assembling a Project

Once you have the clips imported into Windows Movie Maker, you can create your project (that is, your movie) by simply dragging the desired elements onto the storyboard or timeline.

You have two views of the movie to work with: Storyboard and Timeline. Storyboard shows images (video clips and pictures) in a sequence of frames, like movie film; Timeline shows all types of media. To switch between them, choose View ➤ Storyboard or View ➤ Timeline.

Storyboard

Timeline

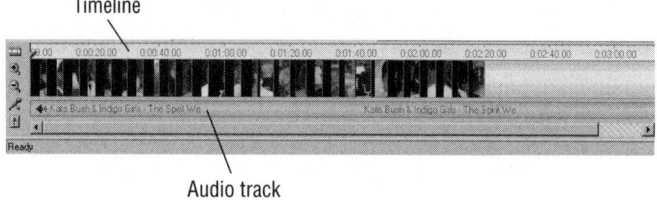

Audio track

To place a clip on the timeline, do the following:

1. Choose View ➤ Timeline, displaying the timeline.
2. Click the collection you want to use a clip from, displaying its clips.
3. Drag the clip onto the timeline in the spot where you want it.
4. Repeat for each clip to add. If desired, open the View menu and choose Storyboard to switch to Storyboard view.

Setting Transitions

Rather than abruptly stopping one clip and starting the next, you can set a transition between the two. This fades out the first clip and fades in the next one, just like the professionals do on TV.

To create a transition effect between two clips, do the following:

1. Display the project as a timeline (View ➤ Timeline).

2. Select the second of the two clips.

3. Drag the selected clip slightly to the left, so that it slightly overlaps the earlier clip. The amount of overlap determines the length of the transition.

Previewing the Movie

After you've created the project, you can preview it to see how it'll appear when you publish it as a movie. To preview it, open the Play menu and choose Play Entire Storyboard/Timeline, or click the Play button. It plays in the preview pane (the pane in the top right part of the Windows Movie Maker window), along with any sounds or music associated with it.

Saving the Movie

When you've finished your movie, you can distribute it to friends and relations on disk or via e-mail. All the recipients need is a player such as Windows Media Player (available free from Microsoft's Web site, in case they don't have Windows Me).

To save a movie, do the following:

1. Click the Save Movie button on the toolbar or choose File ➤ Save Movie. The Save Movie dialog box opens.

2. Open the Setting drop-down list and choose the quality level you want. Medium, the default, is best in most cases.

NOTE The higher the quality, the larger the file, and the longer it takes to send over an Internet or network connection. If you are preparing a movie for a low-speed connection distribution, choose a lower quality setting. For distribution on a high-speed network, choose a higher quality.

3. Enter a title in the Title box and your name in the Author box.

4. (Optional) Enter any other information you want to be saved with the movie in the boxes provided, such as Comments.

5. Choose OK. The Save As dialog box opens.

6. Click Save. The movie is saved. A prompt asks whether you want to watch the movie now. Choose Yes or No.

Saved movies are stored in the folder C:\My Documents\My Videos. You can view a movie at any time by finding it there and double-clicking it. You can attach the movie file to an e-mail or include a link to it on a Web page.

See also   Windows Media Player, Sounds and Multimedia

Windows Radio

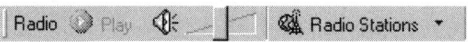
Lets you play a favorite radio station while connected to the Internet. The Windows Radio toolbar is turned off by default; use View ➢ Toolbars ➢ Radio in Explorer, My Computer, or Internet Explorer to turn this feature on.

TIP   Windows Media Player also has radio capability; further, it is more sophisticated and feature-rich than the Windows Radio toolbar, so you may choose it instead to listen to Internet Radio. The method described here is an older, but still functional, method.

To find out what is available and to choose a station, click the down arrow to the right of the Radio Stations icon on the Windows Radio toolbar. Select Radio Station Guide to connect to an Internet guide listing several hundred radio stations representing all radio formats, including news and talk, as well as classical, country, and rock music. You can make your choice from this list.

WARNING   You will need a fast modem or a fast network connection to get decent sound quality. A slower connection will give an interrupted signal as the data are buffered and then played.

Other buttons on the Windows Radio toolbar let you play the selected station, mute the sound completely, or adjust the playback volume level.

Windows Update

Connects to the Windows Update Web site at www.windowsupdate.microsoft.com and keeps your system up-to-date by automatically downloading new device drivers and Windows system updates as they are needed. Choose Start ➢ Windows Update, or choose

Tools ➢ Windows Update from within Internet Explorer. Internet Explorer opens (if it's not already open) and connects to the Web site. The Wizard scans your system looking for items that could be updated. It makes a list of any new device drivers or system patches that you need and then downloads and installs the files you select for any items you want to update.

Winipcfg

A program you can use to find your internet protocol (IP) address when connected to the Internet. To run this program, connect to the Internet using your ISP, and then follow these steps:

1. Choose Start ➢ Run to open the Run dialog box.

2. In the Open text box, type **winipcfg** and then press Enter to open the IP Configuration dialog box.

Much of the information listed here is of a highly technical nature and is of interest only to system administrators who will use Winipcfg when troubleshooting an Internet connection.

See also   Modems

WinPopup

Allows you to send and receive messages to and from other computers on your network. To use WinPopup, it must be active in memory and displayed on the Taskbar of both your computer and the computer with which you are communicating. When a message is received, the WinPopup window will be enlarged for you to see the message and respond if necessary. Messages are stored until you clear one or all of them, or until you shut down WinPopup or Windows.

Loading the WinPopup Window

To load WinPopup into memory so that you can receive and send messages to others on your network, follow these steps:

1. In My Computer or Explorer, navigate to C:\Windows and find `Winpopup.exe` (it will be toward the end of the folder contents), and click it to open the WinPopup window.

WINPOPUP

The WinPopup window has only two menu choices: Messages and Help. Messages provides the following options:

Send   Sends a message to another computer.

Discard   Deletes a received message.

Previous   Displays the previous message.

Next   Displays the next message.

Clear All   Deletes all messages.

Options   Provides the following choices:

Play Sound When New Message Arrives   Warns you with sound. If this option is not selected, no audio notification is given.

Always on Top   Ensures that other screens do not hide the WinPopup window.

Pop Up Dialog on Message Receipt   Displays the WinPopup window when a new message is received. If this option is not selected, no visual notification is given.

2. Minimize the window to an icon on your Taskbar by clicking the Minimize button.

Sending a WinPopup Message

To send a WinPopup Message, follow these steps:

1. Load WinPopup if it is not already in memory.
2. Choose Messages ➤ Send to open the Send Message dialog box.
3. To send a message to a specific user or computer, click User or Computer. To broadcast a message to all users and computers on your workgroup, click Workgroup.
4. Type the name of the user, computer, or workgroup in the text box.
5. Type your message in the Message area and click OK. You will be informed that the message has been successfully sent.

Wireless Link

See Infrared

WordPad

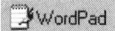 A word-processing program that comes with Windows. To open WordPad, choose Start ➢ Programs ➢ Accessories ➢ WordPad.

WordPad Menus

When you first open WordPad, you will see a typical word-processing window with a menu bar beneath the title bar. Most of the menus contain standard Windows commands, but some commands are unique to WordPad.

File Menu

The File menu contains only one unique command, Page Setup. It displays a dialog box in which you can establish the page size, orientation, margins, and paper source. You can also change the default printer by clicking the Printer button.

Edit Menu

The Edit menu contains these unique options:

Links   Displays a dialog box for managing the maintenance of a linked object. You can choose Update Now for the linked object from the original source, Open or Change the Source, or Break the Link.

Object Properties   Displays a Properties dialog box for the object currently selected in the document.

 TIP   You can double-click an inserted object to activate the program used to create the object. To return to WordPad from the other program, simply click outside the object.

View Menu

The View menu contains the Options command, which opens the Options dialog box. It has six tabs:

Options   Sets the standard measurement units to Inches, Centimeters, Points, or Picas. If you select Automatic Word Selection, WordPad selects a whole word at a time as you drag the mouse pointer over text. If you leave this option unchecked, only one character at a time is selected.

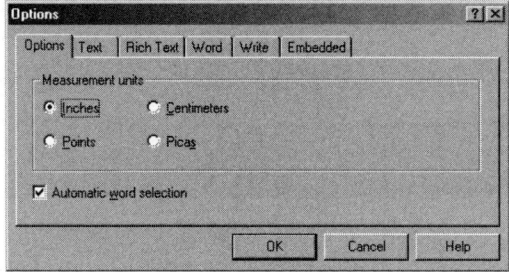

Text, Rich Text, Word, Write   Allow you to set the word wrap and toolbar defaults for each format type. You can set word wrap for No Wrap, Wrap to Window, or Wrap to Ruler. You can display the standard toolbar, the format bar, the ruler, and the status bar.

Embedded   Establishes the word wrap and toolbar defaults for any embedded objects inserted in your document.

Insert Menu

The Insert menu contains the following unique options:

Date and Time   Inserts the date and time into your document according to the format you select from the list box.

Object   Displays a dialog box for selecting the type of object that can be inserted into a document. You have several choices for creating a new object:

Create New   Allows you to select the type of object to be created and to activate the program for creating it. For example, if you choose to create a bitmap image, Paint is activated.

Create from File   Inserts an object from an existing file. It can be embedded or linked.

Link   Links an object to the document. Link is displayed when you select Create from File. In this case, the object is inserted into the document, but any modifications to the original file update the object in the document as well. When Link is not selected, the file is inserted into your document as an embedded object. When you edit the file, the original, creating program's menus and toolbars are activated.

Display as Icon   Inserts an icon of an object into a document, rather than the content of the object itself. When you double-click the icon, the object opens.

Format Menu

The Format menu contains the following unique formatting options for fine-tuning a document:

Font   Allows you to choose font, style, size, color, and special effects, such as strikethrough and underline, to be used in the document.

Bullet Style   Formats a selected paragraph in bullet style.

Paragraph   Allows you to set indentation and alignment for a selected paragraph.

Tabs   Sets the tab stop positions for selected text in the document.

WordPad Toolbars

WordPad has two toolbars—the standard toolbar and the format bar.

Standard Toolbar

The standard toolbar contains these icons:

New   Creates a new document. It can be a Word, Rich Text, or Text Only document.

Open   Allows you to select a document to open.

Save   Stores the current document to disk.

Print   Prints the current document.

Print Preview   Displays the current document as it will print.

Find   Searches for a file containing specified text or an object.

Cut   Moves the selected text to the Clipboard and deletes it from the current file.

Copy   Copies the selected text to the Clipboard.

Paste   Copies the contents of the Clipboard into the current document.

Undo   Removes the results of the last editing action.

Date & Time   Inserts the date and time into the document, according to the format you select.

Format Bar

The format bar contains these icons:

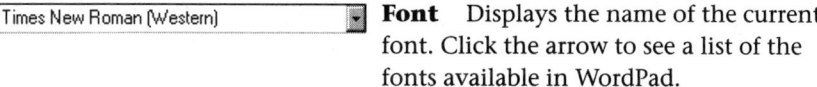

Font   Displays the name of the current font. Click the arrow to see a list of the fonts available in WordPad.

Size   Displays the current font size. Click the arrow to see a list of the point sizes that apply to this font.

Bold   Makes the selected text boldface.

Italic   Makes the selected text italic.

Underline   Underlines the selected text.

Color   Displays a palette of colors for the font.

Align Left   Left-justifies the selected text.

Center   Centers the selected text horizontally.

Align Right   Right-justifies the selected text.

Bullets   Formats the selected paragraph as a bulleted list.

Creating a Document

You can create a WordPad document in several ways. To create a document from scratch, follow these steps:

1. Click in the text area of the window and type your text.
2. Use the toolbars and menus to enhance the text with formatting, color, and other special effects.
3. Click Save to save the document.

To create a document by inserting the contents from the Clipboard, follow these steps:

1. Highlight the text or graphic in another application and click Copy or Cut to place the text or graphics onto the Clipboard.
2. Open WordPad and click where you want the contents of the Clipboard to be placed.
3. Click the Paste icon.

To create a document by inserting an object, follow these steps:

1. Place the pointer where you want the inserted object.
2. Choose Insert ➢ Object.
3. Choose File ➢ Create.
4. Enter the path and name of the object to be inserted. If the object is to be linked, click Link. Click OK.

See also   Notepad

Index

Note to the Reader: Throughout this index *italicized* page numbers indicate illustrations.

Symbols

+, expanding text in Help with, 87, *87*
+, indicating hidden objects in Explorer, 70
.vxd files, disabling, 246
.WAV files, controlling volume and balance, 265, 266
  inserting, 231

A

accessibility, 2, *2. See also* Accessibility Options; Accessibility Wizard; Magnifier
  Access Control tab, 226
  in Internet Explorer, changing, 125, *125*
  On-Screen Keyboard, 169, *169*
  restricting with shared resources, 227, *227*
Accessibility Options, 2, *2. See also* Accessibility Wizard; Magnifier; On-Screen Keyboard
  Display tab for alternative colors and fonts, 2, 4
  General tab to define availability of options, 2, 5
  Automatic Reset, 5
  Notification, 5
  SerialKey Devices, 5
  Keyboard tabs for enhancing keyboard use, 2, 3
  FilterKeys to desensitize the keyboard, 2, 3
  StickyKeys to enhance use of Alt, Ctrl, or Shift, 2, 3
  ToggleKeys plays a tone with Caps Lock, Num Lock, or Scroll Lock keys, 2, 3
  Mouse tab for using numeric keypad instead of mouse, 2, 4–5
  Sound tab for the hearing impaired, 2, 4
  ShowSounds, 4
  SoundSentry, 4
Accessibility Wizard, 6
accessing computers
  on network with My Network Places, 154
  remote, with My Computer, 153
Active Desktop, 6–9. *See also* Desktop; Internet Explorer; Taskbar
  Customize My Desktop, 7, *7*, 74, *75*
  Background, 7, *7*
  Web to organize elements, 8, *8*
  customizing background, 6, 7, *7*, 8–9, *9*
  New Active Desktop Item Wizard, 8–9, *9*
  organizing elements, 8, *8*, 57, *58*
  View as Web Page, 7
Active Desktop Item Wizard, 8
Add or Edit Discussion Servers Wizard, 107
Add New Hardware, 9–11, *10*
  non Plug-and-Play devices, 10, *10*
  Plug-and-Play devices, 9
Add New Modem Wizard, 137
Add Printer Wizard, 192, 197, *197*, 198, *198*
Add User Wizard, 202

ADD/REMOVE PROGRAMS

Add/Remove Programs, 11–14, *11*, *13*
  installing, *11*, 12, 101
  Network Install tab, 14
  Startup Disk tab, *11*, 14
  uninstalling, *11*, 12, 263
  Windows Setup tab, 12–13, *13*
Address Book, 14–18
  AutoComplete in Outlook Express, 173
  creating a new Address Book entry, 16–17, *17*
  importing addresses and Outlook Express, 15
  importing an existing address book, 14–15
  menus, 16
  opening from Outlook Express, 171, *171*
  setting up a new group, 17–18
Address Toolbars, 18, 69
  locations of, 18
addresses, finding on Internet, 116
allowed network protocols
  IPX/SPX Compatible (Internet Packet Exchange/Sequenced Packet Exchange), 44, *44*
  NetBEUI (NetBIOS Extended User Interface), 44, *44*
  TCP/IP (Transmission Control Protocol/Internet Protocol), *44*, 45
America Online, 168, *168*, 169
  AOL NetFind, 224
annotating graphic images, 98, *98*
applications. *See also* Disk Defragmenter; programs; ScanDisk
  accessing data in database management systems, 168, *168*
  installing with Add/Remove Programs, 12, 263
  running automatically with Scheduled Tasks, 221–222, *221*

sharing, 161
  uninstalling with Add/Remove Programs, 12, 263
  vs. deleting with Explorer, 263
windows
  closing, 27, *27*
  maximizing and minimizing, 135–136
archive files, compressed, 28, *28*
area code, using in Dial-Up Networking, 43
arithmetic calculations, 22
audio. *See also* Sounds and Multimedia
  CD Player, 24
  conferencing with, 158, 159
  Windows Media Player, viii, 269–272, *269*, *271*, *272*
audio devices
  connecting to, 272
  recording from. *See* Sound Recorder
Auto Hide and Taskbar, 257
AutoComplete
  changing settings for, 123, *123*
  in Outlook Express, 173
  and URLs, 107, *107*
Automatic Updates, 18–19, *19*
AWD files, 95, 96

B

background on Desktop, customizing, 7, *7*, 8–9, 35, 53, 71
Backup programs, 20
bandwidth, increasing, 46
Bigfoot Internet Directory Service, 224
BMP files, 95, 96
Boot-up disks, creating, 11
briefcase. *See* My Briefcase

browsing
  changing settings for browsing in Internet Explorer, 125, *125*
  in Windows using buttons in dialog boxes, 20, *20*
business cards, adding to e-mail messages, 173, 177
businesses, finding on Internet, 116

C

Calculator, 21–24, *21*
  Calculator Window, 21, *21*
  scientific calculations, 22–23, *23*
  standard arithmetic, 22
  statistical calculations, 23–24, *24*
calendar, *211*, 212
capturing screen images, 24
CD Player, 24, 64, *64*. *See also* Sounds and Multimedia; Windows Media Player
CD players. *See also* Windows Media Player
  adjusting sound quality, 266
  volume and balance control, 265
CD-ROM. *See also* Sound Recorder
  determining memory used by, 243
  extracting files from, 246–247
  optimizing Access Pattern, 243
CD-ROM drive
  optimizing use of, 243
  playing audio from with Windows Media Player, 269
  volume and balance control for audio played through, 265
CD-ROMs, for installing applications, 101
certificates, managing, 123, *123*
Character Map, 25, *25*
chatting
  with MSN Messenger service, 148–149, *148*

with NetMeeting, 159, 160–161
client, definition of, 164
Clipboard, 25–26. *See also* Clipboard Viewer
  using in Notepad, 167
  using while capturing a screen image, 24
Clipboard Viewer, 26, 26–27, *26*. *See also* Clipboard
  Display menu, 27
  Edit menu, 26
  file menu, 26
clips, 270–271, 273. *See also* sound files
  organizing, 273
clock
  displaying, 257
  setting, 33–34, *33*
closing application program windows, 27, *27*. *See also* Shut Down
Collections for Windows Movie Maker, 273–274, *273*
color
  black and white scale for graphic images, 99
  changing for display, 58–59, *58*
  changing for graphic images, 99
  and Web pages, 119, *120*
comma-separated text files, importing to Address Book, 14–15
Communications applet for accessing Windows Me communications tools, 27, *27*. *See also* Dial-Up Networking; Direct Cable Connection; Home Networking Wizard; HyperTerminal; Internet Connection Wizard; modems; MSN Messenger Service; NetMeeting; Phone Dialer

Compressed Folders feature, 28, *28*
conferencing via the Internet. *See* NetMeeting
Conflicting Device List in Device Manager, 39, *39*
connecting to the Internet with Dial-Up Networking, 40–47. *See also* Internet Connection Wizard
connecting to other computers, 91–94, *92*
connection properties in Dial-Up Networking for changing all connections, 47
  Show an icon on Taskbar after connection, 47
  Show a confirmation dialog after connection, 47
connection properties in Dial-Up Networking for changing individual connections, 43–47
  additional communications devices, adding to connection, 46
  changing phone number and modem, 43, *43*
  changing modem, 43, *43*
  changing telephone number to dial, 43, *43*
  choosing to include area code when dialing, 43, *43*
  choosing server type and protocols, 44–45, *44*
  allowed network protocols, 44, *44*
  choosing to record a log file for this connection, 44, *44*
  enabling software compression of incoming and outgoing data, 44, *44*
  specifying server type, 44, *44*
  establishing dial-up connection, specifying how and when, 46–47, *46*
  determining level of automation, 46, *46*
  disconnecting when connection may not be needed, *46*, 47
  enabling idle in order to disconnect after a period of time, *46*, 47
  redialing, specifying number of times, 46, *46*
  script, entering if required by network, 45
  security options, 45, *45*
  changing user name and password, 45, *45*
  choosing automatic connection, 45, *45*
  security options dictated by server, 45, *45*
connection speed in Dial-Up Networking, increasing, 46
Control Panel, 28–29, *28*, *29*. *See also* Folder Options; Printers; Start; Taskbar
Copy Disk command, 31, *31*
copying
  files and folders, 29–30, *30*
  multiple, 30
  Paste command, 186
  using drag-and-drop, 29
  using the Edit menu, 30
  using the right mouse button, 30, *30*
  floppy disks, 31, *31*. *See also* Explorer; My Computer
  text from the Internet, 112
Create Shortcut Wizard, 203, 229, 258, *258*
creating new folders, 32, *32*, 65
currency
  currency symbol, determining position of, 210, *210*
  currency symbol, selecting, 210, *210*

decimal symbol, determining, 210, *210*
negative number format, specifying, 210, *210*
number of digits in a number group, specifying, 210, *210*
symbol to separate number groups, determining, 210, *210*
Customize this Folder Wizard, 71
  Add Folder Comment, 71
  Choose or Edit an HTML Template, 71
  Modify Background Picture and Filename Appearance, 71
  Remove Customization, 71

D

data
  and infrared transmissions, 100–101
  storing, 25–30
data bits, setting number of, *137*, 138
database management systems, accessing data in, 168, *168*
date, 33–34, *33*, 211–212, *211*
  calendar type, changing, *211*, 212
  digits in the date, determining, *211*, 212
  format for date display, determining, *211*, 212
  symbol for displaying a formal date notation, determining, *211*, 212
  symbol to separate the month, day, and year, determining, *211*, 212
default Internet connection, 46, *46*
defaults, establishing for Windows features, 28–29, *28*, *29*

deleting files and folders, 34. *See also* Explorer; Recycle Bin
  undoing deletes, 34
Desktop. *See also* Active Desktop; Control Panel; Display
  arranging icons on, 143
  changing appearance of, 35, 53, *53*
  colors, customizing, 202
  contents, 35
  moving toolbars to, 260
  Online Services folder, 168, *168*, 169
  shortcuts with File menu, 109, *109*
  themes, 35, 36. *See also* Screen Saver
  when the My Briefcase icon does not appear, 149
device drivers
  managing printer drivers, 196
  for telephony, 260, 261
    configuring, 261
    deleting, 261
Device Manager, 36–40, *36*, *37*, *38*, *39*. *See also* Plug-and-Play; System applet
  checkbox for making devices available in all hardware profiles, 37, *37*
  checkbox to disable a device, 37, *37*
  removing and redetecting a device, 40
  viewing device's properties, 37, *37*
    device status information, 37, *37*
    driver files information, 38, *38*
    system resources information, 38–39, *39*
devices
  and availability in multiple profiles, 37, *37*
  disabling, 37, *37*
  displaying the Properties dialog box for devices, 241

DIAL-UP NETWORKING

external sound devices
   and sound quality, 266
   and volume and balance control,
      265
listed by category, *36*, 37
listing by type, 241
removing, 241
removing and redetecting, 40
Dial-Up Networking, 27, *27*, 40–48,
   41. *See also* Internet Connection
   Wizard; Internet Explorer;
   modems; network; Phone Dialer
   accessing remote computers with
      My Computer, 153
   changing connection properties,
      43–47
      changing user name and password and specifying other
         security options, 45, *45*
      choosing server and protocols,
         44, *44*
      communications device, adding
         to connection with Multilink
         tab, 46
      entering a script if required, 45
      phone number and modem,
         changing, 43, *43*
      specifying how and when connection will be established,
         46, *46*
   changing general settings, 47
   changing passwords, 184
   connecting to the Internet with,
      47
   creating new connections, 41, *41*,
      90, 91
   dialing established connections,
      42, *42*
   installing modems, 41
   System Monitor and, 251
dialing configurations, establishing,
   260–261

dialing established connections, 42,
   42
changing settings for, *137*, 138
dialog boxes, Properties on Address
   Book toolbar, 16–17, *17*
digital cameras
   adding a scanner or digital camera,
      218–219, *219*
   connecting to with USB, 263
   setting scanner or digital camera
      properties, 219–220, *220*
   transferring images from a digital
      camera, 220
Digital IDs in Address Book, 17
Direct Cable Connection, 27, *27*,
   48–49, *48*. *See also* Dial-Up Networking; infrared; modems;
   network
disconnect automatically in Dial-Up
   Networking, *46*, 47
Disk Cleanup, 49–50, *50*, 133, 134.
   See also Disk Defragmenter;
   Scheduled Tasks
   displaying amount of space that
      can be recovered, 50, *50*
   Recycle Bin and, 207
   removing applications and components or reconfiguring to use
      less disk space, 50, *50*
Disk Defragmenter, 51–52, *51*, 133,
   134. *See also* ScanDisk; Scheduled Tasks
   checking the driver for errors, 51, *51*
   rearranging program files so programs start faster, 51, *51*
disk space
   finding amount remaining on
      hard disk, 52, *52*
   finding amount used by files or
      folders, 52
   making more available on hard
      disk, 49–50, *50*, 133, 134, *134*

maximizing, 62–63, *62*
Recycle Bin and, 207
vs. speed, 63, *63*
disks. *See also* floppy disks; hard disk
checking for errors. *See* ScanDisk
cleaning up, 49–50, *50*
compressed, 62–63, *62*
defragmenting, 51–52, *51*
formatting, 72, 80–81, *80*
   choosing format type, 80, *80*
   displaying summary on disk space and bad sectors, *80*, 81
   labeling the disk, 80, *80*
   not labeling and removing existing label, *80*, 81
   specifying disk capacity, 80, *80*
naming, 155, *155*
printing from, 195
removable, optimizing settings for, 243
repairing errors, 216–217
setting and changing access passwords, 185
Display, 53–59. *See also* Display Properties dialog box; Screen Saver
options, 4
   changing colors, 4
   changing font, 4
Display Properties dialog box, 53–59
   changing appearance, 56, *56*
   changing the scheme, 56, *56*
   customizing a single item, 56, *56*
   Effects tab, 57, *57*
   Font tab, 56, *56*
   Screen Saver tab, 54–55, *55*
      changing the password, 54, *54*
      determining speed and density of screen saver pattern, 54, *54*
      displaying screen saver for preview, 54, *54*
      list of available screen savers, 54, *54*

Power Management Properties dialog box, 55, *55*
   requiring a password to go beyond the screen saver, 54, *54*
   setting delay before screen saver is activated, 54, *54*
   selecting or modifying the background, 53, *53*
   selecting and organizing Active Desktop elements, 57, *58*. *See also* Active Desktop
   varying resolution and color palette, 58–59, *58*
documents. *See also* files; folders
   access to last 15 used, 59, *59*, 188, 236
   clearing list, 188
   printing, 193
      changing print order, 194
      and print queue, 194
   storing in My Documents, 154, *154*
DOS. *See* MS-DOS prompt
DoubleSpace, 61
downloading data from a laptop, 48, *48*
drag-and-drop, 59–60, 144
   for creating shortcuts, 228
   from Explorer to put shortcuts in the StartUp submenu, 237
Drive Converter, 60–61. *See also* DriveSpace; MS-DOS Prompt
Driver tab in Device Manager, 38, *38*
Driver File Details, 38, *38*
Update Driver, 38, *38*
drivers
   files details, 38, *38*
   installing for home network, 90–91
   managing printer drivers, 196

DRIVES

print properties and print driver, 196
updating, 38, *38*
drives
 checking for errors. *See* ScanDisk
 compressed, 61–63, *62*
 managing, 61–63, *61*, *62*
 DriveSpace, 61–63. *See also* Drive Converter; ScanDisk
  Advanced menu, 62
   choosing compression method, 62
   connecting compressed-volume files to selected drive, 62
   removing a compressed drive, 62
   removing a compressed drive from its volume file, 62
   updating the DriveSpace window, 62
  disk compression settings, 62–63, *62*
   HiPack compression, *62*, 63
   no compression, *62*, 63
   no compression unless drive is at least X% full, *62*, 63
   standard compression, *62*, 63
  Drive menu, 62
   changing the distribution of free space, 62
   formatting compressed drives, 62
  DriveSpace dialog box, 61–62, *61*

E

e-mail. *See also* Address Book; Outlook Express
 accessing with Tools menu, 110, *110*
 addresses, grouping, 17–18
 assigning sounds to receiving, 232–234, *232*
 checking Hotmail with MSN Messenger, 149
 configuring accounts, 133
 encrypting contents, 175, *175*, 177
 in/out boxes in Outlook Express, 171, *171*
 opening from Internet Explorer toolbar, 106, *106*
 options to add
  business cards, 173, 177
  graphic images, 173
  hyperlinks to a Web site, 173
  signatures, 173, 177
 receiving in Outlook Express, 170, *170*, 172–173, *172*
 searching for messages in Outlook Express, 171, *171*
 sending
  sending current page or URL with File menu, 109, *109*
  sending from MSN Messenger, 149
  sending from Outlook Express, 170, *170*, 171, 173–175, *174*
  sending a print file as an attachment, 195
  sending with Send To utility, 225
  sending and receiving to and from network with WinPopup, 278–279
 sent message box in Outlook Express, 171, *171*
 setting default program choice for, 124, *124*
e-mail folders, Synchronization Manager and, 239
embedding, 129–130
 features of, 129
 modifying an embedded object, 130
 OLE (Object Linking and Embedding), 168

steps in, 129
vs. linking, 129
Enable indicator on taskbar to display a language on taskbar, 128
encyclopedia, finding information in from the Internet, 116
encrypting e-mail contents, 175, *175*, 177
entertainment, 64, *64. See also* CD Player; Sound Recorder; Sounds and Multimedia; Windows Media Player; Windows Movie Maker
Eudora Pro or Lite Address Book, importing to Address Book, 14–15
Excite search engine, 224
Exists in All Hardware Profiles checkbox, 37, *37*
Explorer, 64–73. *See also* Explorer toolbar
  about Explorer window, 70
  creating a new My Briefcase folder, 151
  Customize this Folder Wizard, 71
  and customizing folders, 71
  determining disk space and, 52, *52*
  Edit menu for working with contents of a file or folder, 65–66, *66*
  Favorites menu, 67, *67*
  File menu for file management options, 65, *65*
  finding a file or folder, 72
  Help menu, 67, *67*
  loading WinPopup from, 278–279
  mapping and disconnecting network drives, 67, 134, 135
  menus may not have all options, 64
  moving files and folders with Edit menu, 144
  running MS-DOS programs in Windows from, 145
  searching for files or folders in, 223, *223*
  similarity with My Computer, 68
  toolbars. *See also* Explorer toolbar
    Address toolbar, 69
    Links toolbar for links to Microsoft's Web site, 70
    Radio toolbar for selecting a radio station, 70
  Tools menu for customizing Explorer, 67, *67*
  tree structure for viewing, 70, *71*
  uninstalling programs vs. deleting with Explorer, 263
  View menu for choosing how files and folders are displayed, 66–67, *66*
Explorer toolbar
  changing the way information is displayed in Explorer window, 69, *69*
  deleting files or folders, 69, *69*
  displaying graphic files as small previews, 69
  displaying the contents of icons in various ways, 69, *69*
  displaying contents of small icons, 69, *69*
  displaying or hiding folders, 68, *68*
  displaying larger icons, 69, *69*
  moving backwards and forwards, 68, *68*
  moving and copying files or folders, 69, *69*
  moving up the directory tree, 68, *68*
  searching, 68, *68*
  undoing or canceling the previous action, 69, *69*
  viewing all the recent places you've been on the Web (history), 68

F

FAT16, conversion from, 60–61
FAT32, conversion to, 60–61
Favorites in Explorer, 67, *67*, 73–74, *73*
  add to, 73
  creating and moving folders, 73
  displaying, 106, *106*
  organizing, 73–74, *74*
  renaming or deleting items, 74
  similarity with Internet Explorer, 67
  using in various windows, 73
Favorites in Internet Explorer
  displaying Favorites menu from Explorer Bar, 113
  organizing
    creating folders, 114, *114*
    deleting selected items, 114, *114*
    moving folders, 114, *114*
    renaming selected items, 114, *114*
faxes, sending with Send To utility, 225
file extensions, changing association of, 76–77, *77*
file sharing in network, 165, *165*
File Transfer Protocol. *See* FTP
files
  checking for errors, 216, 218
  checking on status in My Briefcase, 151
  compressed, 28, *28*
  controlling advanced settings for, 76–76, *76*
  copying, 29–30, *30*, 66, *66*
    multiple, 30
    Paste command, 186
    using drag-and-drop, 29
    using Edit menu, 30
    using the right mouse button, 30, *30*
  copying to the Briefcase, 151
  creating new in Explorer, 65, *65*
  deleting, 34, 65, *65*
  deleting from Recycle Bin
    bypassing the bin, 207
    emptying the bin, 205
  determining amount of space occupied by, 52, *52*
  and drag-and-drop, 59–60
  errors in
    deleting, 217
    repairing. *See* ScanDisk
  extracting from installation disk, 246–247
  finding with Explorer, 72
  finding with My Computer, 153, *153*
  hidden, 76, *76*
  inserting objects into with WordPad, 281
  management of in Internet Explorer, 109, *109*
  management of, 65, *65*, 72
  moving, 66, *66*, 72
    using drag-and-drop, 144
    using the Edit menu in My Computer, Explorer, or a folder window, 144
    using the right mouse button, 144–145
  naming, 155
  recovering from Recycle Bin, 206–207
  renaming, 156, *156*
  selecting, 66, *66*
  selecting multiple files to move or copy, 144
  sending to destination with Explorer, 65, *65*

FOLDERS

shared
  closing, 157
  displaying currently shared files, 157
  and passwords, 185
  setting sharing properties for a particular file, 226–227
  setting up sharing, 226, *226*
  storing in My Documents, 154, *154*
  synchronizing between two computers. *See* My Briefcase
  transferring between computers, 48, *48*
  transferring with FTP, 81
  transferring to shared resources users, 159, 161
    adding files to transfer list, 159
    deleting files from transfer list, 159
  types, 76
  undeleting, 206–207, 262, *262*
    by selecting in Recycle Bin, 262
    by using Restore All button, 262, *262*
.vxd, disabling, 246
FilterKeys, *2*, *3*
floppy disk drives
  sending with Send To, 225
  specifying that Windows searches for new with each startup, 243
floppy disks. *See also* disks
  copying, 31, *31*. *See also* Explorer; My Computer
  formatting, 72, 80–81, *80*
  for installing applications, 101
  printing from, 195
Folder Options, 74–77
  File Types tab, 76–77, *77*
  General tab for defining systemwide settings, 74–75, *75*
    choosing between Active Desktop and Classic Desktop, 74, *75*
    choosing between enabling Web contents and displaying folder contents in traditional manner, 74, *75*
    choosing between single- and double-clicking, 75, *75*
    choosing how folders are opened, 75, *75*
  View tab for controlling advanced settings for files and folders, 75–76, *76*
    using current settings, 75, *76*
    using original View menu settings, 75, *76*
folders. *See also* Folder Options
  changing passwords, 185
  checking for errors, 216
  checking on status in My Briefcase, 151
  choosing to open in the same window, 75, *75*
  compressed, 28, *28*
  controlling advanced settings for, 75–76, *76*
  copying, 29–30, *30*, 66, *66*
    multiple, 30
    Paste command, 186
    using drag-and-drop, 29
    using the Edit menu, 30
    using the right mouse button, 30, *30*
  creating new, 32, *32*, 65
  customizing appearance of, 71
  deleting, 34
  determining amount of space occupied by, 52, *52*
  and drag-and-drop, 59–60
  finding with Explorer, 72
  finding with My Computer, 153, *153*
  management of with Explorer, 65, *65*, 72

295

moving, 66, *66*
  using drag-and-drop, 144
  using the Edit menu in My Computer, Explorer, or a folder window, 144
  using the right mouse button, 144–145
naming, 156
opening with Run, 214
pasting, 66, *66*
renaming, 157, *157*
searching with Browse, 20, *20*
selecting multiple folders to move or copy, 144
shared
  adding to shared resources, 157
  displaying those currently available, 157
  displaying those currently in use, 157
  and passwords, 185
  Properties dialog box for, 158
  removing from shared status, 157
  setting sharing properties for particular folders, 226–227
fonts, 77–79, *78*. *See also* Character Map
  adding new to computer, 79
  changing on Desktop, 35, 56, *56*
  changing for e-mail messages, 177
  changing size on display, 56, *56*
  changing on Web pages, 119, *120*
  characters available in various, 25, *25*
  controlling which are used in Windows, 79
  customizing, 202
  displaying and printing samples, 79
  List Fonts by Similarity, 78
  managing for printing, 197
  selecting to annotate graphic images, 98, *98*
  setting color, 56, *56*
  setting style, 56, *56*
  TrueType and non-TrueType, 77, 197
free space, adjusting between drives, 62
FTP (File Transfer Protocol), 81–82
  commands (table), 81
  running from MS-DOS, 81

G

gamepads, configuring and testing, 83, *83*
Games, ix, 85
Gaming Options, 83, *83*
  adding a game controller, 83–84, *84*
  calibrating Game Controller, 84
  list of controllers on system, 83, *83*
  list of games that are DirectPlay compatible, 83, *83*
  list of ID assignments for each controller, 83, *83*
  testing Game Controller, 85
GDI (Graphic Device Interface) resources, 214
graphic image files, 95–96
  ignoring, to speed up Internet Explorer, 117
graphic images
  adding to e-mail messages, 173, 177
  annotating, 98, *98*
  displaying as full screen, 99
  modifying, 95–99
  saving as a file, 112
  specifying quality for printing, 197
  storing in My Documents, 154
grouping e-mail addresses, 17–18

H

hard disk. *See also* DriveSpace; ScanDisk
  defragmenting, 51–52, *51*
  finding amount remaining on, 52, *52*
  freeing up space on, 49–50, *50*, 133–134, *134*
  maximizing, 62–63, *62*
  optimizing usage, 243
  space vs. speed, 63, *63*
hardware
  adding new, 9–11, *10*
  enabling and disabling devices, 200
  list of hardware installed on computer, 36, *36*
  and Plug-and-Play, 190
  using System Information to collect information about, 248, *248*
hardware profiles, 199–201, *200*
  copying, 242
  creating new, 200–201, *200*, 242
  deleting, 242
  disabling, 37, *37*
  disabling laptop network connection, 200
  making hardware device available in all, 37, *37*
  renaming, 242
hearing impairment, altering computer for, 2, *2*, 4, 5, 6
Help
  in Explorer, 67, *67*
  from Start menu, 236
  Help button, 268
  for printing, 195
  What's This?, 268
Help online, 86–90, *86*
  available in certain dialog boxes, 90
  browsing by topic, 87–88, *87*
  expanding text in, 87, *87*
  going to a Web page for, 88, *88*
  Help Index, 88, *89*
  Home page, 87, *87*
  printing from, 87, *87*
  right-clicking to find help for an object, 90
  searching with, 88, *88*
  toggling between windows, 87, *87*
  tours and tutorials, 88, *88*, 89–90, 111, *111*
  using, 86, *86*
  using assisted support, 89
    contact support, 89
    more resources, 89
    support communities, 89
  Windows Help and Support window, 86, *86*
hibernation for laptops, 55, *55*, 191
history of documents recently used, clearing list, 188, *188*
history of places visited on the Web, 68, 114–115, *115*, 119, *120*
  accessing folder for, 115
  clearing list, 119, *120*, 188, *188*
  specifying number of days to keep, 119, *120*
  viewing folder contents, 106, *106*, 115, *115*
  when computer used by several people, 115
Home Networking Wizard, 27, *27*, 90–91, 101, 199
home page, choosing, 118–119, *120*
hot swapping, 263
HTML
  for messages in Outlook Express, 173
  selecting HTML documents for Desktop background, 7, *7*

HTML editor, setting default program choice for, 124, *124*
hyperlinks
  adding to e-mail messages, 173
  downloading and playing free content from Internet, 269
  for Help, 87, 88, 89
  to Microsoft's Web site, 70, 269
HyperTerminal, 27, *27*, 91–94
  creating a new connection, 91–93, *92*
  reopening a saved connection, 93
  working with a connection, 93–94, *93*, *94*
    creating, opening, and disconnecting, 93
    modifying, 94
    sending and receiving, 94
    Unique Options in Hyper Terminal Menus (table), 94

I

icons
  adding My Briefcase icon to Desktop, 149
  Arrange Icons on Desktop, 143
  arranging in Explorer, 67, 142, *142*
  changing icon size, *142*, 143
  creating small for Start menu, 257, *257*
  customizing on Desktop, 202
  customizing on Taskbar, 257, *257*
  inserting icon of an object into a document in WordPad, 282
  moving and arranging, 142–143, *142*
    and files and folders, *142*, 143
    sorting in various manners, *142*, 143
    with Thumbnail, *142*, 143
  selecting new for Desktop, 57, *57*
  various on Control Panel, 29
  X through to indicate disabled device, 241
idle
  enabling disconnect after a period of inactivity, 47
  setting time, 46, *47*, 55, *55*, 191
images
  acquiring with Scanner and Camera Wizard, ix, 218
  capturing screen images, 24
Imaging, 95–99, *95*. *See also* Imaging toolbars
  menus, 99
    Unique Imaging Menu Items (table), 99
  toolbars, 96
    annotation toolbar for annotation and drawing tools, 98–99, *98*
    imaging toolbar for working with images and other toolbars, 97–98, *97*, *98*
    standard toolbar for functions associated with opening, closing, and saving images, 96–97, *96*, *97*
    turning on and off, 98, 99
  types of files managed by, 95
    AWD, 95, 96
    BMP, 95, 96
    TIFF, 95, 96
Imaging toolbars
  annotation toolbar for annotation and drawing tools, 98–99, *98*
    drawing lines and rectangles of various types, 98, *98*
    inserting text, 98, *98*
    Rubber Stamp tool, 98, *98*
  imaging toolbar for working with images and other toolbars, 97–98, *97*, *98*

rotating, changing page, 97, *97*
scanning, dragging, annotating, 97, *97*
Thumbnail views, 98, *98*
standard toolbar for opening, closing, and saving images
  best fit, 97
  cutting and pasting, 96, *96*
  opening, closing and saving images, 96, *96*
  printing, 96, *96*
  zooming in and out, 96, *96*
turning on and off, 98, 99
Infoseek, 224
infrared (IR)
  communications, 100–101
  connections, 48
Install New Modem Wizard, 41
installing applications, 101
installing and uninstalling
  from networks, 14
  programs, 11–13, *11*
Internet
  and Help, 86, 88
  listening to radio from, 271, *272*
  option in Search utility, 224
  searching, 106, 224
  signing up for access, 136, *136*
  watching TV broadcasts on computers from, 268
Internet configuration options, 118–125. *See also* Internet; Internet Explorer; Outlook Express
  Advanced tab for changing various Internet Explorer settings, 125, *125*
  Connections tab for specifying how your system connects to the Internet, 123, *124*
  Content tab for restricting access to sites, 122–123

changing settings for Windows AutoComplete, 123, *123*
controlling access to certain sites, 122–123, *123*
managing digital certificates, 123, *123*
General tab, 118–120, *120*
  choosing home page, 118–119, *120*
  choosing how certain information is displayed in Internet Explorer, 120, *120*
  choosing the language used on certain Web pages, 120, *120*
  choosing which colors are used on certain Web pages, 119, *120*
  history of recent links, 119, *120*
  managing stored Web pages for offline access, 119, *120*
  specifying font style and text size for Web pages, 119, *120*
Programs tab, 124–125, *124*
Security tab, 120–121, *121*, *122*
  changing security levels, 121, *121*
  customizing security settings, 121, *121*, *122*
  Internet zone, 120, *121*
  local intranet zone, 120, *121*
  restricted sites, 121, *121*
  trusted sites, 121, *121*
Internet Connection Sharing, viii, 90, 101–102
Internet Connection Wizard, *27*, 41, 102–105, 123, *124*
  creating the connection manually, 103, 104–105
  creating a new connection to the Internet, 102–104, 123, *124*
  establishing a connection to an existing account, 103

299

setting up connections, 102–103, *103*
tutorial, 103
Internet connections
  monitoring with System Monitor, 251
  various types, 101
Internet Explorer 5.5, viii, 105–118.
  See also Dial-Up Networking; Internet options
  and automatic Windows updates, 277–278
  browsing offline, 117
  changing print settings, 125, *125*
  configuring, 112
  connecting to Microsoft's Web site to search, 224
  Explorer bar, 108, *108*
  fitting buttons on toolbars, 107
  information about, 248
  Internet Explorer window, 111–112, *112*
    changing Web pages, 111
    copying text, 112
    opening links, 111
    opening other windows, 111
    printing with pop-up menu, 111
    saving graphic images, 112
    saving images, 111
    status bar, 111, *112*
  logo, 110
  menus
    Edit menu, 109, 109–111, *109*
    Favorites menu, 67, *67*, 110, *110*
    File menu, 109, *109*
    Help menu, 111, *111*
    Tools menu, 110, *110*
    View menu, 109, *110*
  returning to favorite pages, 112–116
    accessing, 113, *113*
    Add to Favorites, 113, *113*
    Favorites, 112–114, *113*
    History list of sites visited, 114–115, *115*
    organizing Favorites, 113–114, *114*
    using Back and Forward buttons, 113
  searching the Web, 116, 224
    changing settings, 125, *125*
    search submitted to search engines, 116
    searching with Internet Explorer Address toolbar, 116
    selecting type of search, 116
  similarity with Windows Explorer, 105
  speeding up, 117, *118*
  starting, 105
  toolbars, 106–108, *106*, *107*, *108*.
    See also Internet Explorer Standard Buttons toolbar
    Address toolbar, 107–108, *107*
    hiding or displaying, 109, *110*
    Links toolbar, 107, *107*
    Radio toolbar, 108, *108*
  Internet Explorer Standard Buttons toolbar, 106–107, *106*, *107*
    Discuss button for connecting to a discussion server, 107, *107*
    Edit button for opening current page in Web page editor, 107, *107*
    Favorites button for displaying Favorites menu contents, 106, *106*
    History button for displaying history, 106, *106*
    Home button to open home page, 106, *106*
    Mail button for mail options, 106, *106*
    Messenger button for running MSN Messenger, 107, *107*

Print button to print current Web page, 107, *107*
Refresh button for updating current page, 106, *106*
Search button for displaying search options, 106, *106*
Stop button to cancel current download, 106, *106*
Internet games, 85
Internet Options and Tools menu, 110, *110*
Internet Protocol (IP) address
  finding, 278
  when using Connection Sharing, 102
Internet service providers (ISP), 40, 47
  collecting mail from, with Outlook Express, 171, *171*
  connecting to, 104, 105, 177
  MSN and, 136
  and online services, 169
  IPX/SPX Compatible (Internet Packet Exchange/Sequenced Packet Exchange)protocol, 44, *44*

J

joysticks, configuring and testing, 83, *83*

K

keyboard, 127–128, *127*
  changing language displayed, 127, *127*
  desensitizing for people with tremors, 3
  Language tab, 128
  Add (a language), 128
  Enable indicator on taskbar for switching default languages quickly, 128
  Properties to change keyboard layout default, 128
  Remove (a language), 128
  Set as Default (a language), 128
  Switch Languages between two or more, 128
  Repeat Key Speed tab, 127–128, *127*
  Click Here and Hold Down a Key to Test Repeat Rate, 127, *127*
  Cursor blink rate, *127*, 128
  Repeat delay, 127, *127*
  Repeat rate, 127, *127*
Keyboard tab in Accessibility Options, 3
keystrokes, eliminating unwanted, 3

L

LAN Manager passwords, disabling sending of, 47
language
  changing in Windows, 128
  selection to use on Web pages, 120, *120*
laptops
  disabling network connection, 200
  downloading from, 48, *48*
  hibernation, 55, *55*, 191
  preventing synchronization when on battery power, 240
  Lightweight Directory Access Protocol (LDAP), 224
  importing to Address Book, 14–15
linking, 129–130
  features of, 129
  making changes in linked objects, 129

LOGGING OFF

modifying a linked file, 130
OLE (Object Linking and Embedding), 168
steps in, 129
using linked objects in WordPad, 280, 282
vs. embedding, 129
logging off, 131–132, 236
of network, 164
logging on
to network, 164
to network vs. logging on to Windows, 183
to Windows, 131, 182, 183
Lycos, 224

M

Magnifier, *2*, 6, 132, *132*
Mail icon on Control Panel, 133
Maintenance Wizard, 133–134, *134*. *See also* Scheduled Tasks
Disk Cleanup and, 221
Disk Defragmenter and, 221
Recycle Bin and, 207
ScanDisk and, 221
Make New Connection Wizard, 41, *41*
mapping network drives, 134–135, *135*
disconnecting a network drive, 135
maps, finding on Internet, 116
Maximize/Minimize buttons, 135–136
Media Library, 271, 272
Media Player. *See* Windows Media Player
meeting with NetMeeting, 161
memory
and drives of various speeds, 243
measured with Resource Meter, 213
menus
personalizing, 186–188, *187*
resetting usage data, 188, *188*
turning off, 187, *187*
microphones
controlling sound quality, 266
controlling volume and balance, 265
recording sound clips, 274
specifying type in Sound Recorder, 234
Microsoft Desktop Gallery, 8, *8*
Microsoft Exchange Personal Address Book, importing to Address Book, 14–15
Microsoft Internet Mail for Windows 3.1 Address Book, importing to Address Book, 14–15
Microsoft Network. *See* MSN
Microsoft Office 2000 clipboard, 26
Microsoft SQL 7 databases and Synchronization Manager, 239
Microsoft's Web site
accessing with Internet Explorer logo, 110
downloading free audio content from, 269
downloading Windows Media Player, 274
hyperlinks to, 70, 269
Links toolbar as connection to, 107, *107*
for radio stations, 108, *108*
searching with, 224
mobility, lack of, configuring computer for, 2, *2*, 4, 6
modems
advanced settings, 137
changing settings, 40, 137–139
controlling sound quality, 266

MY BRIEFCASE

creating new connection, 41, *41*
Diagnostics tab, 139, *139*
   Driver button for information about driver, 139, *139*
   Help button to access Help, 139, *139*
   More Info button for port information and modem testing, 139, *139*
General tab, 137–138, *137*
   dialing properties, 138
   installing a new modem, 137
   Modems Properties dialog box, 137–138, *137*
   removing modem drivers from Windows, 137
installing, 41, 137
managing interaction with computer, 260
specifying port used, *137*, 138
speed required for listening to radio, 277
volume and balance control and, 265
mouse, 139–142
   and drag-and-drop, 59–60
   emptying Recycle Bin with, 205
   mouse button configuration and speed, changing, 140, *140*
      choosing between single- and double-clicking, 75, *75*, 140, *140*
      ClickLock to drag without holding mouse button, 140, *140*
      double-click speed, 140, *140*
      from right-handed to left-handed, 140, *140*
   using right-click to print, 193
pointer
   adding a trail, 141, *142*
   changing appearance of, 141, *141*
   changing speed of, 141, *142*

Movie Maker. *See* Windows Movie Maker
movies. *See* Windows Movie Maker
MP3s, 269, 271
MS-DOS. *See also* MS-DOS Prompt
   Help in, 146
   returning from to Windows, 82
MS-DOS programs, switching between full screen and window, 145
MS-DOS Prompt
   accessing, 60–61
   running FTP (File Transfer Protocol) from, 81–82
   and running MS-DOS programs in Windows, 145–146, *146*
MSN, 136, *136*
   connecting to MSN Internet content, 136
   signing up for Internet access, 136, *136*
MSN Messenger service, 27, *27*, 107, *107*, 146–149, *147*, *148*
   accessing with Tools menu, 110, *110*
   adding a contact to list, 147, *147*
   checking Hotmail e-mail with, 149
   sending e-mail with, 149
   setting temporary online status, 149
   signing up for, 146–147
   using instant messaging (chatting), 148–149, *148*
Multilink Channel Aggregation (MCA), 46
multimedia, changing settings, 125, *125*
multiple users profiles, 202
muting sound devices, 265
My Briefcase, 149–152, *150*
   adding My Briefcase icon, 149
   copying a file to Briefcase, 151

303

files
    choosing not to update a particular file, 151
    updating all files in Briefcase, 151
    updating selected files, 151
    folder, 150–151
    installing, 150
    sending with Send To utility, 225
    synchronizing files in Briefcase, 152
    when icon does not appear on the Desktop, 149
    window, 150
My Computer, 152–153, *153*
    accessing remote computers with, 153
    determining disk space and, 52, *52*
    finding a file or folder with, 153
    folder, 153, *153*
    loading WinPopup from, 278–279
    mapping network drives and, 134, 135
    similarity to Explorer, 68
    using Edit menu to move files and folders, 144
My Documents, 154, *154*
    files, specifying a different destination for, 154
    using to create new folders, 32
My Network Places, 154, *154*
    mapping network drives and, 134, 135

N

naming
    computer, 165–166, *165*
    a new folder, 32, *32*
Net Watcher, 156–158
    monitoring current shared resources users with, 156–157, *157*
    devices and folders, displaying those available for sharing, 157, *157*
    devices and folders, displaying those being shared, 157, *157*
    files, adding to shared resources, 157, *157*
    files, closing shared, 157, *157*
    selecting shared computer to monitor, 157, *157*
    user, disconnecting, 157, *157*
    users, display current, 157, *157*
    Net Watcher menus, 157–158
    Unique Options on the Net Watcher Menus (table), 158
NetBEUI (NetBIOS Extended User Interface) protocol, 44, *44*
NetMeeting, 158–163
    Address Book, entering NetMeeting information into, 17
    call status indicators, 160
        a call in progress, 160
        logged on to a directory server, 160
        no connections available, 160
        not logged on, 160
        unavailable for calls, 160
    File Transfer window, 159
        aborting a file transfer, 159
        adding files to be transferred, 159
        removing files from transfer list, 159
        sending files, 159
        viewing received files, 159
    making a call, 158, *158*, 160–161
        chatting, 159, *159*, 160–161
        seeing a list of those participating in call, 159, *159*
        sending a message, 161
        terminating current call, 158, *158*
    meetings
        hosting a meeting, 161
        joining a meeting, 161

options, 162–163
   audio settings, fine-tuning, 163
   Do Not List My Name in the Directory option, 162
   personal information, detailing, 162
   security and digital certificate, choosing type, 163
   video settings, customizing, 163
other main NetMeeting functions, 158–159
   adjusting volume, 159, *159*
   displaying video image in small window, 159, *159*
   finding persons or companies in directories, 159, *159*
   sharing applications, 161
   starting or stopping a video presentation, 159, *159*
   transferring files, 159, *159*, 162
   Whiteboard, using, 159, *159*, 162
   working with shared application, 159, *159*
NetMeeting in Address Book, 17
Netscape Address Book, importing to Address Book, 14–15
Netscape Communicator Address Book, importing to Address Book, 14–15
Netscape Navigator
   help if changing from, 111, *111*
   and Internet Explorer, 109, *109*
network, 163–166
   monitoring activity. *See* System Monitor
   shared printers, 197–198, *197*, 199
   users, monitoring with Net Watcher, 156–158
   WinPopup, sending and receiving messages with, 278–279
network administration, assigning passwords to shared devices, 185

network connection, disabling connection for laptops, 200
Network dialog box, 163–166. *See also* network administration; security
   Access Control tab, 166, *166*
      passwords, assigning to shared resources, 166, *166*
      users, identifying those allowed to share resources, 166, *166*
      users, listing those with access and no password, 166, *166*
   Configuration tab, 163–165, *163*
      components, displaying properties of, 164, *164*
      file and print sharing, 165, *165*
      logging on and off, displaying options for, 164–165, *164*
      network configuration, adding components to, *163*, 164
      network configuration, removing components, 164, *164*
   Identification tab, 165, *165*
      adding a description, *165*, 166
      computer groups, identifying, *165*, 166
      computers, identifying on the network, 165, *165*
Network Neighborhood, customizing, 202
network use, Home Networking Wizard, viii, 27, *27*, 90–91
networking components, types of, 164
   client software, 164
   protocols, 164
   service software, 164
News, accessing with Tools menu, 110, *110*
newsgroup reader, setting default program choice for, 124, *124*

NEWSGROUPS

newsgroups
  finding information in, 116
  lack of censorship and, 176
  reading and posting news in Outlook Express, 170, *170*, 176
  receiving a listing of from ISP, 176
  setting up an account, 176
Notepad, 167. *See also* WordPad
  retrieving text, 167
  when to use, 167
  window, 167
number systems, using various in the calculator, 23, *23*
numbers settings
  negative number format, establishing, 209, *209*
  negative sign symbol, establishing, 209, *209*
  number of digits after decimal point, specifying, 208, *209*
  number of digits in a group, specifying, 208, *209*
  symbol for decimal point, establishing, 208, *209*
  symbol that will group digits, determining, 208, *209*
  symbol to separate items, specifying, 209, *209*
  U.S. or metric system, determining, 209, *209*
  whether a zero is shown in front of a decimal point, determining, 209, *209*
numeric keypad
  and Calculator, 22
  using as mouse, 4–5

O

ODBC Data Sources (32bit), 168, *168*
OLE (Object Linking and Embedding), 168

On-Screen Keyboard, *2*, 169, *169*
online help. *See* Help
Online Services, signing up with, 168–169, *168*
operating system, optional components, 12–13, *13*
Outlook Express, 170–178
  customizing toolbars, 171, *171*
  dual-pane window, 172, *172*
  establishing management rules for e-mail and newsgroups, 178
  messages, creating and sending, 173–174, *174*, 175, *175*
    attaching files, 174, *174*, 175–176
    checking names in Address Book, 174, *174*
    encrypting, 175, *175*
    placing in Outbox, 174, *174*
    selecting priorities, 175, *175*
    signing digital signatures, 175, *175*
    spell checking, 174, *174*
    toggling between Online and Offline, 175, *175*
    undoing changes, 174, *174*
    Windows Clipboard, copying text to, 174, *174*
    Windows Clipboard, cutting text to, 174, *174*
    Windows Clipboard, pasting contents of a message into, 174, *174*
  options in Outlook Express, 176–177
    business cards, including, 177
    connecting to ISPs, options for, 177
    displaying articles from newsgroups, options for, 176
    fonts, selecting, 177
    format for mail and articles to newsgroups, specifying, 176

general options, 176, *177*
housekeeping options, 177
requesting a receipt, 176
security zones and message encryption, establishing, 177
signature settings control, 176
spell checker configuration, 177
stationary, selecting, 177
Outlook Bar buttons, 171, *171*
  deleted items box, 171, *171*
  drafts of messages box, 171, *171*
  inbox and outbox, 171, *171*
  sent items box, 171, *171*
Outlook Express menus, 172
Outlook Express toolbar, 170–171, *170*, *171*
  messages, creating new, 170, *170*
  messages, finding, 171, *171*
  messages, sending and collecting, 171, *171*
  opening Windows Address Book, 171, *171*
Outlook Express window, 170, *170*
reading mail, 172–173, *172*
  dealing with read messages, 173
  retrieving e-mail, 173
reading the news, 176
sharing addresses with, 15
starting, 170
Tip of the Day, 170
using Identity Manager for multiple users, 178

P

Paint program, 179–182, *179*
  creating images, 181
  Paint menus, 181–182
  tools, 179–181, *179*, *180*
    airbrushes, using, 180, *180*
    color of an object, selecting, 179, *179*
    curved lines, drawing, 180, *180*
    ellipses, drawing, 180, *180*
    enclosed areas, filling with color, 179, *179*
    enlarging a selected area, 180, *180*
    erasing, 179, *179*
    freehand lines, drawing, 180, *180*
    irregular areas to move, copy, or edit, selecting, 179, *179*
    lines of different shapes and widths, drawing, 180, *180*
    modifications of these selections, 180–181
    polygons, creating, 180, *180*
    rectangles with curved corners, creating, 180, *180*
    rectangles, creating, 180, *180*
    rectangular areas to move, copy, or edit, selecting, 179, *179*
    straight lines, drawing, 180, *180*
    text, inserting into a drawing, 180, *180*
  Unique Options in the Paint Menus (table), 181–182
    color inversion, 181
    custom colors, defining, 182
    enlarging viewed objects, 181, 182
    horizontal and vertical options, 181
    images from the screen, removing, 182
    opaque and transparent drawing, 182
    wallpaper options, 181
paper, setting size and orientation for printing, 196
parallel ports, using with Direct Cable Connection, 49
parity setting, *137*, 138
passwords, 182–185, *183*. *See also* Accessibility options; security; user profiles

PATHS

assigning to shared resources, 166, *166*
Change Other Passwords button to work with other passwords, 185
changing in Dial-Up Networking, 45
changing the Windows password, 184, *184*
enabling user profiles, 182–183, *183*
logging on and off and, 130, 131, 182, 183, 184
for other resources, 184–185
  Dial-Up connections, 184
  disks, 185
  folders, 185
  network administration, 185
  printers, 185
  screen savers, 185
  shared resources, 185, 226, 227
screen saver passwords, 185
for security, 54, *54*
specifying a Windows password, 183
and user profiles, 182
paths, about, 186
  specifying, 186
PCs, setting up to work in a small network, 27, *27*, 90–91
personalizing menus, 186–188, *187*
  resetting usage data, 188, *188*
  turning off, 187, *187*
Phone Dialer, 188–189, *189*
  dialing properties, 189, *189*
    area code and country, 189, *189*
    call waiting disabling, 189, *189*
    tone or pulse dialing selection, 189, *189*
  dialing with, 190
  Phone Dialer dialog box, 189, *189*
  setting dialing properties, 189, *189*

specifying modem or telephone line to use, 189, *189*
Speed Dial command, 189, *189*
setting up a Speed Dial number, 189–190
phone numbers, managing, 14–18
Plug-and-Play devices, 190
  installing, 9, *10*
ports
  changing hardware settings, *137*, 138
  FireWire, 273
  managing, 196
  setting levels for receiving and transmitting buffers, *137*, 138
  specifying use for modems, *137*, 138
  traditional vs. using USB, 263
power management, 55, *55*
  hibernation for laptops, 55, *55*, 191
  options, 190–192, *191*
    Hibernate tab for laptops, 191
    idle time, setting length of, 55, *55*, 191
    Power icon, turning on and off, 192
  Power Scheme, saving, 191
printer sharing in network, 165, *165*
printers, 192–199. *See also* printing
  adding a new printer, 197–199
    Add Printer Wizard, 197, *197*, 198, *198*
    adding a local printer, 198, *198*
    adding a network printer, 197, *197*
  changing passwords or sharing status, 185
  connecting to with USB, 263
  default, 193, 194
  differences in icons, *192*, 193
  print queue. *See* printing
  Printers folder, 192–193, *192*
  properties, 195–197, *196*
    fonts management, 197

graphics quality, specifying, 197
Help in dialog box, 195
number of copies to be printed, changing default, 196
paper size and orientation, 196
printer memory options, 197
printer ports and drivers, management options, 196
printing a test page, 196
Properties controls determined by printer driver, 196
shared name and shared password, 196
sharing, 196
shared, 199
  and passwords, 185
  setting sharing properties for particular printers, 226–227
  setting up sharing, 226, *226*
printing. *See also* printers
  current Web page, 107, *107*
  a document, 193
  by dragging file icon to the printer icon, 193
  from File menu, 193
  removing a document from the print queue, 194
  by right-clicking the mouse, 193
  from Explorer, 65, *65*
  from Help, 87, *87*
  from infrared printer, 101
  from Internet Explorer, 109, *109*
    changing settings, 125, *125*
  interrupting, 126, 194, 195
  with printer icon or Printers folder, 195
  with printer icon on Taskbar, 195
  with Start button, 195
  temporarily interrupting, 194
  printing to a disk file, 195
  queue, managing with dialog box, 194, *194*

changing the order of documents in, 194
deleting all print jobs from, 194
setting the default printer, 194
temporarily interrupting the print job, 194
processor activity, tracking of. *See* System Monitor
profiles. *See* hardware profiles; user profiles
programs. *See also* applications
  adding and removing, 11–13, *11*
    Install/Uninstall tab, *11*, 12
    Windows Setup tab, 12–13, *13*
  increasing speed of, 133–134, *134*
  running, 214–215, *214*, *215*
  running automatically with Scheduled Tasks, 221–222, *221*
Programs menu, 202–203. *See also* programs
  adding a new submenu to, 203
  starting programs from, 202
Properties dialog boxes, 203
protocol, definition of, 164

Q

Quick Launch toolbar
  adding shortcuts, 255, 259
  removing shortcuts, 255
  to start Outlook Express, 170
  switching between running applications, 254
  working with, 254–255, *254*, *255*

R

radio. *See also* Windows Media Player; Windows Radio
  listening to from Internet Explorer, 108, *108*

Radio Station Guide, 277
Radio Tuner tab, 272, *272*
stations, connecting to, 277
Read-Ahead Optimization, 243
real mode, 60
recording. *See also* Sound Recorder; Windows Media Player; Windows Movie Maker
  sound or video clips, 274
  varying the volume, 265
Recycle Bin, 34
  accessing, 204
    and drag-and-drop, 60
    using menu, 204
  bypassing the bin, 207
  changing size of, 205–206, *206*
  deleting shortcuts with, 229
  disk space and, 50
  emptying, 205
    automatically deleted files, 207
    from folder, 205
    using mouse, 205
  folder, 204–205
    emptying bin from, 205
    options, 74
    restoring in, 205
  recovering files from (undeleting), 206–207, 262, *262*
redialing in Dial-Up Networking, setting number of retries, 46, *46*
refreshing. *See* Synchronization Manager
Regional Settings, 34, 207–212, *208*
  Currency tab, 209–210, *210*
    currency symbol, determining position of, 210, *210*
    currency symbol, selecting, 210, *210*
    decimal symbol, determining, 210, *210*
    negative number format, specifying, 210, *210*
    number of digits in a number group, specifying, 210, *210*
    symbol to separate number groups, determining, 210, *210*
  Date tab, 211–212, *211*
    calendar type, changing, *211*, 212
    digits in the date, determining, *211*, 212
    format for date display, determining, *211*, 212
    symbol for displaying a formal date notation, determining, *211*, 212
    symbol to separate the month, day, and year, determining, *211*, 212
  general features, 207
  Number tab, 208–209, *209*
    negative number format, establishing, 209, *209*
    negative sign symbol, establishing, 209, *209*
    number of digits after decimal point, specifying, 208, *209*
    number of digits in a group, specifying, 208, *209*
    symbol for decimal point, establishing, 208, *209*
    symbol that will group digits, determining, 208, *209*
    symbol to separate items, specifying, 209, *209*
    U.S. or metric system, determining, 209, *209*
    whether a zero is shown in front of a decimal point, determining, 209, *209*
  Regional Settings tab, 207–208, *208*
    language and country of location, changing, 207–208, *208*

previews of values in other tabs, 208
Time tab, 210–211, *211*
  AM symbol, specifying, 211, *211*
  PM symbol, specifying, 211, *211*
  symbol to separate the hours from the minutes and seconds, determining, 210, *211*
  time formatting, determining, 210, *211*
Registry, 212. *See also* Registry Checker; System Restore
  as central database, 212
  removing programs from, 263
  restoring to an earlier version, 212
Registry Checker for troubleshooting Registry, 212–213
remote access. *See* Dial-Up Networking; NetMeeting
Resource Meter, 213–214, *213*, *214*
  general features, 213
  reading, 214, *214*
  using, 213–214, *213*, *214*
Resources tab in Device Manager, 38–39, *39*
rich text. *See* HTML
Run, 214–215, *215*, 236

S

Save As command, and naming files and folders, 155
ScanDisk, 133, 134, 216–218, *216*. *See also* Disk Cleanup; Disk Defragmenter; Maintenance Wizard
  Advanced options, 217–218
  cross-linked files, deleting, 217
  errors, choosing whether or not to automatically fix, 218
  file fragments, deleting, 217
  files, checking for invalid names and dates, 218
  information about repairing scanned drive, displaying, 217
  recording the results of a scan, 217
  reporting errors in filenames, 218
  closing, 218
  general features, 216
  running, 216–217, *216*, 218
    checking only Windows and system files portion of disk, 216
    checking portion of disk occupied by applications and data files they create, 217
    errors, Automatically Fix Errors checkbox, 217
    errors, checking entire disk for, 216
    preventing ScanDisk from repairing and moving hidden or system files, 217
    restricting write-testing, 217
    simple file and folder errors, testing for, 216, *216*
    test thoroughly, 216, *216*
Scanner and Camera Wizard, ix, 218
scanners
  adding a scanner, 218–219, *219*
  connecting to with USB, 263
  setting configuration, 99
Scanners and Camera utility, 218–220, *219*, *220*
  adding a scanner or digital camera, 218–219, *219*
  setting scanner or digital camera properties, 219–220, *220*
  transferring images from a digital camera, 220
Scheduled Task Wizard, 221

SCHEDULED TASKS

Scheduled Tasks, 133, 220–222, *221*
  adding a new scheduled task, 221–222, *221*
    customizing task configuration, 222
    selecting the name program you want to schedule, *221*, 222
    selecting the time the program will run, *221*, 222
  general features, 220–221
  halting a scheduled task in progress, 222
  running, 221
  for running Disk Defragmenter, 52
  using the advanced options, 222
   notification of missed tasks, 222
   pausing, 222
    turning application off and halting scheduled tasks, 222
    viewing Scheduled Tasks log file, 222
scientific calculations, 22–23, *23*
screen images, capturing, 24
screen resolution, setting, *58*, 59
screen savers
  changing, 54, *54*, 222
  changing image, 222
  changing password, 185
  determining speed and density of pattern, 54, *54*
  general features, 222
  previewing, 35, 54, *54*
  Screen Saver utility, 222–223
  and security level, 185
  setting time before activation, 54, *54*
screens
  changing colors on Desktop, 35
  enlarging a portion of, 132, *132*
search engines, 116
Search utility, 223–224, *223*
  replaces the Find feature, 223

searching for audio clips, 271
searching for files or folders, 223–224, *223*. *See also* My Computer
  using Explorer, 223, *223*
  using Windows, 224
searching for people, 224–225, *224*
searching on the Internet, 224
security
  Dial-Up Networking, 45, *45*
  Internet Explorer
    changing security level, 121, *121*
    changing settings, 125, *125*
    custom security level, 121, *122*
    four levels in four zones, 120–121, *121*
  for multiple users, 178
  network, 163, 183
    determining access with passwords, 166, *166*
    determining access without passwords, 166, *166*
    network vs. Windows passwords, 183
  passwords and other resources, 184–185
  and user profiles, 182, *183*
  Windows
    changing passwords, 54, *54*, 184, *184*
    creating passwords, 54, *54*, 183
    vs. network passwords, 183
Send To utility, 225, *225*
servers, 40
  specifying type to access, 44, *44*
service software, definition of, 164
settings, establishing for Windows features, 28–29, *28*, *29*
Settings utility, 225, *225*
shared drives, 134
shared files, Uninstall and, 12
shared printers, 197–198, *197*, 199

SOUND RECORDER

shared resources, 226–227, *226*, *227*. *See also* network
  general information, 226
  limiting access to, 226, 227, *227*
  monitoring users with Net Watcher, 156–158
  setting global sharing, 226, *226*
  setting individual sharing properties, 226–227, *227*
    comments about resources, 227, *227*
    specifying name of resource, 227, *227*
    specifying type of access, 227, *227*
shortcuts, 228
  adding a shortcut to the Programs menu, 228–229
  changing properties, 228
  creating, 228
    by dragging the item, 228
    in Explorer, 65, *65*, 228
    from Explorer, My Computer, or Desktop, 228
    in My Computer, 228
  deleting, 229
  general description, 228
Show Web Content on My Active Desktop box, 8, *8*
ShowSounds, 4
Shut Down utility for closing Windows, 229–230, *229*, 236
  dangers of not using, 229
  procedure for using, 229–230, *229*
  restarting, 229
signatures, sending to e-mail messages, 173, 177
slide shows. *See* Windows Movie Maker
snapshots. *See* System Monitor; System Restore

software
  client, 164
  enabling compression for incoming and outgoing data, 44, *44*
  service, 164
  System Information for collecting information about, 248, *248*
sound card and volume control, 265
sound clips, 269, 271
sound devices, muting, 265
sound files, 232. *See also* Sound Recorder
Sound Recorder, 64, *64*, 230–232, *230*
  Edit menu, 231
    copying from, 231
    deleting, 231
    displaying audio properties, 231
    inserting .WAV files, 231
    mixing sounds, 231
    pasting in, 231
  Effects menu to produce special effects, 232
  File menu for special options, 231
    creating or recording a new sound file, 231
    displaying properties for current sound file, 231
    removing changes made to sound files, 231
  general features, 230
  Sound Recorder dialog box, 230–231, *230*, *231*
    getting a visual image of the sound quality, 230, *230*
    locating position on sound track, 230, *230*
    playing, 231, *231*
    recording, 231, *231*
    repositioning sound track at the beginning or end, 231, *231*

SOUND TAB IN ACCESSIBILITY

seeing length of sound track, 230, *230*
stopping, 231, *231*
Sound tab in Accessibility Options, 2, 4
sound tracks, creating. *See* Sound Recorder
sounds
  assigning to system events. *See* Sounds and Multimedia
  changing for Desktop, 35
Sounds and Multimedia, 232–235. *See also* CD Player; Sound Recorder; Windows Media Player
  Audio tab for establishing default setting for multimedia devices, 234, *234*
    MIDI Music Playback, 234, *234*
    Sound Playback, 234, *234*
    Sound Recording, 234, *234*
  Device tab for list of multimedia recording and playback devices on the system, 235
  general features, 232
  Sounds tab to assign sounds, 232–234, *232*
    browsing available sounds, 233
    naming the sound to assign, 233
    playing the sound, 233
    schemes, listing, 233
    volume control, showing on Taskbar, 233
    volume, setting master, 233
    Windows events to which sounds can be assigned, listing, 233
  Voice tab for controlling voice recording and playback, 235
SoundSentry, 4
speakers
  balance between two, controlling, 265

type in Sound Recorder, specifying, 234
volume, controlling, 265
speed vs. disk space, 63, *63*
spelling, checking in Outlook Express, 174, *174*, 177
Start button, 235–236
Start menu, 235–236
  automatic updates to Windows operating system, 236
  changing size of, 257, *257*
  displaying smaller icons, 257, *257*
  documents, accessing last 15 documents, 236
  Help, 236
    searching, 236
    setting various options, 236
  logging off, 236
  programs, accessing, 236
  programs, adding to, 258–259, *258*
    by dragging, 258
    using Create Shortcut Wizard, 258, *258*
  programs, running, 236
  shutting down, 236
start-up disks, creating, 14
Startup menu for identifying and isolating system problems, 238
  getting to the menu, 238
  options, 238
    confirming each step of start-up, 238
    creating a system log while rebooting, 238
    normal start-up for regular operation of Windows, 238
    Safe Mode, 238
StartUp submenu for shortcuts, 236–238. *See also* Startup menu
  placing a program on the StartUp menu, 237, *237*
  removing a shortcut, 237–238

Station Finder, 272, *272*
stationary in e-mail messages, 177
statistical calculations, 23–24, *24*
StickyKeys, *2*, 3
stop-bits, setting, *137*, 138
Storyboard, 275, *275*
Switch languages, 128
Synchronization Manager, 239–240, *239*
  changing options, 239–240
    specific time for synchronization, specifying, 240
    synchronization during idle time, specifying, 239–240
    synchronized items when you log on, specifying, 239
  starting
    from Help system, 239
    from programs, 239
synthesizers
  controlling sound quality, 266
  controlling volume and balance, 265
Sysedit. *See* System Configuration Editor
system
  optimizing for best performance, 133–134, *134*
  returning to an earlier configuration. *See* System Restore
System applet, 240–244
  Device Manager tab for listing devices installed in or attached to computer, 241–242, *241*
    devices, removing from the list, 241
    devices, selected, displaying Properties dialog box for, 241, *241*
    devices, viewing by connection, 241, *241*
    devices, viewing by type, 241, *241*
    hardware resources, printing summary of, *241*, 242
    refreshing or redisplaying the list, 241, *241*
  General tab for general information about system, 240, *240*
  hardware profiles, 242
    copying, 242
    deleting, 242
    renaming, 242
  opening the System Properties dialog box, 240, *240*
  Performance tab for information about memory, 242–244, *242*
    disk-related hardware, settings, 243
    graphic speed acceleration, setting, 243
    virtual memory settings, specifying, 243–244
system clock, setting, 33–34, *33*
System Configuration Editor (Sysedit), 244, *244*
  accessing with Run command, 244
  recommendation of experience before using, 244
System Configuration Utility, 245–247, *245*
  installation disk, extracting files from, 246–247, *247*
  recommendation of experience to use, 245
  running, 245–246, *245*
    non-USA installation and usage, specifying settings, 246
    non-USA installation environment variables, 246
    programs that load automatically at Windows start-up, disabling, *245*, 246

SYSTEM CONFIGURATION

Startup mode, selecting with
  General tab, *245*, 246
Static VXDs to disable .vxd files,
  246
System.ini for troubleshooting,
  246
Win.ini for troubleshooting, 246
system configuration, displaying
  information about, 248
System Information advanced
  reporting tool, 247–249
  displaying data, 248–249, *248*
  advanced data, *248*, 249
  applications, 248, *248*
  components, 248, *248*
  hardware resources, 248, *248*
  Internet Explorer, 248, *248*
  software environment, 248, *248*
  general features, 247
  opening, 248, *248*
  technical nature of information
    collected, 247
System Monitor, 249–251
  adding other graphs to the System
    Monitor display, 251
  controlling some aspects of the
    graphical display, 251
  displaying new items, 251
  general features, 249
  installing, 249
  System Monitor dialog box,
    250–251, *250*
  toolbar, 249–250, *250*
  adding items to be monitored
    with Add, 249, *249*
  deleting items to be monitored
    with Remove, 250, *250*
  displaying in bar-chart form with
    Bar Charts, 250, *250*
  displaying data numerically with
    Numeric Charts, 250, *250*
  displaying monitored data in
    line-chart form with Line
    Charts, 250, *250*
  editing monitoring charts with
    Edit, 250, *250*
  halting storage of System Monitor information with Stop
    Logging, 250, *250*
  storing System Monitor information in a file with Start Logging, 250, *250*
system performance, optimizing. *See*
  System applet
System Restore, viii, 251–253
  configuring, 50
  restoring configurations, 252–253,
    252
  saving configuration snapshots,
    251–252
  starting, 251
  undoing restorations, 253
System Tray, 253, 255
  closing programs with, 253
  location of, 253
  opening programs with, 253
System.ini for troubleshooting, 246

T

Task Scheduler. *See* Scheduled Tasks
Taskbar, 254–255
  adding toolbars, 259. *See also*
    Address Toolbars; Quick
    Launch
  Address for opening Internet
    addresses, 259
  Desktop for adding icons, 259
  Links with a set of Internet
    addresses, 259
  Quick Launch, 259
  changing menu properties,
    256–257, *257*

TIME

Auto Hide, choosing to display Taskbar as a small thin line, 257
clock, choosing to show, 257
making always visible, 257
redisplaying when Auto Hide is selected, 257
shrinking by dragging edge, 257
Taskbar and Start menus, changing properties, 256, *257*
changing size and position of, 256, *256*
adding an additional line of buttons, 256, *256*
moving to the top or either side of the screen, 256, *256*
icons, 254
applications currently active represented by rectangular buttons, 254
Bring the Desktop to the front, 254
Open Internet Explorer, 254
Open Outlook Express, 254
Open Windows Media Player, 254
Start button, 254
switching between running applications with, 254
system tray icons, 254
language, displaying on, 128
open applications, temporarily placing on, 136
Quick Launch toolbar, 254–255
opening Internet Explorer from, 254, *254*
opening Outlook Express, 255, *255*
opening Windows Media Player, 255, *255*
shortcuts, placing on, 255
shortcuts, removing from, 255

windows, minimizing all open, 254, *254*
System Tray, location of on, 253
System Tray, working with the, 253
toolbars, creating custom, 260
volume controls, 233
windows, switching with, 255
Taskbar and Start menu, customizing, 255–261. *See also* Start menu; Taskbar
TCP/IP (Transmission Control Protocol/Internet Protocol), *44*, 45, 47. *See also* FTP (File Transfer Protocol)
telephone
allowing control by computer, 260
managing equipment connection with computer, 260
telephone number, changing in Dial-Up Networking, 43, *43*
Telephony applet, 260–261, *260*
configuring, adding, or removing device drivers with Drivers tab, 261
dialing configuration, setting up with My Locations tab, 260–261, *261*
general features, 260
terminal programs, 91
text, copying from the Internet, 112
themes for Desktop, 35, *36*
thumbnails
displayed as previews, 69
specifying size and aspect ratio for, 99
TIFF files, 95, 96
time
AM symbol, specifying, 211, *211*
changing zone, 34
PM symbol, specifying, 211, *211*
setting, 33–34, *33*

317

symbol to separate the hours from the minutes and seconds, determining, 210, *211*
time formatting, determining, 210, *211*
Timeline, 275, *275*
Tip of the Day in Outlook Express, 170
ToggleKeys, *2*, 3
toggling between Online and Offline in Outlook Express, 175, *175*
tone, turning on for Caps Lock, Num Lock, or Scroll Lock, 3
toolbars. *See also* Taskbar
  Address, 18, *18*
  Address Book, 16–17
  including or excluding, 66, *66*
  moving to the Desktop, 260
  in Outlook Express, 171, *171*
troubleshooting
  graphic speed acceleration and, 243
  hardware problems, 242
  Registry, 212–213
  with ScanDisk, 216–218, *216*
  with Startup Menu, 238
  from System Properties, 243
  System.ini for, 246
  using System Information, 248, *248*
  Win.ini for, 246
TV broadcasts, receiving with WebTV for Windows, 268
TV Viewer. *See* WebTV for Windows
Typical Role for This Machine, 243

U

undoing deletes of files or folders, 34
Universal Serial Bus. *See* USB

unmapping network drives. *See* mapping network drives
Update Device Driver Wizard, 38, *38*
Updating. *See also* Synchronization Manager
Windows Millennium automatically, 18–19, *19*, 236
URL
  in address toolbar, 107, *107*
  and AutoComplete, 107, *107*
  management with File menu, 109, *109*
USB (Universal Serial Bus), 263
user profiles, 201–202
  creating, 201–202, *201*
  Desktop settings for multiple users, customizing, 202
  icons, customizing, 202
  Program menu options, customizing, 202
  Start menu, customizing, 202
  user profiles, customizing, 202
  and logging on and off, 130
usernames, 182, 183
  changing, 45
users, 264, *264*. *See also* logging on; passwords; user profiles

V

VCRs, importing video footage from, 273
Video. *See also* Windows Media Player; Windows Movie Maker
  conferencing, 158, 159
  copying footage from video camera or VCR to hard disk, 273
  editing video footage, 273
video cameras, importing video from, 273

video clips. *See also* Windows Movie Maker
  ignoring to speed up Internet Explorer, 117
  recording, 274
videocapture devices, 273
  and recording video clips, 274
Virtual Memory, 243–244
Virtual Private Network (VPN) connection, requiring secure, 47
vision, reduced, altering computer for, 2–3, *2*, 5, 6
voice-command devices, controlling volume and balance for, 266
volume control, 64, *64*, 265–266, *265*
  playback sound quality, adjusting, 266
  recording volume, varying, 265–266
  in Sound Recorder, 232, 234
  for voice-command devices, 266
  volume and balance control, 265
    audio CDs from CD-ROM drive, 265
    external devices, 265
    master control, 265
    microphones, 265
    modems, 265
    synthesizers, 265
    .WAV files, 265

W

wallpaper on Desktop, changing, 6, 7, *7*, 8, 35, 53, *53*
warning dialog boxes, assigning sounds to, 232–234, *232*
Web
  Active Desktop and, 6, 7, 8
  free content with MSN, 136
  Microsoft Desktop Gallery, 8–9
  searching from Internet Explorer, 116
  searching from Start menu, 116
Web pages. *See also* Favorites
  changing colors, 119, *120*
  changing fonts, 119, *120*
  displaying, *See also* Favorites; history; Internet Explorer; Internet options
  finding, 116
  Home page, 106, *106*
    choosing, 118–119, *120*
  language selection on, 119, *120*
  location shown on Address toolbar, 107, *107*
  moving to new, 111
  refreshing, 106, *106*
  stored
    checking for newer versions, 119, *120*
    managing for offline access, 119, *120*
  Synchronization Manager and, 239
Web Publishing Wizard, 267–268
  features, 267
  requirements for use, 267
    connection to a Web server, 267
    knowing the URL for the Web Server, 267
    knowing where on the server to place files, 267
    permission to copy files to server, 267
  steps in using, 267–268
Web sites
  allowed content control, 122–123, *123*
  downloading free audio content from, 269
  history, 114–115, *115*
  opening from various places in Windows, 114

319

approved sites, 122, *123*
ratings, 122, *123*
tracking favorites, 73–74, *73*, *74*
Windows Update Web site, 277–278
WebTV for Windows, 268
　closing, 268
　connecting to the Internet and, 268
　requirement of TV tuner adapter, 268
　starting with Add/Remove Programs in Control Panel, 268
What's This?, 90, 268. *See also* Help
Whiteboard, 162
Windows
　fonts used in, controlling, 79
　opening and closing sounds, changing, 232–234, *232*
　opening Web sites from various places in, 114
　operating system, optional components, 12–13, *13*
　password security and, 182, 183
　printing and, 193
　searching for files or folders. *See* Search utility
Windows Address Book, importing to Address Book, 14–15
Windows Clipboard and e-mail messages, 174, *174*
Windows Clipboard Viewer, 12
Windows Explorer. *See* Explorer
Windows Me. *See* Windows Millennium Edition
Windows Media Player, viii, 64, *64*, 269–272, 272. *See also* CD-ROM; radio
　audio CDs, playing, 269–271, *270*
　　clip name, 270–271
　　equalizer and other sound controls, displaying or hiding, 270, *270*
　　muting, 270, *270*
　　playing, pausing, and stopping, 270, *270*
　　rewinding and fast forwarding, 270, *270*
　　shuffling, 270, *270*
　　skipping backwards and forwards, 270, *270*
　　track list for the CD, playing, displaying, or hiding, 270, *270*
　　troubleshooting, 269
　　volume, adjusting, 270, *270*
　CD audio clips, copying, 272
　changing the look of Windows Media Player, 272
　downloading from Microsoft's Web site, 274
　general features, 269
　listening to Internet radio, 271–272, *272*
　　Radio Tuner tab, 272
　　Station Finder, 272
　　Windows Media Player superior to Windows Radio, 277
　playing free content from the Internet, 269, *269*
　playing music clips from hard disk, 271, *271*
　　controlling the clip play, 271
　　searching for clips, 271
　　using Media Library to organize and play, 271
　playing radio on, 108, *108*
　playlists on Media Library, creating, 272
　portable audio devices, connecting to, 272
　starting, 269
Windows Me
　automatic updates, 18–19, *19*
　as evolutionary step, viii
　new features of, viii–ix

Windows Movie Maker, viii, 273–277, *273*, *275*
  assembling a project, 275, *275*
    Storyboard, 275, *275*
    Timeline, 275, *275*
  basic procedures, 273–274
  distributing to friends and relations, 276
  general features, 273
  importing video footage, 273, 274
    into Collections, 273, 274
    from digital video cameras, 273
    from video cameras or VCRs, 273
  previewing movies, 273, 276
  quality, deciding on, 276
  recording clips, 274
  saving movies, 276
  setting transitions, 275–276
  storing movies, 277
  viewing movies, 277
Windows operating system
  installing or uninstalling elements of with Add/Remove Programs, 11–14, *11*
  optional components, 12–13, *13*
  Windows Millennium Edition (Me) as evolutionary step, viii
Windows Radio, 277. *See also* Windows Media Player
  Media Player as more sophisticated program, 277
  modem speed required, 277
  selecting stations, 277
Windows Update
  device drivers downloaded automatically, 277
  Web site address for, 277
  Windows system updates downloaded automatically, 277
Windows Update Wizard, 277–278
Windows Update Web site, 277–278
Windows Update Wizard, 277–278

Windows word processing programs. *See* WordPad
windows, closing application program, 27, *27*
Win.ini for troubleshooting, 246
Winipcfg for finding Internet protocol (IP) address, 278
WinPopup, 278–279
  loading the window into memory, 278
  receiving messages from other computers on the network, 278
  sending a message, 279
wireless link. *See* Infrared
Wizards, viii
  Accessibility, 6
  Active Desktop Item Wizard, 8
  Add or Edit Discussion Servers Wizard, 107
  Add New Hardware Wizard, 9–10, *10*
  Add New Modem Wizard, 137
  Add Printer Wizard, 192, 197, *197*, 198, *198*
  Add User Wizard, 202
  Create Shortcut Wizard, 203, 229, 258, *258*
  Customize this Folder Wizard, 71
    Add Folder Comment, 71
    Choose or Edit an HTML Template, 71
    Modify Background Picture and Filename Appearance, 71
    Remove Customization, 71
  Home Networking Wizard, viii, 27, *27*, 90–91, 101, 199
  Install New Modem Wizard, 41
  Internet Connection Sharing Wizard, 101–102
  Internet Connection Wizard, *27*, 41, 102–105, 123, *124*

creating a new connection to the Internet, 102–104, 123, *124*
creating the connection manually, 103, 104–105
establishing a connection to an existing account, 103
setting up connection, 102–103, *103*
Tutorial, 103
Maintenance Wizard, 133–134, *134*, 221. *See also* Scheduled Tasks
  Disk Cleanup and, 221
  Disk Defragmenter and, 221
  Recycle Bin and, 207
  ScanDisk and, 221
Make New Connection Wizard, 41, *41*
NetMeeting Wizard, 158
New Active Desktop Wizard, 8
Scanner and Camera Wizard, ix, 218
Scheduled Task Wizard, 221
Update Device Driver Wizard, 38, *38*
Web Publishing Wizard, 267–268
Windows Update Wizard, 277–278
word processing programs. *See* WordPad
WordPad, 280–284, *280*. *See also* Notepad
  documents
    cutting, copying, and pasting, 283, *283*
    inserting date and time, 281
    inserting date and time according to the format selected, 283, *283*
    paragraphs, formatting as bulleted list, 284, *284*
    printing and print preview, 283, *283*
    undoing, 283, *283*

documents, creating, 282, *282*, 284
  by inserting from the Clipboard, 284
  margins and paper source, selecting, 2
  page size and orientation, establishing, 280
  from scratch, 284
  tab, paragraph, or bullet style, selecting, 282
  font, selecting, 282, 283, *283*
  aligning text to left, center, or right, 284, *284*
  boldface, italic, or underline, 283, *283*
  current font, size displayed, 283, *283*
  palette of colors for the font, displaying, 283, *283*
linked objects, edit menu for managing the maintenance of, 280
objects, inserting into documents, 281
  icons of objects, 282
  linking an object, 282
  objects from existing files, 281
  objects, selecting and creating different types for insertion, 281
Options command, 280–281, *281*
  standard measurement units, setting, 280–281, *281*
  text, rich text, Word and Write formats, setting the word wrap and toolbar defaults for, 281
  word wrap and toolbar defaults for embedded objects, establishing, 281
  standard toolbar, 282–283, *282*, *283*

workgroups
    broadcasting messages to with
        WinPopup, 279
    identifying, *165*, 166

X

X through an icon to indicate disabled device, 241

Y

Yahoo!, 224

Z

zip files, 28, *28*

PC Confidential

Secure Your PC and Privacy from Snoops, Spies, Spouses, Supervisors, and Credit Card Thieves

by Michael A. Banks • $24.99
0-7821-2747-9

Get the essential information you need to protect your privacy on your PC—at home and at work!

Did you know that your computer keeps track of
- Data you've deleted?
- Where you've been on the Internet?
- When and how long you've been working?
- And more…

Find out how and why hackers may be using your PC. Learn how to hide and encrypt private information. *PC Confidential* offers solutions to improving your personal PC security.

Bonus software for extra security: CD-ROM includes valuable software that can be used for added levels of security beyond the basics, including Windows 95 and 98 security patches, Internet Explorer encryption patch, PowerToys, LockIt and AppLock PC password programs, PGP demo software, Encrypted Magic Folders, eSafe to quarantine downloads, KlikLock, SpamHater, Cookie Crusher, and more.

www.sybex.com

SYBEX®

The PC Problem-Solving Wonder!

Completey revised and updated by Mark Minasi and a team of gurus, the 11th edition now includes easy-to-find Troubleshooting and QuickSteps sections in addition to valuable instructional videos by the engaging author.

ISBN: 0-7821-2800-9
$59.99 US
Available August 2000

Includes A+ certification test engines with more than 350 practice questions!

Check out this valuable bonus material:

- An extensive major hardware vendor resource guide
- Chapter on using the Internet to upgrade PCs and peripherals
- An online chapter that covers storage devices
- A comprehensive glossary

www.sybex.com   SYBEX®

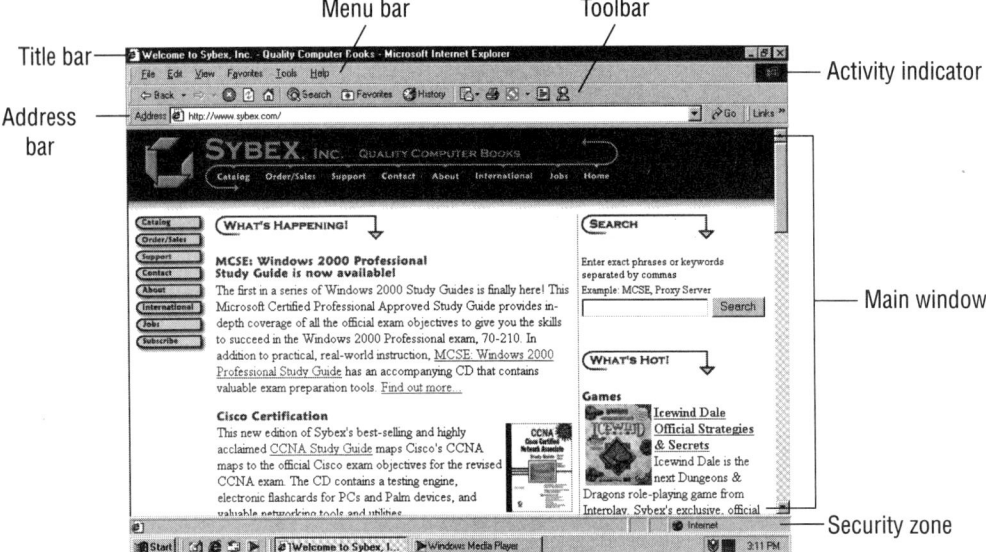